Jesus Was a Feminist

Jesus Was a Feminist

What the Gospels Reveal about
His Revolutionary Perspective

Leonard J. Swidler

SHEED & WARD
Lanham, Chicago, New York, Toronto, and Plymouth, UK

Published by Sheed & Ward
An imprint of Rowman & Littlefield Publishers, Inc.
A wholly owned subsidary of The Rowman & Littlefield Publishing Group, Inc.
4501 Forbes Boulevard, Suite 200
Lanham, MD 20706

Estover Road
Plymouth PL6 7PY
United Kingdom

Distributed by National Book Network

Library of Congress Cataloging-in-Publication Data

Swidler, Leonard J.
  Jesus was a feminist : what the Gospels reveal about his revolutionary perspective /
Leonard Swidler.
     p. cm.
  Includes index.
  ISBN-13: 978-1-58051-218-3 (pbk. : alk. paper)
  ISBN-10: 1-58051-218-6 (pbk. : alk. paper)
  1. Feminism—Religious aspects—Christianity. 2. Women—Religious aspects—
Christianity. 3. Jesus Christ. 4. Bible. N.T. Gospels—Criticism, interpretation, etc.
I. Title.

BT704.S95 2007
232.082—dc22   2007014224

Printed in the United States of America

For my wife, Arlene Anderson Swidler,
the First Feminist in my life

Contents

A Conclusion Sneak Preview

$\mathcal{T}$o save the reader the bother of having to look at the back of the book for the answer, let me say up front in very brief fashion the most dramatic conclusions I come to here in this volume after many decades of research and reflection.

The first one is, as the title of the book indicates, that Jesus was a feminist—and that presumably his followers should imitate him in that. However, as the following introductory section notes, I published that claim over a third of a century ago. Still, it remains news to many Christians, including the leaders of the Catholic and Orthodox churches.

The second dramatic conclusion that I draw is that Jesus—contrary to a two-thousand-year mistranslation of a key Gospel passage—did *not* reject divorce and remarriage!

The third is that proto versions of two of the canonical Gospels, namely, Luke's and the Fourth Gospel, were written by women. Actually, I made the argument in 1979 for there being a "Luka" author of the Proto-Luke Gospel, but the claim was not commented on, to my knowledge. Here I also further claim that the time has come for us to recognize publicly that the penultimate version of the Fourth Gospel was written by a woman, namely, Mary Magdalene. It is also clear that the version of Matthew's Gospel that we have also doubtless had a multitude of women sources, and perhaps even organizers, behind it.

The fourth, and most sweeping, conclusion is that we would not have Christianity today if all the materials on Jesus' teaching and life that were gathered and handed on by women were missing. One could imagine, *per impossibilem*, that if all the other material—not handed on by women—about Jesus' teaching and life were nevertheless gathered together and written down, and the other missionary activities we learn about by Paul, Barnabas, Silas,

Timothy, and others (but sans the work of all the women listed by name, and not, in the New Testament), did in fact occur, doubtless some kind of religion around Jesus would have grown up. However, it would have been rather anemic, and doubtless would have faded from all but human memory, like Mithraism and numberless other cults popular for a few centuries.

The proof for these four claims? For that you will have to read the book.

§1 The Plan

This book grew out of an article that was published in the January 1971 issue of the *Catholic World* titled "Jesus Was a Feminist." The article in turn grew out of an undergraduate course I offered in the fall of 1970 at Temple University (a state university) called Women and Religion. I had become a conscious feminist after I saw my wife Arlene Anderson Swidler—who was smarter than 99 percent of men (and I have yet to meet any of the 1 percent), being constantly slighted in the academic world simply because she was a woman. I realized later that I had always been an unconscious feminist because my mother was a strong woman who held her own—and in the worst days of the 1930s had to carry our whole family financially—in that grim world of the Great Depression (I was born in the auspicious year, 1929. I guess like Louis XIV, *Apres moi l'deluge!*). The Religion Department of Temple University was in 1970 perhaps the greatest in the world, but it did not have any women faculty. Indeed, there were precious few women scholars trained in theology or religious studies then. In fact, I was probably the first Catholic layperson in modern times to receive a degree in Catholic theology (1959 from the Pontifical Catholic Theology Faculty of the University of Tübingen); now there are thousands, and I helped create many of them.

With the support of Arlene, I set about preparing for the fall 1970 course, but when I came to Christianity, I could not find any books on the attitude of Jesus toward women. There were many books on Paul's attitude toward women, but concerning Jesus I could find only a paragraph or two in a few books. So, I did what any good undergraduate would do: I sat down with the only primary materials that dealt with Jesus, the four Gospels, and carefully went through them, taking notes on every scrap that in any way related to women.

The first difference between the Gospels and the rest of the New Testament I noticed is the attitude toward women. There is not only a large

1

amount of evidence of a positive attitude by Jesus toward women exhibited in the Gospels, there is also a complete lack of any evidence of a negative attitude toward women by Jesus. The same could not, of course, be said of the followers of Jesus in the rest of the New Testament. There are a number of negative statements about women to be found in the New Testament outside of the Gospels. These generally are very familiar to hundreds of millions of people, having been read and preached on in churches for millennia, having had thousands of books written on them, and having been incarnated in church laws, structures, and customs.

The result of looking through the Gospels was astonishingly clear and abundant—Jesus was a feminist! It was so obvious that I hesitated to even think about submitting my material for possible publication, but I finally did. When it was published, it turned out to be a kind of mini–Nobel Prize in religion! It was reproduced dozens and dozens of times and was translated and reproduced in many languages in all continents. I still encounter women who tell me how important that article was in their life.

As a historian, I continued to gather material in the field, and in 1976 I published *Women in Judaism: The Status of Women in Formative Judaism*[1] and in 1979 I published my last book, *Biblical Affirmations of Woman*,[2] in the area of women and religion. By then, many highly qualified women were entering the field, and so I decided that I was no longer needed there. Now, almost two decades later, after that volume has gone through some eight printings, I thought that it would, nevertheless, be helpful to pull together all the material that I had gathered in the past forty years on Jesus—I have published quite a lot on him over the decades—and offer a more full-blown presentation of the evidence that Jesus was indeed a feminist. This fact ought to have consequences for the two billion Christians in the world today, and for the other four billion persons they are likely to encounter—the current world population. Had Arlene not fallen victim to Alzheimer's disease starting over a dozen years ago, I am sure that this would be another of our joint publications—but she is here within me.

The plan here is that after providing

1) a historical context, and then
2) a psychological setting, I will present in rather terse fashion
3) an overview of the evidence that Jesus was a feminist, including
4) a sustained argument, with evidence, that he was also an "androgynous" person, followed by
5) a more complete analysis of the Gospel and related materials bearing on the topic. Then will follow
6) an analysis of the role the four Gospel writers played in all this—including
7) an argument that almost certainly two of the "Proto" Evangelists were women!—as well as

8) the pertinent apocryphal materials. Finally there will be
9) a "representative" sampling of the largely negative misdirection the Christian Fathers took Christianity in regard to women, and
10) a conclusion.

§2 THE NAME JESUS-YESHUA

A word here about the name of Jesus: The name *Jesus* is simply a Latin form of the Greek *Iesous*. Actually *Iesous* is not originally a Greek name, but rather a Greek form of a Hebrew name, *Yehoshua* (the biblical *Yoshua*), which means "*YHWH* (probably pronounced *Yahweh*) is salvation." It is not difficult to see how the movement from *Yehoshua*, which in colloquial parlance would sometimes be abbreviated as *Yeshua* or even *Yeshu*, was transliterated into the Greek *Iesous* and the Latin *Jesus*. Unfortunately, in the movement of the name *Yeshua* from its original forms into the various languages used by Christians, and others, something important was lost. First of all, Jews no longer use the name *Yeshua*, nor indeed do Christians. In fact, both the Hebrew and Greek forms, as proper names, disappeared from usage after the first century.[3] As a result, both Christians and Jews automatically think of Jesus as the name of someone other than a Jew. This simple fact tends to cut Christians off from the taproot of their religion, the Hebrew-Jewish tradition. On the other side, it also tends to cut Jews off from a very important son of their tradition, one who has become the most influential Jew of all history, surpassing in historical impact even such giants as Moses, David, Marx, Freud, and Einstein.

The name of *Yeshua* is made up of two parts. The first part, "Ye," is an abbreviated form of the Hebrew proper name for God, *YHWH*. The second part, *shua*, is the Hebrew word for salvation. Where the root meaning of the Indo-European words for salvation is fullness, wholeness, the root meaning of the Semitic word used here, "*shua*," is that of capaciousness, openness. Salvation then means the opposite of being in straits; it means being free in wide-open space. This makes it close to, though not precisely the same as, the Indo-European root meaning. The word *salvation*, however, is one that, to a large extent, has been significantly altered in the Christian tradition from its meaning in Israelite religion and its root meaning in Greek and Latin. It has for the most part been given a restricted meaning since the third century C.E., namely, that when believers in Jesus Christ die, if they have remained faithful, they will go to heaven. But that is not at all what the word basically means. In its Latin form, *salvatio*, it comes from the root "*salus*" (the Greek form is *soterion/soteria* from *saos*), meaning wholeness, health, or well-being—hence, "salutary" and "salubrious" in English. The same is true of the Germanic root of the word, *Heil*, which adjectivally also means whole, hale, healed, healthy. Indeed, this is also where the English word "holy" comes from. To be holy means to be whole, to lead a whole, a full life. When we lead a whole, full life, we are holy, we attain salvation, wholeness.

The Jewish scholar Geza Vermes confirmed this Semitic understanding of salvation as being current with Yeshua and his contemporaries when he pointed out that they linked together physical and spiritual health: "In the somewhat elastic, but extraordinarily perceptive religious terminology of Jesus and the spiritual men of his age, 'to heal', 'to expel demons' and 'to forgive sins' were interchangeable synonyms."[4]

The name Yeshua, then, means *YHWH* is salvation, wholeness; and the name *YHWH* (it most probably means "I will be who I will be") is the Hebrew proper name of the one and only God who created everything that exists. We are so used to the concept of monotheism today that we do not realize what an extraordinary breakthrough this insight was in the history of humankind. It had massive immediate implications for how one related to all other human beings and all reality.

If I lived in a nation which had its own god or gods, and all other nations also had their own god or gods, then the ethical rules that were developed by my god's religion would not necessarily be applicable to those persons and things under other gods. Hence, there was not one ethic which was valid for all human beings and for all the earth—until the insight developed that there was, in fact, one creator God of all human beings and of all reality. So, then, the very name Yeshua is an assertion that *YHWH* is the source of wholeness for all human beings, for all things. It is a name which carries the very heart of the great contribution of the Hebrew people to humanity, ethical monotheism. Of course, there were many Jewish men who were named Yeshua besides Yeshua of Nazareth. However, there is a special appropriateness in the fact that Yeshua of Nazareth was given this name, for it is through him that billions of non-Jews came to the Jewish insight of ethical monotheism, came to *YHWH*, came to salvation, wholeness.

For all these reasons I will, in this book, use the original Hebrew name, Yeshua.

NOTES

1. Leonard Swidler, *Women in Judaism: The Status of Women in Formative Judaism* (Metuchen, NJ: Scarecrow Press, 1976).

2. Leonard Swidler, *Biblical Affirmations of Woman* (Philadelphia: Westminster Press, 1979).

3. See "Iesous" in Gerhard Kittel, ed., *Theological Dictionary of the New Testament* (Grand Rapids, MI: Eerdmans, 1966), 3:284ff.

4. Geza Vermes, *Jesus and the World of Judaism* (Philadelphia: Fortress Press, 1983), 10.

I

YESHUA AND WOMEN:
AN OVERVIEW

§3 Prologue: Women in the Ancient World

The land of Israel/Palestine lies in the center of the fertile crescent of the ancient Near East. The fertile crescent extended from the lower end of the Tigris and Euphrates rivers in the east (Sumer, in present-day Iraq), up through present-day Syria and Lebanon, and down through Israel/Palestine, with Egypt and the Nile Valley at its western tip. Civilization developed about the same time at the two extremities, Sumer in the east and Egypt in the west, and the status of women in both civilizations was relatively high in their early periods. Before 2400 B.C.E. in Sumer, polyandry (more than one husband to a wife) was at times practiced; some women also owned and controlled vast amounts of property, enjoyed some laws that in effect prescribed something like equal pay for equal work, and were able to hold top rank among the literati of the land, and to be spiritual leaders of paramount importance. In Egypt, during the third and fourth, and into the fifth dynasties (2778–2423 B.C.E.), when the highest level of culture of the Old Kingdom was reached, daughters had the same inheritance rights as sons, marriages were strictly monogamous (with the exception of royalty) and tended to be love matches; in fact, it can be said that in the Old Kingdom the wife was the equal of the husband in rights, although her place in society was not identical with that of her husband.

However, in the east, in the land of Mesopotamia, "Between the Rivers," the Sumerian civilizations gave way gradually during the last quarter of the third millennium B.C.E., bowing to successive conquerors, Akkadia, Babylon, and Assyria. Here the lot of women declined drastically. For example, the Babylonian Code of Hammurabi (1728–1636 B.C.E.) and similar codes permitted men to repudiate their wives for any or no reason, though the woman was able to divorce the husband only for very serious cause; indeed, even if in such a case a wife were a "gadabout," her life was forfeit: "If she was not careful, but was a gadabout, thus neglecting her house [and] humiliating her husband, they shall throw that woman into the water."[1] This general trend was confirmed by the analyses of the excavations of the ancient Mesopotamian city of Mari, where, for a short period in the first half of the eighteenth century B.C.E., some women enjoyed a relatively high status.

> There can be no doubt that men were culturally dominant. . . . A cultural bias against women is revealed by incidental disparaging remarks sprinkled throughout these texts about the weak, unheroic character of women.

> In the matter of male dominance, Mari was in accord with the general Mesopotamian culture. The surprising fact, then, is not that women were regarded as inferior but that they were able to attain the great prominence that they did.

> This political prominence of women in Mari and upper Mesopotamia stands in contrast both to their role in succeeding periods in Mesopotamian history and to the role of their contemporaries in lower Mesopotamia. . . . Lamentably, the cultural standing of women deteriorated in succeeding periods of Mesopotamian history.[2]

The status of women also declined at the western tip of the fertile crescent, in Egypt, with the disintegration of the Old Kingdom in 2270 B.C.E. Eventually, however, it rose again, so that in Egypt, over the almost three-thousand-year history before the coming of Alexander the Great in 330 B.C.E., the status of women was quite high for about fifteen hundred years, corresponding with strong central governments. The periods of high status were, broadly speaking, 3000–2270 B.C.E., 1580–1085 B.C.E., and from 663 B.C.E. into the Greco-Roman period until the dominance of Christianity around 375 C.E. Thus, Jacques Pirenne could write:

> We have arrived at the epoch of total legal emancipation of the woman. That absolute legal equality between the woman and the man continued to the arrival of the Ptolemies [Hellenistic successors to Alexander the Great] in Egypt.[3]

Though taking a somewhat more pessimistic view, Jean Vercoutter is largely in agreement when after his extensive history of women in ancient Egypt, he concluded:

> If all the sources are in agreement that, everything considered, the woman in Egypt was subordinate to the man, that her duty was to please him, give him children and care for his house, it also appears that in turn custom allowed women a large freedom: they could go out freely and if perchance they owned some goods they would become the equal of the man in order

to assure its management. In this sense the condition of the female Egyptian was superior to that of the Greek, for example, and when with the Macedonian conquest Hellenistic customs and then Roman penetrated the Nile valley the female Egyptian lost many of the privileges which she had acquired little by little. It would indeed take centuries for that relative liberty which Egyptian women enjoyed to again be their lot.[4]

When we shift our focus to the world of Hellas, we also find women enjoying a relatively high status in the early period of Greek civilization, as in the Minoan culture of Crete (3000–1100 B.C.E.) and the Greece of the time of the Homeric poems (before 900 B.C.E.). But, there too, women's status declined, reaching a low point during the Golden Age of Greece, in the fourth and fifth centuries B.C.E., though a distinction would have to be made between Athens, where women had a very inferior status, and Sparta, where they had great freedom.

But after the spread of Greek culture by Alexander the Great around 330 B.C.E. from Egypt to the Indus River, the lot of women gradually improved. We can trace a growing movement for women's liberation with the passage of time in this Hellenistic world, so that, in general, women were more nearly equal to men in rights by the time of the New Testament than they had been in 300 B.C.E. Likewise, in general, greater freedom for women could be found the farther west one traveled. Naturally, these are overall descriptions which admit variations in details, but they are basically valid.

Let us look at least at some of the most important indicators of this women's liberation movement in Hellenistic culture. In fifth-century Greece, marriage was monogamous, but the husband was allowed sex with *hetaerae* (courtesans) and concubines. By 311 B.C.E. we find a marriage contract from the Greek island of Cos:

> Contract of Heracleides and Demetria. . . . He is free, She is free. . . . It is not permitted to Heracleides to take another woman, for that would be an injury to Demetria, nor may he have children by another woman, nor do anything injurious to Demetria under any pretext. If Heracleides be found performing any such deed, Demetria shall denounce him. . . . Heracleides will return to Demetria the dowry of 1000 drachmas, which she contributed, and he will pay an additional 1000 drachmas in Alexandrian silver as an additional fine.[5]

Women in Hellenistic times also exercised extensive rights in the economic sphere. A woman could inherit a personal patrimony equally with her sons—buy, own, and sell property and goods, and will them to others. Indeed, in Hellenistic times there were wealthy Greek women, some of whom were greatly honored for their philanthropy. Klaus Thraede summed the matter up when he wrote: "The emancipation of the woman in private law was decisive for the development which began already in the classical period: the equalization in inheritance and property rights as well as the de facto independence in marriage and divorce."[6]

Unlike the Greek (Athenian) wives of the classical period, who did not even eat with male guests when they were in their own homes, let alone go out in mixed gatherings, the wives of the Hellenistic period were quite likely to turn up at social gatherings (*symposia*), and women went on long journeys. Whereas earlier it was customary for only Spartan women to participate in sports, including the Olympics, women's involvement in this area advanced in later Hellenistic times to the point where there were women professional athletes, as, for example, the three daughters Tryphosa, Hedea, and Dionysia of Hermesianax of Tralles, who engaged in foot and chariot races in the years 47 to 41 B.C.E. Many women pursued music as a profession. Asia Minor was known for its women physicians, though according to Pliny the Elder, much of the information about these women physicians was deliberately suppressed. On the level of skilled artisans, a woman often pursued a craft similar to her husband's, for example, a woman goldsmith and a man armorer—or think of Priscilla, who, with her husband Aquila, was a tentmaker.[7]

In an advanced civilization the key to advanced status is education; by itself it will not accomplish everything, but usually little is possible without it. Whereas in classical Athens, among women usually only the *hetaerae* had any kind of education, education for young girls became ever broader and more widespread throughout the Hellenistic period, and one result was that more and more wives as well as husbands were educated. In fact, in Hellenistic Egypt there were more women who could sign their names than men, and thus Hellenistic literature, particularly the novel, was written for a feminine public. Another result of the broader Hellenistic education of women was the appearance of a flood of Hellenistic women poets.

It is perhaps most of all in that discipline of the spirit for which the Greeks are most renowned, philosophy, that one can see the striving for women's liberation. In the seventh century many women were students of Pythagoras. But by the fourth century, Plato and Aristotle paid only lip service to equality for women. However, in the Hellenistic period women again took up the study of philosophy. For example, we know that one of Aristotle's followers, Theophrastus (d. 287 B.C.E.), had both a woman disciple, Pamphile (some of whose writing is extant), and a woman opponent, unfortunately anonymous. Thereafter to some extent the Cynics also spoke out in favor of equal rights for women, and women played a prominent role in the school of Epicurus (343–270 B.C.E.), not only as disciples but even as favorite teachers.

But the philosophical school which did most to promote the improved status of women was that of the Stoics. These grassroots philosophers stressed the worth of the individual woman, the need for her education (consequently there were many women followers of Stoicism), strict monogamy, and a notion of marriage as a spiritual community of two equals. The Roman knight C. Musonius Rufus, a contemporary of Philo the Jew and the apostle Paul, discussed at length whether women should also pursue philosophy and whether daughters should be brought up the same as sons; he answered yes to both questions.

In religion and cult, women in classical Greece, namely, during the fifth century B.C.E., experienced restrictions that were broad, but by no means absolute. There were a number of religious activities or places that they could not enter upon, as, for example, the very important oracle of Delphi or the cult of Hercules; and usually only maidens, not married women, could watch the sacred games at Olympia. Women were also almost entirely absent from, or were kept in the background of, the activities of state religion. Still, in some cults, such as those of Artemis and Dionysus, women did play a significant role.

In the Hellenistic period, however, the extraordinary popularity of the eastern cults and mystery religions and the burgeoning women's liberation movement dramatically changed the situation. Women not only took part in these religious cults, they often did so in great numbers and often in leading and even priestly roles, as, for example, in the Eleusinian, the Dionysian, and the Andanian mysteries. The cult of the goddess Isis, which came from Egypt but spread all over the Hellenistic and Roman world, was at the beginning of its popularity exclusively a women's cult, and even after men were admitted it still provided women with leading religious roles and justly had the reputation of being a vigorous promoter of women's equality and liberation.

The Hellenistic world was largely conquered by the Romans a century or so before the birth of Yeshua. Although it was the Hellenistic cultural world that exercised the greatest outside influence on Judaism and Christianity, the influence of Rome was also present in its own way, that is, mostly political, legal, and military, from the time of Pompey's conquest of Palestine in 63 B.C.E. Hence, it is proper to note briefly the condition of women among the Romans.

Behind the culture of Rome there stood the extraordinarily developed culture of the Etruscans, stretching in space from Rome up to Pisa, and in time from before the seventh into the third century B.C.E. We find in Italy, as in Minoan Crete, a civilization characterized by a preeminence of women. Everywhere women were at the forefront of the scene, playing a considerable role and never blushing from shame, as Livy says of one of them, when exposing themselves to masculine company. In Etruria, it was a recognized privilege for ladies of the most respectable kind, and not just for *hetaerae* as in Greece of the contemporary classical period, to take part with men in banquets, where they reclined as the men did. They attended dances, concerts, and sports events and even presided, as a painting in Orvieto shows, perched on a platform, over boxing matches, chariot races, and acrobatic displays.

Women, of course, did not enjoy such a high status in contemporary Greece, nor did they in early Rome. But by the third century B.C.E., Rome moved to improve the property rights of women. Somewhat later in the republic, doubtless because of the influence of the Etruscan culture and the growing pressure of the women's liberation movement in Hellenism, the condition of women improved to the point where a woman could, in general, marry and divorce on her own initiative and even choose her own name. During the same period, the image of leading women appeared on coins—for the first time. The Roman Cornelius Nepos (d. 32 B.C.E.) even felt that the advanced status of Roman women was something to boast about: "What Roman would find it annoying to be accompanied by his wife to a banquet? Or what housewife does not take the first place in her house or go about in public?"[8]

The status of women continued to improve dramatically under the empire. Indeed, the political activity of women of the senatorial class developed so vigorously that we find on the walls of Pompeii the names of women running for office, a definite advance over Egyptian and Greek women, who had few political rights; women were sent on imperial missions to proconsuls; the possibility of a woman consul was even discussed. Nevertheless, it is basically true to say that "only the men exercised the political rights of citizens: military service, voting at the assemblies of the people, access to magistratures."[9]

Women were everywhere involved in business and in social life, namely, theaters, sports events, concerts, parties, traveling—with or without their husbands. They took part in a whole range of athletics and even bore arms and went into battle.

In family affairs one would have to speak of a certain equality of the sexes in daily life. The woman's consent was necessary for marriage; in an increasing number of marriages (*non in manu*) she had no obligation to obey, nor did the husband have any legal power over his wife. Speaking of this kind of marriage, one scholar noted that "the married woman without *manus* was without doubt the most emancipated wife in the history of law!"[10] From the point of view of money, the pattern increasingly was one of equality and of separation. The equality of the spouses was in effect total, whether concerning the full liberty of divorce in classical law, the limiting causes of that liberty in the late empire, or the sanctions of an unjustified divorce.

Republican Rome, acting originally under the influence of Etruscan culture, took up the impulse of women's liberation from Hellenism and carried it forward to where the empire (30 B.C.E. onward) also made it its own and continued to promote it ever further throughout the first several centuries of the Common Era. This evolving liberation of women in Roman society was expressed in the legal forum by that extremely influential Roman jurist in the second century of the Common Era, Gaius:

> It would appear that there is scarcely any very persuasive reason for women of adult age to be in tutelage. For the common notion that, because of the levity of their minds, they are often deceived and that, therefore, it is fitting that they be placed under the authority of tutors, would appear to be more specious than true. In fact, women of adult age conduct their own business for themselves, and in certain cases, for the sake of form, only the tutor gives his authorization. Indeed, even if he refuses it, he is often forced to grant it by the praetor.[11]

In sum: The status of women in the ancient world of the fertile crescent after the early Sumerian period was almost uniformly low, except in Egypt, where it was early and often quite high. In the classical Greco-Roman world (after the Minoan and pre-Homeric Greek periods) the condition of women was varied, but often quite restricted, with the clear exception of Etruscan culture. It nevertheless improved, particularly during the Hellenistic period, so vigorously and continually that one must speak of a women's liberation movement which had a massive and manifold liberating impact on the lot of women—not everywhere and not in every class or at every period equally effective, of course. This improving impulse was picked up and carried forward by Rome. In fact, the general rule in this matter is that the farther west one goes, the greater is the freedom of women, though in detail there are the greatest possible variations—and that also, in general, there is a progression in the freedom for women according to time. Thus, as the women of Rome tended to be freer than those of Greece, who were more liberated than women of the oriental world, so also the women of the time of the Roman Empire had greater freedom than those of the time of the Roman republic, and their sisters in the Hellenistic world and period were less restricted than those of Greece at the time of the Athenian Empire. Due account must be taken, of course, of the unsympathetic vagaries of all human history, and the fact that in so many ways the liberation of women was long since anticipated in ancient Sumer, Egypt, Minoan Crete, and later also in Etruria.

It is in this context and under this surrounding and pervading influence that the biblical traditions, Jewish and Christian, developed.

NOTES

1. Codex Hammurabi, 143. For complete documentation see Leonard Swidler, *Women in Judaism: The Status of Women in Formative Judaism* (Metuchen, NJ: Scarecrow Press, 1976), 4ff.

2. Bernard Frank Batto, *Studies on Women at Mari* (Baltimore, MD: Johns Hopkins University Press, 1974), 136–38.

3. Jacques Pirenne, "Le Statut de la femme dans l'ancienne Egypte," *La Femme. Recueil de la Société Jean Bodin*, 11, no. 1 (1959): 76.

4. Jean Vercoutter, "La Femme en Egypt ancienne," in *Histoire mondiale de la femme*, ed. Pierre Grimal (Paris: Nouvelle Librairie de France, 1965), 1:152.

5. O. Rubensohn, *Elephantine-Papyri*, no. 1 (Berlin, 1907).

6. Klaus Thraede, "Frau," *Reallexikon für Antike und Christentum* (1973), col. 199.

7. Acts 18:3.

8. Thraede, "Frau," *Reallexikon* BAW, 16, col. 200.

9. Jacques-Henri Michel, "L'Infériorité de la condition féminine en droit romain," *Ludus Magistralis*, no. 46 (1974): 7.

10. Michel, "L'Infériorité de la condition féminine en droit romain," 6.

11. Gaius, *Institutes* 1.190. Quoted in Latin and French by Michel, in "L'Infériorité de la condition féminine en droit romain," 13, who remarks, "perhaps this text, which deserves to be better known . . . should figure one day in some feminist pantheon." For an excellent overview of the history of women in Greco-Roman society, see Sarah B. Pomeroy, *Goddesses, Whores, Wives, and Slaves: Women in Classical Antiquity* (New York: Schocken Books, 1975).

§4Yeshua, A Feminist, Androgynous—
An Integrated Human

In a certain sense the whole of human life is a complex series of encounters on a variety of levels and in manifold directions: the encounter of the human being with its own self, with nature around it, with its fellow human beings, and with ultimate reality—in the Judeo-Christian tradition called God. This complex of encounters redound on and influence each other: whoever leaves the encounter of the human with ultimate reality aside, for example, will distort the human relationship to itself, to nature, and to fellow humanity. Only in the present day are we becoming fully aware that the encounter with our environment and nature is rapidly transforming the world into a place where humans can no longer meet each other in a human manner; indeed, we may soon no longer be able to exist at all if we do not succeed in reversing the pollution of our environment.

History is the story of the encounters of humans with themselves and their fellow humans—and it is too infrequently a joyful account. Often humans appear to flee from an encounter with their true selves and appear, all too seldom, really to encounter their fellow humans; far too often they meet them as objects, but do not encounter them as persons. That, however, means that they do not meet them as they really are. Still worse is the long history of the dehumanizing of humans by one another, a dehumanizing in various ways and in various degrees. Fortunately, one of the crassest forms of the "exploitation of man by man," slavery, has been largely eliminated. Even the elimination of economic slavery has made significant progress in recent centuries, although the remaining task in this area is staggeringly great.

However, even the complete elimination of economic exploitation in the customary sense would still leave half of the human race in conditions which systematically distort and degrade their humanity. Which half of the human race? The female half. Women are thought almost by nature to be submissive,

15

subordinate, second class—not as slaves in the usual sense, but rather as something humanly even more unworthy: voluntarily submissive, willing slaves. They are often trained, programmed so that they are eager to be only half-humans, and specifically the "passive" half. Of course, as in every master-slave relationship, the humanness of the master is distorted as well as that of the slave. Men, too, are often trained, programmed to be half-humans, the "aggressive" half.

It is no solution, as one is wont to suggest, that the sexes naturally mutually complete each other so that a human whole is formed when the two half-humans are united, as for example, in marriage. Even our colloquial speech tells us that this notion is false. To be "passive" is not normally thought of as virtuous, any more than being "aggressive" is. In the relationship of one human being to another the passivity of one does not complement the aggressiveness of the other, but abets it. To be sure, all human beings must combine receptivity and assertiveness, softness and firmness, feeling and clear thinking. However, this combination must be present in *every* person. Every woman and every man must be receiving as well as giving, soft and firm, emotional and rational, in order to be a complete human. However, the structures of almost all societies tend to split the human person into two halves, the male and female, and even to insist that this is prescribed in natural law. Biology is transformed into ontology! But, in fact, women are no more constituted primarily by their sex than are men; they are primarily human, *persons*—just as men are.

Christians are not distinguished from others because they are anti-human, un-human, or super-human. As all other people, Christians strive to be complete in their humanity, but they believe that they have found in Yeshua the model of full humanity. Yeshua is the Christians' model of the encounter with God, nature, with one's self, one's fellow human beings, especially the oppressed, that is, the physically sick, the poor, the ignorant—and women. For centuries, Christians have attempted to imitate Yeshua in all these encounters, except the last named one. And yet, the encounter between man and woman is the most basic, pervasive of all the exploitative encounters in the history of humanity. It is the encounter which most pressingly needs the liberating model of Yeshua. Perhaps because it is the most fundamental, final bastion of sinful humanity, that is, of unfree humanity, that it is the last to yield to the liberating grace in Yeshua.

Put in one word, the model that Yeshua provided, the burden of everything that he thought, taught, and wrought, was "liberation." According to Luke 4:18, he quoted Isaiah of himself: "He has sent me to bring the good news to the poor, and to proclaim *liberty*," and according to John 8:32–36, he said, "if you make my word your home . . . you will learn the truth and the truth will make you *free*. . . . If the son makes you *free*, you will be *free* indeed."

Fundamentally this liberation is a freeing from ignorance and hence from a bondage to a false self and a false perception of reality, that is, first of all of our own selves, then our fellow human beings, expanding out to all things around us, and through them the Source of all reality. Then the human being is free to reach out in love to her or his own true self, fellow humans, nature, and the Source of all.

If indeed the most exploitative encounter between human beings is the encounter of men with women, and hence is most in need of Yeshua's liberating model, so too is the encounter with the self in a similar need in a very closely related manner. As the Jungian psychologist Hanna Wolff put it:

> Yeshua is the first male who broke through the androcentricism of antiquity. The despotism of the solely male values is deposed. Yeshua is the first one who broke with the solidarity of men, that is, of non-integrated men, and their anti-feminine animus. Yeshua stands before us as the first man without animus.[1]

The so-called feminine and masculine characteristics were exemplified in Yeshua in integrated, liberating androgynous fashion, and he presented a similar mutual, liberating model in the encounter with nature and with God. It is on the first two of those encounters—men with women, and with self— that we will focus through the model Yeshua presented.

§5 YESHUA WAS A FEMINIST

Perhaps today is the *Kairos*, the key moment, when this last rampart will finally yield to the power of the combination of the model of Yeshua and the grace of the moment, the contemporary secular movement toward a full, equal human development of women—feminism. What is the model of Yeshua's encounter with women? If we look at the Gospels not with the eyes of male chauvinism or the "eternal feminine," we will see that the model Yeshua presents is that of a feminist—Yeshua was a feminist.

> *A feminist is a person who is in favor of, and promotes, the equality of women with men, who advocates and practices treating women primarily as human persons (as men are so treated) and willingly contravenes social customs in so acting.*

To prove the thesis it must be demonstrated that, so far as we can tell, Yeshua neither said nor did anything which would indicate that he advocated treating women as intrinsically inferior to men, but that, on the contrary, he said and did things which indicated that he thought of women as the equals of men, and that, in the process, he willingly violated pertinent social mores.

The negative portion of the argument can be documented quite simply by reading through the four Gospels. Nowhere does Yeshua treat women as "inferior beings." In fact, it is apparent that Yeshua understood himself to be especially sent to the typical classes of "inferior beings" such as the poor, the lame, the sinner—and women—to call them all to the freedom and equality of the "Reign of God." But there are two factors which raise this negative result exponentially in its significance: the status of women in Palestine at the time of Yeshua, and the nature of the Gospels. Both need to be recalled here in some detail, particularly the former.

§6 The Status of Women in Palestine

The status of women in Palestine during the time of Yeshua was very decidedly that of inferiors. Despite the fact that there were several heroines recorded in the Hebrew Scriptures, according to most rabbinic customs of Yeshua's time, and long after, women were not allowed to study the Scriptures (the Torah—In rabbinic writings, e.g., the Mishnah [codified 200 C.E.], the Tosephta [codified just afterward], the Palestinian Talmud [400 C.E.], the Babylonian Talmud [500 C.E.], there are many references to persons and things as far back as 200 B.C.E). Thus, in many matters we can know what the rabbis of the time of Yeshua taught, even though caution must be exercised since the later codifier might have adjusted texts for his own purposes. Nevertheless, until cogent arguments and evidence are given, that substantial revision did occur in the pertinent passages, good scholarship dictates that the available texts be utilized with due care.[2] One first-century rabbi, Eliezer, put the point sharply: "Rather should the words of the Torah be burned than entrusted to a woman. . . . Whoever teaches his daughter the Torah is like one who teaches her lasciviousness."[3]

In the vital area of prayer, women were so little thought of as not to be given obligations of the same seriousness as men. For example, women, along with children and slaves, were not obliged to recite the *Shema*, the morning prayer, or prayers at meals.[4] In fact, the Talmud states: "Let a curse come upon the man who (must have) his wife or children say grace for him."[5] Moreover, in the daily prayers there was a threefold thanksgiving: "Praised be God that he has not created me a gentile; praised be God that he has not created me a woman; praised be God that he has not created me an ignorant man."[6] It was clearly a version of this rabbinic prayer that Paul controverted in his letter to the Galatians: "There is neither Jew nor Greek, there is neither slave nor free, there is neither male nor female; for you are all one in Christ Yeshua."[7]

Women were also greatly restricted in public prayer. It was not even possible for them to be counted toward the number necessary for a quorum to form a congregation to worship communally (a *minyan*).[8] They were again classified with children and slaves, who similarly did not qualify (there is an interesting parallel to the canon 93 of the 1917 Roman Catholic Code of Canon Law, the *Codex Juris Canonici* (CIC)—valid until 1983—which grouped married women, minors, and the insane). In the great temple at Jerusalem they were limited to one outer portion, the women's court, which was five steps below the court for the men.[9] In the synagogues the women were also separated from the men, and, of course, were not allowed to read aloud or take any leading function.[10] (The same is still true in many Orthodox synagogues today—and Catholic canon 1262 of the 1917 CIC, also states that "in church the women should be separated from the men." Doubtless Islam also took its practice of separating women and men at prayer from this prior Jewish custom.)

Besides the disabilities women suffered in the areas of prayer and worship there were many others in the private and public forums of society. The "Proverbs of the Fathers" contain the injunction: "'Speak not much with a woman.' Since a man's own wife is meant there, how much more does not this apply to the wife of another? The wise men say: 'Who speaks much with a woman draws down misfortune on himself, neglects the words of the law, and finally earns hell.'"[11] If it were merely the too free intercourse of the sexes which was being warned against, this might signify nothing derogatory to woman. But since a man may not speak even to his own wife, daughter, or sister in the street,[12] then only male superiority can be the motive, for intercourse with uneducated company is warned against in exactly the same terms: "One is not so much as to greet a woman."[13] In addition, save in the rarest instances, women were not allowed to bear witness in a court of law.[14] Some Jewish thinkers, as for example, Philo, a contemporary of Yeshua, thought women ought not leave their households except to go to the synagogue (and that only at a time when most of the other people would be at home)[15] and girls ought even not cross the threshold that separated the male and female apartments of the household.[16]

In general, the attitude toward women was epitomized in the institutions and customs around marriage. For the most part the function of women was thought of rather exclusively in terms of childbearing and rearing; women were almost always under the tutelage of a man, either the father or husband, or if a widow, the dead husband's brother. Polygamy—in the sense of having several wives, but *not* in the sense of having several husbands—was legal among Jews at the time of Yeshua, although probably not heavily practiced. Moreover, divorce of a wife was very easily obtained by the husband—he merely had to give her a writ of divorce; women in Palestine, on the other hand, were not allowed to divorce their husbands.

Rabbinic sayings about women also provide an insight into the attitude toward women: "It is well for those whose children are male, but ill for those whose children are female."[17] "At the birth of a boy all are joyful, but at the birth of a girl all are sad."[18] "When a boy comes into the world, peace comes into the world: when a girl comes, nothing comes."[19] "Even the most virtuous of women is a witch."[20] "Our teachers have said: Four qualities are evident in women: They are greedy at their food, eager to gossip, lazy, and jealous."[21]

The condition of women in Palestinian Judaism was that of inferiors.

§7 The Nature of the Gospels

The Gospels are not the straight factual reports of eyewitnesses of the events in the life of Yeshua of Nazareth as one might find in the columns of the *New York Times* or the pages of a critical biography. Rather, they are four different faith statements reflecting at least four primitive Christian communities who believed that Yeshua was the Messiah. They were composed from a variety of sources, written and oral, over a period of time and in response to certain needs felt in the communities and individuals at the time; consequently they are many-layered. Since the Gospel writer-editors were not twenty-first-century critical historians, they were not particularly intent on recording the very words of Yeshua, the *ipsissima verba Christi*, nor were they concerned about winnowing out all of their own cultural biases and assumptions. Indeed, it is doubtful that they were particularly conscious of them.

This modern critical understanding of the Gospels, of course, does not impugn the historical character of the Gospels; it merely describes the type of historical documents they are so their historical significance can more accurately be evaluated. Its religious value lies in the fact that modern Christians are thereby helped to know much more precisely what Yeshua meant by certain statements and actions as they are reported by the first Christian communities in the Gospels. With this new knowledge of the nature of the Gospels it is easier to make the vital distinction between the religious truth that is to be handed on and the time-conditioned categories and customs involved in expressing it.

§8 Yeshua as Source and as Jew

When the fact that no negative attitudes by Yeshua toward women are portrayed in the Gospels is set side by side with the recently discerned "communal faith-statement" understanding of the nature of the Gospels, the importance of the former is vastly enhanced. For whatever Yeshua said or did comes to us only through the lens of the first Christians. If there were no very special religious significance in a particular concept or custom, we would expect that current concept or custom to be reflected by Yeshua. The fact that the overwhelmingly negative attitude toward women in Palestine did not come through the primitive Christian communal lens by itself underscores the clearly great religious importance Yeshua attached to his positive attitude—his feminist attitude—toward women: Feminism, that is, personalism extended to women, is a constitutive part of the Gospel, the Good News, of Yeshua.

It should also be noted here that, although in the analysis that follows it is the image of Yeshua as it emerges from the four Gospels that will be dealt with, the feminist character that is found there is ultimately to be attributed to Yeshua himself and not to the church, the evangelists, or their sources. Basically the "principle of dissimilarity" operates here. That principle, devised by contemporary New Testament scholars, states that if a saying or action attributed to Yeshua is contrary to the cultural milieu of the time, then it most probably had its origin in Yeshua. In this case the feminism of Yeshua could hardly be attributable to the primitive church.

As is seen already in the later New Testament writings, the early church quickly became not only non-feminist, but also anti-woman. For example: "The women should keep silence in the churches. For they are not permitted to speak, but should be subordinate, as even the law says."[22] "Let a woman learn in silence with all submissiveness. I permit no woman to teach or to have authority over men; she is to keep silent."[23] The misogynist slide continued after the New Testament: In the second century Tertullian, the "father of theology," said:

> And do you not know that you are (each) an Eve? The sentence of God on this sex of yours lives in this age: the guilt must of necessity live, too. You are the devil's gateway; you are the unsealer of that (forbidden) tree: you are the first deserter of the divine law: you are she who persuaded him whom the devil was not valiant enough to attack. You destroyed so easily God's image, man. On account of your desert—that is, death—even the Son of God had to die.[24]

In the next century Origen wrote: "What is seen with the eyes of the creator is masculine, and not feminine, for God does not stoop to look upon what is feminine and of the flesh."[25] in the fourth century Epiphanius wrote: "For the female sex is easily seduced, weak, and without much understanding. The devil seeks to vomit out this disorder through women. . . . We wish to apply masculine reasoning and destroy the folly of these women."[26]

In the Jewish culture women were held to be, as the first century Jewish historian Josephus put it, "in all things inferior to the man."[27] Since it was out of that milieu that the evangelists were writing and from which they drew their sources, neither of them could have been the source of the feminism found in the Yeshua of the Gospels. Its only possible source was Yeshua himself. In fact, given the misogynist tendency exhibited both in the Judaism of Yeshua's time and in the early Christian Church, there is every likelihood that the strong feminism of Yeshua has been muted in the Gospels, as can be seen, for example, by the fact that the story of the woman taken in adultery[28] is absent from the earliest Greek manuscripts and almost did not make it into the canon of the New Testament at all. See §50 for a fuller treatment.

A further word of caution is needed here. The Jewish culture of the time of Yeshua indeed treated women as inferior to men, as did many of the surrounding cultures, and Yeshua did in this matter run counter to that culture. In the case of women, as in that of other marginalized groups, Yeshua raised a powerful prophetic voice of protest. But it needs to be remembered that raising a prophetic voice was precisely a Jewish thing to do; in this Yeshua was not acting in a non-Jewish manner, but in a specifically Jewish tradition. Moreover, after the first enthusiastic response of women followers to this liberating feminist move by Yeshua, the Christian Church quickly sank back into a non-feminist, even misogynist, morass until our time. There is no ground here for Christians to claim superiority over Jews, but rather just the opposite. Christians claim to be followers of Yeshua, whereas Jews do not. Christians, therefore, had far more reason to be, like Yeshua, feminists. But they—we—failed miserably.

This whole book, of course, attempts to present evidence sustaining this point. In this regard it is interesting to note that there are at least two early New Testament textual variants which directly accuse Yeshua of running counter to the culture and "leading women astray." In Luke 23:5 there is a variant manuscript reading attested to by the fourth-century Palestinian-born Church Father Epiphanius: The chief priests said to Pilate of Yeshua, "he is inflaming the people with his teaching all over Judea; it has come all the way from Galilee, where he started, down to here"—to which Epiphanius' attested text adds, "and he has turned our children and wives away from us for they are not bathed as we are, nor do they purify themselves (*et filios nostros et uxores avertit a nobis, non enim baptizantur sicut nos nec se mundant*)." The second text is even earlier, from the first half of the second century, when some of the New Testament itself was still being written. It is attested to by Marcion (d. 160 C.E.) and occurs in Luke 23:2: "They began their accusation by saying, 'We found this man inciting our people to a revolt, opposing payment of the tribute to Caesar'"—to which Marcion's attested text adds, "leading astray the women and the children (*kai apostrephonta tas gynaikas kai ta tekna*)."[29]

§9 Women Disciples of Yeshua

One of the first things noticed in the Gospels about Yeshua's attitude toward women is that he taught them the Gospel, the meaning of the Scriptures, and religious truths in general. When it is recalled that in Judaism it was considered improper, and even "obscene," to teach women the Scriptures, this action of Yeshua was an extraordinary, deliberate decision to break with a custom invidious to women. Moreover, women became disciples of Yeshua not only in the sense of learning from him, but also in the sense of following him in his travels and ministering to him. A number of women, married and unmarried, were regular followers of Yeshua. In Luke 8:1ff. several are mentioned by name in the same sentence with the twelve apostles: "He made his way through towns and villages preaching and proclaiming the Good News of the Reign of God. With him went the Twelve as well as certain women . . . who ministered to (*diekonoun*) them out of their own resources."[30] A fascinating second-century Gnostic document referred to the seven holy women named in the Gospels as disciples on a par with the twelve apostles: "After he had risen from the dead, when they came, the twelve disciples (*mathetes*) and seven women who had followed him as disciples (*matheteuein*), into Galilee . . . there appeared to them the Redeemer."[31] The significance of this phenomenon of women following Yeshua about, learning from and ministering to him, can be properly appreciated only when it is recalled that not only were women not to read or study the Scriptures, but in the more observant settings, they were not even to leave their household, whether as a daughter, wife, or member of a harem.

§10 Women and Resurrection from the Dead

Within this context of women being disciples and ministers, Yeshua quite deliberately broke another custom disadvantageous to women. According to the Gospels, Yeshua's first appearance after his resurrection to any of his followers was to a woman (or women), who was then commissioned by him to bear witness of the risen Yeshua to the Eleven.[32] In typical male Palestinian style, the Eleven refused to believe the women since, according to Judaic law, women were not allowed to bear legal witness. Clearly, this was a dramatic linking of a very definite rejection of the second-class status of women with the central element of the Gospel—the resurrection. The effort centrally to connect these two points is so obvious—an effort certainly not attributable to the male disciples or evangelists—that it is an overwhelming tribute to male intellectual myopia not to have discerned it effectively in two thousand years. In this case the source obviously was the women followers of Yeshua.

The intimate connection of women with resurrection from the dead is not limited in the Gospels to that of Yeshua. There are accounts of three other resurrections in the Gospels—all closely involving a woman. The most obvious connection of a woman with a resurrection account is that of the raising of a woman, Jairus' daughter.[33] A second resurrection Yeshua performed was that of the only son of the widow of Nain: "And when the Lord saw her, he had compassion on her and he said to her, 'Do not weep.'"[34] The third resurrection Yeshua performed was Lazarus', at the request of his sisters Martha and Mary.[35] From the first, it was Martha and Mary who sent for Yeshua because of Lazarus' illness. But when Yeshua finally came Lazarus was four days dead. Martha met Yeshua and pleaded for his resurrection: "Lord, if you had been there, my brother would not have died. And even now I know that whatever you ask from God, God will give you." Then followed Yeshua's raising of Lazarus from the dead. Thus, Yeshua raised one woman from the dead, and raised two other persons largely because of women.

There are two further details that should be noted in these three resurrection stories. The first is that only in the case of Jairus' daughter did Yeshua touch the corpse—which made him ritually unclean. In the cases of the two men Yeshua did not touch them, but merely said, "Young man, I say to you, arise," and, "Lazarus, come out." One must at least wonder why Yeshua chose to violate the laws for ritual purity in order to help a woman, but not a man. The second detail is in Yeshua's conversation with Martha after she pleaded for the resurrection of Lazarus. Yeshua declared himself to be the resurrection ("I am the resurrection and the life."), the only time he did so that is recorded in the Gospels. Yeshua here again revealed the central element in the Gospel—the resurrection—to a woman.

§11 Women as Sex Objects

There are, of course, numerous occasions recorded in the Gospels where women are treated by various men as second-class citizens. There are also situations where women were treated by others not at all as persons but as sex objects, and it was expected that Yeshua would do the same. The expectations were disappointed. One such occasion occurred when Yeshua was invited to dinner at the house of a skeptical Pharisee[36] and a woman of ill repute (*harmatolos*, a sinner) entered and washed Yeshua's feet with her tears, wiped them with her hair and anointed them. The Pharisee saw her solely as an evil sexual creature: "The Pharisee . . . said to himself, 'If this man were a prophet, he would know who this woman is who is touching him and what a bad name she has.'" But Yeshua deliberately rejected this approach to the woman as a sex object. He rebuked the Pharisee and spoke solely of the woman's human, spiritual actions; he spoke of her love, her unlove, namely, her sins, her being forgiven, and her faith. Yeshua then addressed her (it was not "proper" to speak to women in public, especially "improper" women) as a human person: "Your sins are forgiven. . . . Your faith has saved you; go in peace."

A similar situation occurred when the scribes and Pharisees used a woman reduced entirely to a sex object to set a legal trap for Yeshua.[37] It is difficult to imagine a more callous use of a human person than the "adulterous" woman was put to, by the enemies of Yeshua. First, she was surprised in the intimate act of sexual intercourse (quite possibly a trap was set up ahead of time by the suspicious husband), and then dragged before the scribes and Pharisees, and then by them before an even larger crowd that Yeshua was instructing: "making her stand in full view of everybody." They told Yeshua that she had been caught in the very act of committing adultery and that Moses had commanded that such women be stoned to death.[38] "What have you to say?" The trap was partly that if Yeshua said yes to the stoning he would be violating Roman law, which limited capital punishment, the *jus gladii*, to itself, and if he said no, he would appear to contravene Mosaic law. It could also partly have been to place Yeshua's reputation for kindness toward, and championing the cause of, women in opposition to the law and the condemnation of sin.

Yeshua, of course, eluded their snares by refusing to become entangled in legalisms and abstractions. Rather, he dealt with both the accusers and the accused directly as spiritual, ethical, human persons. He spoke directly to the accusers in the context of their own personal ethical conduct: "If there is one of you who has not sinned, let him be the first to throw a stone at her." To the accused woman he likewise spoke directly with compassion, but without approving her conduct: "'Woman, where are they? Has no one condemned you?' She said, 'No one, Lord.' And Yeshua said, 'Neither do I condemn you; go, and do not sin again.'"

One detail of this encounter provides the basis for a short excursus related to the status of women. The Pharisees stated that the woman had been caught in the act of adultery and according to the Law of Moses was therefore to be stoned to death. Since the type of execution mentioned was stoning, the woman must have been a "virgin betrothed," as referred to in Deuteronomy 22:23–24. There provision is made for the stoning of *both* the man and the woman, although in the Gospel story only the woman is brought forward. However, the reason given for why the man ought to be stoned was not because he had violated the woman, or God's law, but "because he had violated the wife of his neighbor." It was the injury of the man through the misuse of his property—wife, or betrothed wife-to-be—that was the great evil.

§12 Yeshua's Rejection of the Blood Taboo

All three of the Synoptic Gospels (Mark, Matthew, and Luke) insert, into the middle of the account of raising Jairus' daughter from the dead, the story of curing the woman who had an issue of blood for twelve years.[39] What is especially touching about this story is that the affected woman was so reluctant to project herself into public attention that she, "said to herself, 'If I only touch his garment, I shall be made well.'" Her shyness was not because she came from the poor, lower classes, for Mark pointed out that over the twelve years she had been to many physicians—with no success—on whom she had spent all her money. It was probably because for twelve years, as a woman with a flow of blood, she was constantly unclean,[40] which not only made her incapable of participating in any cultic action and made her in some sense "displeasing to God," but also rendered anyone and anything she touched (or anyone who touched what she had touched!) similarly unclean. (Here was the basis for the Catholic Church's not allowing women in the sanctuary during Mass until after Vatican II—she might be menstruating, and hence unclean.) The sense of degradation and contagion that her "womanly weakness" worked upon her over the twelve years doubtless was oppressive in the extreme. This would have been especially so when a religious teacher, a rabbi, was involved.

But not only does Yeshua's power heal her, in one of his many acts of compassion on the downtrodden and afflicted, including women, but Yeshua also makes a great to-do about the event, calling extraordinary attention to the publicity-shy woman: "Yeshua, perceiving in himself that power had gone forth from him, immediately turned about in the crowd, and said, 'Who touched my garments?' And his disciples said to him, 'You see the crowd pressing around you, and yet you say, 'Who touched me?'" And he looked around to see who had done it. But the woman, knowing what had been done to her, came in fear and trembling and fell down before him and told him the whole truth. And he said to her, 'Daughter, your faith has made you well; go in peace, and be healed of your disease.'"

It seems clear that Yeshua wanted to call attention to the fact that he did not shrink from the ritual uncleanness incurred by being touched by the "unclean" woman (on several occasions Yeshua rejected the notion of ritual uncleanness), and by immediate implication rejected the "uncleanness" of a woman who had a flow of blood, menstruous or continual. Yeshua apparently placed a greater importance on the dramatic making of this point, both to the afflicted woman herself and the crowd, than he did on avoiding the temporary psychological discomfort of the embarrassed woman, which in light of Yeshua's extraordinary concern to alleviate the pain of the afflicted, meant he placed a great weight on teaching this lesson about the dignity of women.

§13 Yeshua and the Samaritan Woman

On another occasion Yeshua again deliberately violated the then common code concerning men's relationship to women. It is recorded in the story of the Samaritan woman at the well of Jacob.[41] Yeshua was waiting at the well outside the village while his disciples were getting food. A Samaritan woman approached the well to draw water. Normally a Jew would not address a Samaritan, as the woman pointed out: "Jews, in fact, do not associate with Samaritans." But also normally a man would not speak to a woman in public (doubly so in the case of a rabbi). However, Yeshua startled the woman by initiating a conversation. The woman was aware that on both counts, her being a Samaritan and being a woman, Yeshua's action was out of the ordinary for she replied: "How is it that you, a Jew, ask a drink of me, a woman of Samaria?" As much as the Jews hated the Samaritans, it is nevertheless clear that Yeshua's speaking with a woman was considered a much more flagrant breach of conduct than his speaking with a Samaritan: "His disciples returned, and were surprised to find him speaking to a *woman*, though none of them asked, 'What do you want from her?' or, 'Why are you talking to her?'" However, Yeshua's bridging of the gap of inequality between men and women continued further, for in the conversation with the woman, according to the Fourth Gospel, he revealed himself in a straightforward fashion as the Messiah for the first time: "The woman said to him, 'I know that Messiah is coming.' Yeshua said to her, 'I who speak to you am he.'"

Just as when Yeshua revealed himself to Martha as "the resurrection," and to Mary Magdalene as the "risen one" and bade her to bear witness to the disciples, Yeshua here also revealed himself in one of his key roles, as Messiah, to a woman (all these instances recorded in the Gospel of John; why specifically in that Fourth Gospel will be discussed below when I argue that the Fourth Gospel was initially written by a woman—Mary Magdalene) who immediately *bore witness* of the fact to her fellow villagers. It is interesting to note that apparently the testimony of women carried greater weight among the Samaritans than among the Jews, for the villagers came out to see Yeshua: "Many Samaritans of that town believed in him on the strength of the woman's testimony." It would seem that the Fourth Gospel writer—Mary Magdalene—deliberately highlighted this contrast in the way she wrote about this event, and also that she clearly wished thereby to reinforce Yeshua's stress on the equal dignity of women.

This stress on the witness role of the Samaritan woman is further underscored by the Gospel's language. It says the villagers "believed . . . because of the woman's word" (*episteusan . . . dia ton logon*), almost the identical words recorded in Yeshua's "priestly" prayer at the Last Supper when Yeshua prays not only for his disciples "but also for those who believe in me through their word" (*pisteuont ōn dia tou logou*).[42] As Raymond E. Brown notes, "the Evangelist can describe both a woman and the [presumably male] disciples at the Last Supper as bearing witness to Yeshua through preaching and thus bringing people to believe in him on the strength of their word."[43] If, as I argue below, the penultimate author of the Fourth Gospel is Mary Magdalene, the great similarity of the wording is not likely mere coincidence.

One other point should be noted in connection with this story. As the crowd of Samaritans was walking out to see Yeshua, Yeshua was speaking to his disciples about the fields being ready for the harvest and how he was sending them to reap what others had sown. He was clearly speaking of the souls of humans, and most probably was referring directly to the approaching Samaritans. Such exegesis is standard. It is also rather standard to refer to "others" in general and only to Yeshua in particular as having been the sowers whose harvest the apostles were about to reap (e.g., in the twentieth-century Jerusalem Bible). But it would seem that the evangelist also meant specifically to include the Samaritan woman among those sowers, for immediately after she recorded Yeshua's statement to the disciples about their reaping what others had sown she added the above-mentioned verse: "Many Samaritans of that town had believed on the strength of the woman's testimony." The Samaritan woman preached the "Good News," the *euangelion*, of Yeshua, that is, she was an "evangelist."

§14 Yeshua Says "Yes," on Divorce

One of the most important stands of Yeshua in relation to the dignity of women was his position on marriage. His unpopular attitude toward marriage[44] presupposed a feminist view of women; they had rights and responsibilities equal to men. It was quite possible in Jewish law for men to have more than one wife (although this was probably not frequently the case in Yeshua's time, there are recorded instances, e.g., Herod, Josephus), though the reverse was not possible. Divorce also was a simple matter, to be initiated only by the man. In both situations women were basically chattel to be collected or dismissed as the man was able and wished to; the double moral standard was flagrantly apparent.

Yeshua rejected both by insisting on monogamy and restricting divorce in general; both the man and the woman were to have the same rights and responsibilities in their relationship toward each other.[45]

The key to properly understanding Yeshua's position on divorce lies in a rabbinic dispute at the time which raged between the School of Shammai, who said a wife can be divorced only for adultery (Yeshua here agreed with Shammai), and the School of Hillel, who said a wife can be divorced for any reason (here Yeshua disagreed with Hillel); this latter became the accepted position in subsequent Judaism.[46]

In the Mishnah (written down around the year 200 C.E.) we find the following:

The School of Shammai say: A man may not divorce his wife unless he has found something unseemly in her, for it is written, Because he hath found in her *indecency* in anything. And the School of Hillel say (He may divorce her) even if she spoiled a dish for him, for it is written, Because he hath found in her indecency in *anything*. Rabbi Akiba says: Even if he found another more beautiful than she, for it is written, And it shall be if she find no favour in his eyes.[47]

The recent work done by Ann Nyland, a professor of Greek and other ancient languages is extremely enlightening here. She has published a new translation of the New Testament based on the recent publication of thousands of first-century Greek papyri and inscriptions, which clarified many previous puzzles. Her work merits lengthy quotation:

In Matthew 19:3, the Pharisees asked Jesus, "Is it legal for a person to divorce his wife on the grounds of 'Any Matter'" [*pasan aitian*]? The Rabbis were asking Jesus about his interpretation of Deuteronomy 24:1 ["If a man marries a woman who becomes displeasing to him because he finds something indecent about her. . . ."]. The "Any Matter" is a technical term from Jewish divorce law, a form of divorce introduced by the Rabbi Hillel. The other type of divorce, on the ground of "General Sexual Immorality", was available to both men and women, both of whom were able to divorce the partner on the specific grounds based on Exodus 21:10–11 ["If a man marries another woman, he must provide. . . . If he does not provide her with these three things, she is to go free."]. This traditional divorce was becoming rarer by the start of the first century, being replaced by the "Any Matter" divorce, which was for men only, and popular as no grounds had to be shown and there was no court case. For an "Any Matter" divorce, the man simply had to write out a certificate of divorce and give it to his wife. By Jesus' time, the "Any Matter" was the more popular form of divorce, but the rabbis were still arguing about the legalities of it. The disciples of Shammai were particularly opposed to it. See Josephus, *AJ* 4.253, "He who desires to be divorced from his wife who is living with him on the grounds of 'Any Matter' must certify in writing. . . "; Philo, *Special Laws* 3.30, ". . . if a woman is parting from her husband on the grounds of 'Any Matter'"; see also the Rabbinic Commentary *Sifre/Deuteronomy* 269.

Jesus replied that a divorce on the grounds of "Any Matter" was not legal, that "whoever divorces his wife, unless it's on the grounds of 'General Sexual Immorality' [*epi porneiai*] and marries someone else, commits adultery". Jesus is simply saying that if someone divorces by a form other than the grounds of "General Sexual Immorality" form of divorce, they are not properly divorced and thus not free to remarry, and thus are committing adultery if they do so. He is continuing his statement that he disagrees with the "Any Matter" form of divorce.

It is most important to note the significance of the above. The way the passage has traditionally been translated implies that Jesus was asked the question, "Is it ever legal to divorce?" and he answered, "No, except on the grounds of sexual immorality." This is not the case. Jesus was asked if it was legal divorce on the grounds of "Any Matter" and he answered, "No, only on the grounds of General Sexual Immorality". In other words, he was disagreeing with the form of "Any Matter" form of divorce. He certainly was not saying that at that time, or in the time to come, people were never to divorce except for sexual immorality.[48]

This misunderstanding of the stance of Yeshua was one that was rather thoroughly assimilated by the Christian Church with disastrous effect. It was applied in an overly rigid way concerning divorce in Western Catholic Christianity, where divorce eventually was almost never allowed, even in the case permitted by Yeshua according to Matthew 19:9: "Whoever divorces his wife, except for unchastity"—*mē epi porneiai*.[49] Fortunately, the overly rigid position of Western Catholic Christianity was not taken by Eastern Orthodox Christianity, where divorce continues to be allowed.

§15 The Intellectual Life for Women

Perhaps the strongest and clearest affirmation on the part of Yeshua that the intellectual and "spiritual" life was just as proper to women as to men is recorded in Luke's Gospel in the description of a visit of Yeshua to the house of his friends Martha and Mary.[50] The first thing to be noted is that Yeshua allowed himself to be served by a woman, which was contrary to strict custom, although it might have been somewhat mitigated because it took place in the less rigid village area. This may seem strange today. However:

> There is an interesting corollary to the restrictions on conversing with women within the household, which, among other things, limited their role as a "serving being," albeit with a somewhat demeaning motivation. First, women did not eat with the men whenever there was a guest. This is made clear in two stories about Rabbi Nahman (third century C. E.), who, when at meal with a guest, asked him to send greetings to his (Nahman's) wife Yaltha. One story . . . is as follows: "Ulla was once at the house of Rabbi Nahman. They had a meal and he said grace, and he handed the cup of benediction to Rabbi Nahman. Rabbi Nahman said to him: "Please send the cup of benediction to Yaltha," (bBer. 51b) but Ulla refused to do so. At this point [author P.] Billerbeck comments: "women normally did not partake at a meal for guests; in order to honor them, the cup of benediction with some left over wine was sent to them." (H. L. Strack and P. Billerbeck, *Kommentar zum Neuen Testament aus Talmud und Midrasch*,

1926, vol. I. p. 882.) The same custom persists in the villages of Palestine today. While in Israel in 1972 I was in a number of houses of Arabs, Christian, Druze and Muslim, for meals, and never met the wives, or any other women; my friends had many similar experiences.

The separation of women, or rather, females, from the meals of the men was carried even further; the men were not even to be served by women. When the same Rabbi Nahman wanted to have his daughter, who was only a child, serve him and his guest a drink, he was rebuked with the clear quotation of the earlier Rabbi Samuel: "One must not be served by a woman." When Nahman argued that she was only a child, he was told: "Samuel said distinctly, that one must not be served by a woman at all, whether adult or child." (*Talmud*, bKid. 70a.)

Again, a similar custom persists among contemporary Palestinians; at all the meals I was at, we were never served by girls or women. The women did all the work of preparing the food and usually brought it as far as the door of the dining area, whether it was a room or house roof or whatever, and there it was taken by the youngest males and brought to the guests.[51]

Yeshua here clearly rejected the prevalent notion that the only proper place for women was "in the home." Martha took the woman's typical role and "was distracted with much serving." Mary, however, took the supposedly male role: she "sat at the Lord's feet and listened to his teaching." To sit at someone's feet is a rabbinic phrase indicating studying with that person. (It should be noted that this is a *terminus technicus* for being a disciple—which is even reflected in contemporary English speech when we say: I sat at the master's feet.) That phrase, coupled with the second half, "listened to his teaching," makes it abundantly clear that Mary was acting like a disciple of a teacher, a rabbi. Martha apparently thought Mary was out of place in choosing the role of the "intellectual," for she complained to Yeshua. But Yeshua's response was a refusal to force all women into the stereotype; he treated Mary first of all as a person (whose highest faculty is the intellect, the spirit) who was allowed to set her own priorities, and who in this instance had "chosen the better part." And Yeshua applauded her: "It is not to be taken from her." Again, when one recalls the Palestinian restriction on women studying the Scriptures or studying with rabbis, that is, engaging in the intellectual life or acquiring any "religious authority," it is difficult to imagine how Yeshua could possibly have been clearer in his insistence that women were called to the intellectual, the spiritual life just as were men.

In the course of their journey he came to a village, and a woman named Martha welcomed him into her house. She had a sister called Mary, who sat down at the Lord's feet and listened to him speaking. Now Martha who was distracted with all the serving said, "Lord, do you not care that my sister is leaving me to do the serving all by myself? Please tell her to help me." But the Lord answered: "Martha, Martha," he said, "you worry and fret about so many things, and yet few are needed, indeed only one. It is Mary who has chosen the better part; it is not to be taken from her."[52]

There is at least one other instance recorded in the Gospels when Yeshua clearly taught that the intellectual and spiritual life was definitely for women. One day as Yeshua was preaching, a woman from the crowd apparently was very deeply impressed and, perhaps imagining how happy she would be to have such a son, raised her voice to pay Yeshua a compliment. She did so by referring to his mother, and did so in a way that was probably not untypical at that time and place. But her image of a woman was sexually reductionist in the extreme (one that largely persists to the present): female genitals and breasts. "Blessed is the womb that bore you, and the breasts that you sucked!" Although this was obviously meant as a compliment, and although it was even uttered by a woman, Yeshua clearly felt it necessary to reject this "baby machine" image of women and insist again on the personhood, the intellectual and moral faculties, being primary for all: "But he said, 'Blessed rather are those who hear the word of God and keep it!'"

It is difficult to see how the primary point of this text could be anything substantially other than this. Luke and the sources he depended on (I argue below that he depended on a "Proto-Luke Gospel written by an unknown woman, whom I, for convenience, name Luka) must also have been quite clear about the sexual significance of this event. Otherwise, why would he (and they) have kept and included such a small event from all the months of Yeshua's public life? It was not retained *merely* because Yeshua said those who hear and keep God's word are blessed, for Luke had already recorded that statement of Yeshua in 8:21.[53] Rather, it was probably retained because keeping God's word was stressed by Yeshua as being primary in comparison to a woman's sexuality. Luke ("Luka") seems to have had a discernment here, as well as elsewhere, concerning what Yeshua was about in his approach to the question of women's status that has not been shared by subsequent Christians (and not shared by many of Luke/Luka's fellow Christians), for, in the explanation of this passage, Christians for two thousand years apparently have not seen its plain meaning—doubtless because of unconscious presuppositions about the status of women inculcated by their cultural and religious milieu.

Now as he was speaking, a woman in the crowd raised her voice and said, "Happy the womb that bore you and the breasts you sucked!" But he replied, "Blessed rather are those who hear the word of God and keep it!"[54]

§16 God as a Woman

Yeshua's attitude toward women was also reflected in the very language attributed to him in the Gospels. This fact was manifested in a variety of ways, which will be detailed below. For now, however, I wish to focus solely on another fact, namely, that the positive images of women that Yeshua employed were often very exalted, at times being associated with the Reign of Heaven, likened to the chosen people, and even to God herself!

As noted, Yeshua strove in many ways to communicate the notion of the equal dignity of women, and in one sense that effort was capped by his parable of the woman who found the lost coin: here Yeshua projected God in the image of a woman.[55] Luke/Luka recorded that the despised tax collectors and sinners were gathering around Yeshua, and consequently the Pharisees and scribes complained. Yeshua, therefore, related three parables in a row, all of which depicted God's being deeply concerned for that which was lost. The first story was of the shepherd who left the ninety-nine sheep to seek the one lost—the shepherd is God. The third parable is of the prodigal son—the father is God. The second story is of the woman who sought the lost coin—the woman is God! Yeshua did not shrink from the notion of God as feminine. In fact, it would appear that Luke/Luka's Yeshua included this womanly image of God quite deliberately at this point, for the scribes and Pharisees were among those who most of all denigrated women—just as they did the "tax-collectors and sinners."[56]

> The tax collectors and the sinners, meanwhile, were all seeking his company to hear what he had to say, and the Pharisees and the scribes complained. "This man," they said, "welcomes sinners and eats with them." So he spoke this parable to them:
>
> (1) "What person among you with a hundred sheep, losing one, would not leave the ninety-nine in the wilderness and go after the missing one till he found it? . . .
>
> (2) "Or again, what woman with ten drachmas would not, if she lost one, light a lamp and sweep out the house and search thoroughly till she found it? And then, when she had found it, call together her friends and neighbors? 'Rejoice with me,' she would say, 'I have found the drachma I lost.' In the same way, I tell you, there is rejoicing among the angels of God over one repentant sinner."
>
> (3) He also said, "A man had two sons. The younger said to his father, 'Father, let me have the share of the estate that would come to me.'"[57]

§17 Interim Conclusion

From this evidence it should be clear that Yeshua vigorously promoted the dignity and equality of women in the midst of a very male-dominated society: *Yeshua was a feminist*, and a very radical one.

§18 AN "ANDROGYNOUS" YESHUA

There is, however, also another message about Yeshua's attitude toward women and men to be found in the psychological image of Yeshua that is projected by the Gospels. That image is of an androgynous person, not in the sense of a combination of physical male and female characteristics, but rather the fusion and balance of so-called masculine and feminine psychological traits.

The notion that the significance of Yeshua lay in his humanity rather than specifically in his maleness is one that was stated clearly and even officially already in early Christianity. In the Nicene creed (325 C.E.) ancient Christians said of Yeshua, "et *homo* factus est," "and he became *human*." It did *not* say, "et *vir* factus est," "and he became *male* [*virile*]." There was even a limited amount of Christian painting of Yeshua as physically androgynous, but it was not very fully developed. However, if the question is asked whether the image of Yeshua in the Gospels reflects the psychologically so-called masculine or feminine traits, abundant material for an answer is at hand.

One of the humanly very destructive things our culture does is popularly to divide up various human traits into feminine and masculine ones, as if women naturally had one set and men the other. Such a division is scientifically unfounded; in fact scientific data is piling up which tend to indicate that such a division of traits as allegedly inborn is largely fallacious. Hence, even to continue to use the terms feminine characteristics and masculine characteristics tends to perpetuate the problem. So, until sexually neutral terms are developed and widely used, I will refer to these two sets of characteristics as *so-called* feminine and masculine characteristics.

Certain ways of acting, thinking, speaking, and so on, then, are popularly said to be specifically manly or their opposites, womanly. 1) Men are supposed to be reasonable and cool—women are to be persons of feeling and emotion; 2) men are to be firm, aggressive—women, gentle, peaceful; 3) men should be advocates of justice—women, of mercy; 4) men should have pride and self-confidence—women should have humility and reserve; 5) men are said to be the providers of security (food, clothing, shelter)—women, are the ones who need security; 6) men are supposed to be concerned with organization and structure—women with persons, especially children. In which of these divisions did Yeshua fit?

§19 Reasonable and Cool—Feeling and Emotion

Yeshua had a large number of vigorous, at times even extremely vicious, enemies, both in debate and in life-and-death situations. In debate: After Yeshua criticized the chief priests and scribes, "they waited their opportunity and sent agents to pose as men devoted to the Law to fasten on something he might say and so enable them to hand him over to the jurisdiction and authority of the governor. They put to him this question, 'Master, we know that you say and teach what is right; you favor no one, but teach the way of God in all honesty. Is it permissible for us to pay taxes to Caesar or not?'"[58] They were a clever lot, for Israel was occupied by Roman troops and the Jews, in general, consequently hated everything Roman with a passion, and especially the publicans (native tax collectors for Rome). If Yeshua said straight out to pay Roman taxes, he would have immediately lost his influence with the people, which would have suited his enemies. But if he said do not pay taxes, he would have immediately ended up in a Roman jail, or perhaps worse, which also would have suited his enemies.

"But he was aware of their cunning and said, 'Show me a denarius. Whose head and name are on it?' 'Caesar's,' they said. 'Well, then,' he said to them, 'give back to Caesar what belongs to Caesar—and to God what belongs to God.'" A most *reasonable* response: "As a result, they were unable to find fault with anything he had to say in public; his answer took them by surprise and they were silenced."[59]

In life-and-death situations: "When they heard this everyone in the synagogue was enraged. They sprang to their feet and hustled him out of the town, and they took him up to the brow of the hill their town was built on, intending to throw him down the cliff." Yeshua's reaction? "But he slipped through the crowd and walked away."[60] Real *cool.*

More examples could be given, but these would seem sufficient to place Yeshua in the "masculine" camp for category one.

On the other hand, once when Yeshua came to the little town of Nain he saw a funeral procession for a young man, "the only son of his mother, and she was a widow." The widow was in a desperate situation for in that culture women had almost no legal or economic standing except through a man: father, husband, or son. Understandably, the woman was weeping. A pitiable sight. But here Yeshua's reaction wasn't "cool." "When the Lord saw her he *felt* sorry for her. 'Do not cry' he said. Then he went up and put his hand on the bier and the bearers stood still, and he said, 'Young man, I tell you to get up.' And the dead man sat up and began to talk, and Yeshua gave him to his mother."[61] Yeshua responded with *feeling.*

Another time when Yeshua visited his friends Martha and Mary, two sisters, he learned that their brother Lazarus had died. Mary came to Yeshua and "when Yeshua saw her weeping, and the Jews who had accompanied her also weeping, he was troubled in spirit and *moved by the deepest emotions.* 'Where have you laid him?' he asked. 'Lord, come and see,' they said. *Yeshua began to weep,* which caused the Jews to remark, 'See how much *he loved* him!'"[62] Yeshua was clearly a person with deep emotions and showed them publicly.

Hence, it would seem that in category one Yeshua had not only the so-called masculine characteristics, but also the feminine ones.

§20 Firm and Aggressive—Gentle and Peaceful

There is no question but that Yeshua was *firm*. He certainly was firm when he said to his chief follower Peter in front of the rest of his followers: "Get behind me, Satan!"[63]

Yeshua's *aggressiveness* was expressed in several inflammatory statements: "I have come to bring fire to the earth, and how I wish it were blazing already!"[64] "Do not suppose that I have come to bring peace to the earth: it is not peace I have come to bring, but a sword."[65] "From John the Baptist's time until now the Reign of God has suffered violence, and the violent take it by force."[66] Yeshua was most aggressive in his verbal attack on his enemies among the scribes and Pharisees. *Six times* in a row he denounced them to their faces as frauds: "Alas for you, scribes and Pharisees, you frauds!" And he went on: "Alas for you, blind guides! . . . You blind men! . . . You blind guides! Straining out gnats and swallowing camels! . . . Alas for you, scribes and Pharisees, you hypocrites! You are like whitewashed tombs that look handsome on the outside, but inside are full of dead men's bones and every kind of corruption. In the same way you appear to people from the outside like good honest men, but inside you are full of hypocrisy and lawlessness. . . . Serpents, brood of vipers!"[67]

Yeshua's firmness and aggressiveness was not simply in his word, but in his actions as well:

> So they reached Jerusalem and he went into the Temple and began driving out those who were selling and buying there; he upset the tables of the money changers and the chairs of those selling pigeons. Nor would he allow anyone to carry anything through the Temple. And he taught them and said, "Does not scripture say: My house will be called a house of prayer for all peoples? But you have turned it into a robber's den."[68]

On the other hand Yeshua spoke of *gentleness*. He described himself in an image that was the epitome of gentleness: "Jerusalem, Jerusalem, you that kill the prophets and stone those who are sent to you! How often have I longed to gather your children, as a hen gathers her brood under her wing"[69]—note, Yeshua did not hesitate to use the feminine image of the hen to describe himself. In the Sermon on the Mount he said, "blessed are the *gentle*: they shall have the earth for their heritage."[70] With extraordinary gentleness Yeshua spoke to the weary and weighted: "Come to me, all you who labor and are overburdened, and I will give you rest. Shoulder my yoke and learn from me, for I am *gentle* and humble in heart, and you will find rest for your souls. Yes, my yoke is easy and my burden light."[71]

If a word other than "liberation" could also be used to sum up the life and message of Yeshua, it might be that pregnant Hebrew word, *shalom*, the fullness of active peace. In fact, it is recorded that at his birth angels sang, "Glory to God in high heaven, *peace* on earth to those on whom his favor rests."[72] Time and again when Yeshua healed someone he said, "Your faith has saved you, go in *peace*."[73] He instructed his disciples in peace: "Whatever house you go into, let your first words be, '*Peace* to this house!' And if a person of *peace* lives here, your *peace* will go and rest thereon."[74] Yeshua went "far out" on peace; he taught, "when someone slaps you on one cheek, turn the other!"[75] He promised much to the peace makers: "Blessed are the *peacemakers*: They shall be called the sons of God."[76] To his followers he gave more: "I have told you this so that you may find *peace* in me. . . . *Peace* I bequeath to you, my own *peace* I give you, a *peace* the world cannot give, this is my gift to you."[77]

Obviously Yeshua was firm, aggressive *and* gentle and peace loving; in category two he was both masculine and feminine.

§21 Justice—Mercy

Yeshua was a strong advocate of justice. To be just is to do what is right, and in society it is to follow the law (assuming the law is just). Yeshua insisted on scrupulously following the law: "Do not imagine I have come to abolish the Law or the Prophets. I have come not to abolish but to carry them out. I tell you solemnly, till heaven and earth disappear, not one dot, not one little stroke, shall disappear from the Law until its purpose is achieved. Therefore, whoever infringes even one of the least of these commandments and teaches others the same will be considered the least in the Reign of Heaven; but whoever keeps them and teaches them will be considered great in the Reign of Heaven."[78] In the Beatitudes Yeshua promised, "Blessed are those who hunger and thirst for *justice*; they shall have their fill."[79] Several times Yeshua spoke of the last judgment—where final justice would be meted out: "So will it be at the end of time. The Son of Humanity [Yeshua] will send his angels and they will gather out of his realm all things that provoke offenses and all who do evil, and throw them into the blazing furnace, where there will be weeping and grinding of teeth. Then the *just* will shine like the sun in the realm of their Father."[80] Again: "This is how it will be at the end of time: the angels will appear and separate the wicked from the *just* to throw them into the blazing furnace where there will be weeping and grinding of teeth."[81] And still again: "When the Son of Humanity comes in his glory . . . and all the nations will be assembled before him. Then he will separate them into two groups, as a shepherd separates sheep from goats. The sheep he will place on his right hand, the goats on his left. . . . These will go off to eternal punishment and the *just* to eternal life."[82] The epitaph on Yeshua's life, spoken by the Roman Centurion as Yeshua hung dead on the cross was: "Certainly this was a *just* man."[83]

Nevertheless, Yeshua also said, "It is not the healthy who need the doctor, but the sick. Go and learn the meaning of the words: What I want is *mercy*, not sacrifice. And indeed I did not come to call the *just*, but sinners."[84] Yeshua carried these words out, many times, just as we saw that he did with the woman who was caught in the act of adultery, an act punishable by death.[85] He said: "'Has no one condemned you?' She said, 'No one, Lord.' And Yeshua said, 'Neither do I condemn you; go, and do not sin again.'"[86] In the Beatitudes Yeshua promised: "Blessed are the merciful: They shall have *mercy* shown them."[87] In a similar vein he also taught: "Be *merciful*, even as your Father is merciful. Judge not, and you will not be judged; condemn not, and you will not be condemned; *forgive*, and you will be forgiven."[88] And how often should we forgive? That's what Peter wanted to know: "'Lord, how often shall my brother sin against me, and I *forgive* him? As many as seven times?' Yeshua said to him, 'I do not say to you seven times, but seventy times seven.'"[89]

Yeshua told many powerful parables, but perhaps his most moving was that of the prodigal son who took his inheritance before his father died, wasted it on wild living, and then finally crawled home in shame: "While he was still a long way off, his father caught sight of him and was deeply moved with *mercy*. He ran out to meet him, threw his arms around his neck, and kissed him. The son said to him, 'Father, I have sinned against God and against you; I no longer deserve to be called your son.' The father said . . . 'Let us eat and celebrate, because this son of mine was dead and has come back to life. He was lost and is found.'"[90]

But in this matter of mercy and forgiveness Yeshua went beyond all his predecessors—and successors. He preached the unheard-of doctrine of loving one's enemies: "You have learnt how it was said: You must love your neighbor and hate your enemy. But I say this to you: Love your enemies and pray for those who persecute you."[91] Incredible *words*. But Yeshua *did* just that at the most critical moment of his life—his death: "When they reached the place called The Skull, they crucified him there and the two criminals also, one on the right, the other on the left. Yeshua said, 'Father, *forgive them*; they do not know what they are doing.'"[92] To the bitter end, Yeshua was a man of mercy.

As in the first two categories, so also in this, Yeshua strongly exemplified both the so-called masculine and feminine traits. Yeshua was a person of justice, mercy, and forgiveness.

§22 Pride and Self-Confidence—Humility and Reserve

It might be thought that pride was foreign to Yeshua. But there is a kind of pride which, like its counterpart, humility, is simply truthfulness, affirming the good seen in oneself. A striking example of this pride occurred when a woman anointed Yeshua with some expensive perfumed ointment; there were complaints among his followers that the ointment should rather have been sold and the money given to the poor. "But Yeshua said, 'Leave her alone. Why are you upsetting her? What she has done for me is one of the good works. You have the poor with you always, and you can be kind to them whenever you wish, but you will not always have me.'"[93]

A perhaps even clearer example of this pride appeared when Yeshua made his triumphant entry into Jerusalem: "Great crowds of people spread their cloaks on the road, while others were cutting branches from the trees and spreading them in his path. The crowds who went in front of him and those who followed were all shouting: 'Hosanna to the Son of David! Blessings on him who comes in the name of the Lord! Hosanna in the highest heaven!' And when he entered Jerusalem, the whole city was in turmoil. . . . Some Pharisees in the crowd said to him, 'Teacher, rebuke your disciples.' He replied, 'If they were to keep silence, I tell you the very stones would cry out.'"[94] The self-assurance and self-confidence Yeshua exhibited when dragged before the chief council of Israel was extraordinary. Only in someone who had a very firm grasp on himself could such be found; despite the violence and threats involved, Yeshua was clearly in control, in a way that usually happens only in spy thrillers: After being beaten "he was brought before their Council and they said to him, 'If you are the Messiah, tell us.' 'If I tell you,' he replied, 'you will not believe me, and if *I* question *you*, you will not answer. But from now on, the Son of Humanity will be seated at the right hand of the Power of God.' [a quotation from Ps 110:1] Then they said, 'So, you are the Son of God then?' He answered, 'It is you who say I am.'"[95]

If possible, even more self-assured was Yeshua's attitude later before Pilate, the notoriously cruel and bloodthirsty Roman governor of the area. The man had the power of release and a vicious death, and yet Yeshua had a steel control over himself—and his judge: "Pilate said to Yeshua, 'Are you the king of the Jews?' Yeshua replied, 'Do you ask this of your own accord, or have others spoken to you about me?' Pilate answered, 'Am I a Jew? It is your own people and the chief priests who have handed you over to me: what have you done?' Yeshua replied, 'Mine is not a kingdom of this world; if my kingdom were of this world, my men would have fought to prevent my being surrendered to the Jews. But my kingdom is not of this kind.' 'So you are a king then?' said Pilate. 'It is you who say it,' answered Yeshua. 'Yes, I am a king. I was born for this; I came into this world for this: to bear witness to the truth;

and all who are on the side of truth listen to my voice.' [Pilate said:] 'Surely you know I have power to release you and I have power to crucify you?' 'You would have no power over me,' replied Yeshua, 'if it had not been given you from above.'"[96]

And yet, Yeshua is, rightly, known for teaching humility. As noted above, he said, "Learn from me, for I am gentle and *humble* in heart."[97] He put flesh on this teaching with a story: "When someone invites you to a wedding feast, do not take your seat in the place of honor. A more distinguished person than you may have been invited, and the person who invited you both may come and say, 'Give up your place to this person.' And then, to your embarrassment, you would have to go and take the lowest place. No; when you are a guest, make your way to the lowest place and sit there, so that, when your host comes, he may say, 'My friend, move up higher.' In that way, everyone with you at the table will see you honored. For everyone who exalts himself will be humbled, and the one who *humbles* himself will be exalted."[98]

Another story Yeshua told had much the same message. He spoke of a Pharisee in the temple who bragged to God about all his virtues, and of a hated tax collector who beat his breast and said, "God, be merciful to me, a sinner." "This man, I tell you, went home again at rights with God; the other did not. For everyone who exalts himself will be humbled, but the one who *humbles* himself will be exalted."[99]

Yeshua paradoxically also often taught his followers *reserve*. For example, he said: "Be careful not to parade your good deeds before people to attract their notice." Or, "When you give alms, do not have it trumpeted before you ... but when you give alms, your left hand must not know what your right is doing; your almsgiving must be secret." And further, "When you pray, do not imitate the hypocrites; they love to say their prayers standing up in the synagogues. ... But when you pray, go to your private room and, when you have shut your door, pray to your Father who is in that secret place."[100]

From this evidence, and still more in the Gospels, we would have to conclude that Yeshua combined the so-called masculine traits of pride and self-confidence with the supposedly feminine characteristics of humility and reserve.

§23 Provider of Security—Need for Security

The pattern that has emerged by now is so clear it hardly seems necessary to continue with a thorough analysis. Let us make it even briefer than above.

It was to Yeshua that his many followers flocked to find the *security* of the meaning of human life; of whom Peter said: "Lord, to whom shall we go? You have the words of eternal life";[101] who said of himself, "I am the bread of life. He who comes to me will never be hungry."[102] Yet it was also the same

Yeshua who sent his disciples out with "no purse, no haversack, no sandals";[103] who said to them, "that is why I am telling you not to worry about your life and what to eat, nor about your body and how you are to clothe it";[104] who said of himself, "foxes have holes and the birds of the air have their nests, but the Son of Humanity has nowhere to lay his head";[105] and who in the end felt a crushing need for security in his God: "My God, my God, why have you forsaken me?"[106] Yeshua both provided, and needed, security.

§24 Organization—People

Briefly, in the final category, note Yeshua's concern with *organization and structure* by recalling his carefully choosing his followers, his apostles—twelve to match symbolically the twelve tribes of Israel ("You will sit on thrones to judge the twelve tribes of Israel."[107]), the painful and painstaking instruction of his followers, his sending out of the seventy disciples like "lead men" in a political campaign today "to all the towns and places he himself was to visit."[108] But there is also Yeshua's intense concern with individual *persons*, his healing of numerous miserable people, lepers, blind, lame, paralytics, and so on (even the dead!), his affection for despised individuals, like the tax collector Zacchaeus,[109] the "sinful" woman,[110] and the adulterous woman.[111] There is also Yeshua's special concern for *children*, in fact, the holding of them up as a model: "People were bringing little children to him, for him to touch them. The disciples turned them away, but when Yeshua saw this he was indignant and said to them, 'Let the little children come to me; do not stop them; for it is to such as these that the Reign of God belongs. I tell you solemnly, anyone who does not welcome the Reign of God like a child will never enter it.' *Then he put his arms around them*, laid his hands on them and gave them his blessing."[112]

§25 Interim Conclusion

There is no question: the evidence shows overwhelmingly that Yeshua had the full range of so-called feminine and masculine characteristics in all the categories. What conclusion does that suggest? For one, it suggests that the division of characteristics by sex is quite artificial and false. Yeshua would have been less than a full human being if he had only the so-called masculine set. In fact, if he had had only one set exclusively he would have been so lopsided as to have been an inhuman monster. Unfortunately, this sex-role distortion has too often happened to the image of Yeshua in Christianity, past and present. At different times and places Yeshua has been seen solely as the great ruler of the world, a stern just judge whose favor must be curried through his more sympathetic mother. At other times Yeshua has been projected as all-feeling, "loving," or according to the "Jesus freaks," a person who "saves," without any just judgment involved. But Yeshua was not just so-called masculine or feminine. He was fully human.

The model of how to live an authentically human life, of how to attain "salvation"—to be "whole" (*Heil* in German, whence our English cognates like heal, hale, health), that is, to be "holy" (*heilig* in German, whence our English cognates like healthy, wholly, [w]holy)—that the Yeshua of the Gospels presents is not one that fits the masculine stereotype, which automatically relegates the "softer," "feminine" traits to women as being beneath the male—nor indeed is it the opposite stereotype. Rather, it is an egalitarian model. Thus, the same message that Yeshua taught in his words and dealings with women, namely, egalitarianism between women and men, was also taught by his own androgynous lifestyle.

What has often happened to the image of Yeshua in our society also tends to happen to most of us to a greater or lesser degree. Women are made to think they must cultivate only their "womanly" traits and avoid their "manly" ones, and the converse for men. But the liberating "Good News" of what Yeshua thought, taught, and wrought is that to be authentic humans, we must reject the false division of traits by sex. Thus, we will come to know, and love, our true, integrated self and will thereby be able to see our oneness with all our fellow humans (and most especially the oppressed), with all nature, and ultimately with the Source of all.

NOTES

1. Hanna Wolff, *Yeshua der Mann* (Stuttgart: Radius, 1979), 80–81.

2. For a broad treatment of this subject, see Leonard Swidler, *Women in Judaism: The Status of Women in Formative Judaism* (Metuchen, NJ: Scarecrow Press, 1976) and Leonard Swidler, *Biblical Affirmations of Woman* (Philadelphia: Westminster Press, 1979).

3. Mishnah, Sota 3, 4.

4. Talmud, bKid. 33b and Mishnah, Ber. 3, 3.

5. Talmud, bBer. 20b.

6. Tosephta, Ber. 7, 18 and Talmud, pBer. 13b; bMen. 43b.

7. Gal 3:28.

8. Mishnah, Abot 3, 6.

9. See Josephus, *Antiquities*, 15:418–19; *Jewish War*, 5, 5, par. 198–99; and Mishnah, Middoth 2, 5.

10. See Eliezer L. Sukenik, *Ancient Synagogues in Palestine and Greece* (London: 1934), 47ff. See also Bernadette J. Brooten, *Women Leaders in the Ancient Synagogue* (Chico, CA: Scholars Press), 1982.

11. Mishnah, Aboth 1, 5.

12. Talmud, bBer. 43b.

13. Talmud, bBer. 43b.

14. Mishnah, Shab. 4,1; Talmud, bB.K. 88a; and Josephus, *Antiquities*, 4:219.

15. Philo, *Flaccus*, 89; *De specialibus legibus*, 3:172.

16. Philo, *De specialibus legibus*, 3:169.

17. Talmud, bKid. 82b. Cf. Talmud, bSan. 100b.

18. Talmud, bNid. 31b.

19. Talmud, bNid. 31b.

20. Mishnah, Terum 15; Talmud, pKid. 4,66b, 32; and Soferim 41a in *The Minor Tractates of the Talmud*, ed. A. Cohen (London, 1971), 288.

21. Midrash, GnR. 45, 5.

22. 1 Cor 14:34.

23. 1 Tim 2:11–12.

24. *De cultu feminarum* 1.1, in *The Fathers of the Church*, 40:117–18.

25. Origen, *Selecta in Exodus* 28.17, in Migne, *Patrologia Graeca*, vol. 12, col. 296–97.

26. *Adversus Collyridianos*, in Migne, *Patrologia Graeca*, vol. 42, col. 740–41.

27. *Against Apion*, 2:201.

28. Jn 8:2–11.

29. For these variant texts and references, see Eberhard Nestle, ed. *Novum Testamentum Graece et Latine* (Stuttgart, 1954), 221, and Roger Gryson, *The Ministry of Women in the Early Church* (Collegeville, MN: Liturgical Press, 1976), 126.

30. See also Mk 15:40–41 and Mt 27:55–56 where the women are also reported to have "ministered" (*diekonoun*) to Yeshua.

31. *Sophia Jesu Christi*, in E. Hennecke and W. Schneemelcher, *New Testament Apocrypha* (Philadelphia: Westminster Press, 1963), 1:246. See Swidler, *Biblical Affirmations*, 195–96 for further similar texts.

32. Jn 20: 11ff.; Mt 28:9–10; and Mk 16:9ff.

33. Mt 9:18ff.; Mk 5:22ff.; and Lk 8:41ff.

34. Cf. Lk 7:11ff.

35. Cf. Jn 11.

36. Lk 7:36ff.

37. Jn 8:2–11.

38. Dt 22:22ff.

39. Mt 9:20ff.; Mk 5:25ff.; and Lk 8:43ff.

40. Lv 15:19ff.

41. Jn 4:5ff.

42. Jn 17:20.

43. Raymond E. Brown, "Roles of Women in the Fourth Gospel," *Theological Studies* (December 1975): 691.

44. Cf. Mt 19:10: "The disciples said to him, 'If such is the case of a man with his wife, it is not expedient to marry.'"

45. Cf. Mk 10:2ff. and Mt 19:3ff.

46. One should remember that Yeshua might well have had both Hillel and Shammai as his teachers in Galilee, and most of the time agreed with the School of Hillel. See Leonard Swidler, *Yeshua: A Model for Moderns* (Kansas City, MO: Sheed & Ward, 1988). Also, the School of Shammai was dominant until the destruction of Jerusalem in 70 C.E., after which the School of Hillel became dominant to the present.

47. Mishnah 1 Git. 9, 10. For a full discussion, see Leonard Swidler, *Women in Judaism: The Status of Women in Formative Judaism* (Metuchen, N.J.: Scarecrow Press, 1976), 198.

48. Ann Nyland, *The Source: New Testament with Extensive Notes on Greek Word Meaning* (Parramatta, Australia: Stirling and Smith, 2004), 192–93.

49. Cf. Mt 5:28.

50. Lk 10:38ff.

51. Swidler, *Women and Judaism*, 125.

52. Lk 10:38–42.

53. Cf. Mt 12:46–50 and Mk 3:31–35.

54. Lk 11:27–28.

55. Lk 15:8ff.

56. It should be noted that although Matthew has the story about the lost sheep (Mt 18:12–14), only Luke/Luka has the stories of the prodigal son and the woman whom God is like.

57. Lk 15:1–5, 8–12.

58. Mt 22:33; Mk 12:17; Lk 20:40.

59. Lk 20:20–26.

60. Lk 4:28–30.

61. Lk 7:11–15.

62. Jn 11:33–36.

63. Mk 8:33.

64. Lk 12:49.

65. Mt 10:34.

66. Mt 11:12.

67. Mt 23:13–33.

68. Mk 11:15–17.

69. Lk 14:34.

70. Mt 5:4.

71. Mt 11:28–30.

72. Lk 2:14.

73. Lk 7:50. See also Lk 8:48 and Mk 5:34.

74. Mt 10:5–6.

75. Lk 6:29.

76. Mt 5:9.

77. Jn 14:27, 16:33.

78. Mt 5:17–19.

79. Mt 5:6.

80. Mt 13:41–43.

81. Mt 13:49–50.

82. Mt 25:31–33, 46.

83. Lk 23:47.

84. Mt 9:13.

85. Dt 22:22ff.

86. Jn 8:7–11.

87. Mt 5:7.

88. Lk 6:36–37.

89. Mt 18:21–22.

90. Lk 15:20–24.

91. Mt 5:43 44.

92. Lk 23:33–34.

93. Mk 14:6–9.

94. Mt 21:8 10 and Lk 19:39–40.

95. Lk 22:67–70.

96. Jn 18:33–37; 19:10

97. Mt 11:29.

98. Lk 14:7–11.

99. Lk 18:9–14.
100. Mt 6:1–6.
101. Jn 6:67.
102. Jn 6:35.
103. Lk 10:4.
104. Lk 12:22.
105. Lk 9:58.
106. Mk 15:34.
107. Lk 22:30.
108. Lk 10:1.
109. Lk 19:1ff.
110. Lk 7:36ff.
111. Jn 8:1ff.
112. Mk 10:13–16.

• 3 •

§26 Women in Yeshua's Language

*H*aving made the initial case for Yeshua being both a feminist and an androgynous person, I would now like to present a more in-depth analysis of the evidence supporting the argument that Yeshua was a feminist.

Yeshua's positive attitude toward women is, as noted only very briefly earlier, also reflected in the language attributed to him in the Gospels. First, Yeshua often used women in his stories and sayings, something most unusual for his culture. Secondly, the images of women Yeshua used were never negative, but rather always positive, in dramatic contrast to his predecessors and contemporaries. Thirdly, these positive images of women were, as we saw in chapter 1, often very exalted, even likening women to God herself! Fourthly, Yeshua often taught a point by telling two similar stories or using two images, one of which featured a man and one a woman. This balance, among other things, indicated that Yeshua wanted it to be abundantly clear that his teaching, unlike that of other rabbis, was intended for both women and men—and he obviously wanted this to be clear to the men as well as the women, since he told these stories to all his disciples and at times even to crowds. These sexually parallel stories and images also confirm the presence of women among his hearers; they were used to bring home the point of a teaching in an image that was familiar to the women.

The sexually parallel stories and images used by Yeshua range from very brief pairings to lengthy parables. Their frequency in the Synoptic Gospels is impressive—there are nine of them. For example, the Reign of Heaven was likened to a mustard seed which a man sowed and to leaven which a woman put in her dough,[1] or, in the final days one man of two in the field and one woman of two grinding corn will be taken.[2] The ultimate in sexually parallel stories told by Yeshua, however, was the one in which God was cast in the likeness of a woman. It is worth gathering these parallel stories together here where the focus will be mainly on what they can tell us about Yeshua's attitude toward women. The significance of the variations in the recording of the stories and what they tell us of the attitude of the several evangelists and their sources toward women will be analyzed later.

§27 LAMP ON A LAMP STAND

In chapter 8 of his Gospel, Luke/Luka recorded that Yeshua taught in parables, stories with a message.[3] Luke/Luka then related two parables. It is very likely they are sexually parallel stories: the first is about a sower in a field; the second, about a person placing a lamp on a lamp stand instead of covering it with a bowl or putting it under a bed. The first story is in the context of the outdoor worker; the second is set indoors. In the first, the masculine gender is used all the way through: the sower (*ho spearōn*), his seed (*sporon autou*), he sowed (*en tō speirein auton*). In the second story the Greek uses no genders at all: "no one" (*oudeis*) is the sole subject of the sentence, with no personal pronouns, which would reflect gender, being used. Since in the first, the occupation is culturally male and the gender of the language is masculine, and since the context of the second is culturally female and no gender is reflected in the language, we may conclude that the stories were almost certainly meant by Luke/Luka to be sexually parallel stories, and, in the light of other sexually parallel stories and images used by Yeshua, were also most probably so meant by Yeshua. The first story would immediately be understood existentially by the men of the time, and the second likewise by the women. Both were clearly among Yeshua's listeners. He spoke to each of them.

Though both Mark and Matthew record the saying about putting a lamp on a lamp stand (and indeed Luke/Luka repeats it in another context—Lk 11:33–36), their report of it does not have the clearly sexually parallel quality that it so manifestly does in Luke 8.[4]

§28 THE WIDOW AND THE UNJUST JUDGE

In one pair of stories illustrating the need for perseverance in prayer, Yeshua used two tales remarkably similar in structure—and recollected and recorded by Luke/Luka. The one about the man is given so it can be compared with the one about the woman; the man is given no qualities superior to the woman. It will be helpful in this instance to review these two stories together here:

He also said to them, "Suppose one of you has a friend and goes to him in the middle of the night to say, 'My friend, lend me three loaves, because a friend of mine on his travels has just arrived at my house and I have nothing to offer him,' and the man answers from inside the house, 'Do not bother me. The door is bolted now, and my children and I are in bed; I cannot get up to give it to you.' . . . I tell you, if the man does not get up and give it to him for friendship's sake, persistence will be enough to make him get up and give his friend all he wants. So I say to you: Ask, and it will be given to you; search, and you will find."[5]

In the parallel story about the woman, Yeshua uses the image of a widow. She is up against the powerful male establishment, self-confessedly corrupt, at that; her opponent most probably was also a male property holder—of her property! Yeshua commends her for her popularly tagged "masculine" traits of aggressiveness and stick-to-itiveness. This is a comparison story and the widow is the image of, and is like, the chosen people (*tōn eklektōn*).[6]

Then he told them a parable about the need to pray continually and never lose heart. "There was a judge in a certain town," he said, "who had neither fear of God nor respect for humans. In the same town there was a widow who kept on coming to him and saying, 'I want justice from you against my enemy!' For a long time he refused, but at last he said to himself, 'Maybe I have neither fear of God nor respect for humans, but since she keeps pestering me I must give this widow her just rights, or she will persist in coming and worry me to death.'"

And the Lord said, "You notice what the unjust judge has to say? Now will not God see justice done to his chosen who cry to him day and night, even when he delays to help them? I promise you, he will see justice done to them, and done speedily."[7]

§29 A PROPHET IN HIS OWN COUNTRY

In illustrating his statement, "no prophet is ever accepted in his own country," Yeshua again used two brief stories, one centering on women and the other on men. Again the widow is the most down-and-out example of women, matched in the male realm only by outcast lepers. Not only is Luke/Luka the only recorder of this sexually paired set of stories, but s/he also relates the women's story first, both subtle signs of Luke/Luka's sympathy for the women's cause.

And he went on, "I tell you solemnly, no prophet is ever accepted in his own country. There were many widows in Israel, I can assure you, in Elijah's day, when heaven remained shut for three years and six months and a great famine raged throughout the land, but Elijah was not sent to any one of these: he was sent to a widow at Zarephath, a Sidonian town. And in the prophet Elisha's time there were many lepers in Israel, but none of these was cured, except the Syrian, Naaman."[8]

§30 WOMEN AT THE "END OF DAYS"

Three of the pairs of sexually parallel stories concern aspects of the end of the world. One point of the first pair is that there is no ultimate importance in the distinction between men and women; important human distinctions are founded on bases other than sex. "It will be like this when the Son of Humanity comes. Then of two men in the fields, one is taken, one left. Of two women at the millstone grinding, one is taken, one left."[9] Luke/Luka, with slightly different pairings, makes the same point.[10] In the Greek it is clear that the two persons in verse 34 are male and the two in verse 35 are female. "I tell you, on that night two [men] will be in one bed: one will be taken, the other left. Two women will be grinding corn together: one will be taken, the other left. [There will be two men in the fields: one will be taken, the other left.]"[11]

§31 THE QUEEN OF THE SOUTH

The second pair of images concerning the final day is an interesting but strange coupling. The image of the men of Nineveh condemning Yeshua's generation fits well with the preceding reference to Jonah. But the reference to the Queen of the South (Sheba) can be connected only because of a similar condemnation of Yeshua's generation for not accepting him. Yeshua would not have made these two statements at the same time. But the statement about the Queen of the South probably was on a list of sayings of Yeshua which both Luke/Luka and Matthew had access to. It is likely that Yeshua actually made something like both statements—otherwise why would the Queen of Sheba be brought up by Luke/Luka or his predecessor at all?—and it is likely that the two statements were linked together here partly because of the similar condemnation. But again, it is still another example of sexually parallel stories that probably go back to Yeshua, even if the evangelists, or their sources, are responsible for putting them together here. It is also interesting to note that pro-feminist Luke, or rather Luka, places the image of the women first, while Matthew gives first place to the man.[12]

§32 WISE AND FOOLISH BRIDESMAID

The unknown or uncertain quality of the final day is likewise illustrated by the third pair of images concerning the end of time, but it focuses on the uncertainness of when that day will be. The first story is of an honest and dishonest male servant:

> What sort of servant, then, is faithful and wise enough for the master to place him over his household to give them their food at the proper time? Happy that servant if his master's arrival finds him at his employment. I tell you solemnly, he will place him over everything he owns. But as for the dishonest servant who says to himself, "My master is taking his time," and sets about beating his fellow servants and eating and drinking with drunkards, his master will come on a day he does not expect and at an hour he does not know. The master will cut him off and send him to the same fate as the hypocrites, where there will be weeping and grinding of teeth."[13]

Immediately following is the second story, about the wise and foolish bridesmaids. The structure of the story is almost exactly the same as the one about the men, again illustrating the parity women and men held in Yeshua's eyes. It is difficult to believe that these two stories, or something very like them, were not told by Yeshua, for who else would have been at such pains to compose two such similar stories illustrating the same point, with one focusing on women, if not Yeshua? Of course Matthew, or the source Matthew used, might well be credited with setting down this parallel pair together:

> The Reign of Heaven will be like this: Ten bridesmaids took their lamps and went to meet the bridegroom. Five of them were foolish and five were sensible: the foolish ones did take their lamps, but they brought no oil, whereas the sensible ones took flasks of oil as well as their lamps. The bridegroom was late, and they all grew drowsy and fell asleep. But at midnight there was a cry, "The bridegroom is here! Go out and meet him." At this, all those bridesmaids woke up and trimmed their lamps, and the foolish ones said to the sensible ones, "Give us some of our oil: our lamps are going out." But they replied, "There may not be enough for us and for you; you had better go to those who sell it and buy some for yourselves." They had gone off to buy it when the bridegroom arrived. Those who were ready went in with him to the wedding hall and the door was closed. The other bridesmaids arrived later. "Lord, Lord," they said, "open the door for us." But he replied, "I tell you solemnly, I do not know you." So stay awake, because you do not know either the day or the hour.[14]

It is interesting to note that here Luke does not have the story of the ten bridesmaids, but rather one of servants waiting for the master to return from a wedding feast. Luke uses the generic *anthrōpois* for men and the "generic" masculine gender for servants (*douloi*), so that there is no clear indication if men or both men and women were involved; it could not have been just women. In Mark, almost certainly, just men are involved in the single brief story of the servants (masculine *doulois*) and the doorkeeper (masculine *thyrōroi*).[15]

§33 HEAVEN THE LEAVEN IN DOUGH

Even the Reign of Heaven is depicted in a pair of sexually parallel images: one is a man sowing mustard seed, and the other a woman mixing leaven in flour. The main point of the second comparison is that the Reign of Heaven, like leaven in flour, is initially very small, but in the end it transforms the whole. Yeshua was clearly telling women that though they might seem insignificant in this world, they could by association with the Reign of Heaven share in the transformation of the whole world. Another dimension of meaning is also possible. In that religious culture, leaven was seen as an agent of corruption, and *un*leaven was a sign of God's purity and rule—this can be best seen in the Feast of the Passover. Yeshua's use of leaven, not as a sign of corruption and the lack of God's rule, but the opposite, as a sign of the Reign of Heaven, was probably a deliberate choice on his part to show that what often was thought to be a source of sin was really a source of salvation—and this was done with the intimate association of a woman as the provider of the key image, leaven. Meaning: woman is not the provider of the source (or occasion) of sin, as was usually thought, but the provider of the source of salvation.

Luke/Luka apparently thought this second dimension was intended in Yeshua's saying, for s/he immediately followed it with another set of sayings of Yeshua which make that point—or a similar one—primary: that is, those who thought they certainly would find salvation do not, and those who were not expected to, do.

> He put another parable before them, "The Reign of Heaven is like a mustard seed which a man took and sowed in his field. It is the smallest of all the seeds, but when it has grown it is the biggest shrub of all and becomes a tree so that the birds of the air come and shelter in its branches."
>
> He told them another parable, "The Reign of Heaven is like the leaven a woman took and mixed in with three measures of flour till it was leavened all through."[16]

§34 GOD IS LIKENED TO A WOMAN

As detailed in §16, the ultimate in sexually parallel stories told by Yeshua included one in which God was cast in the likeness of a woman. Yeshua told three stories about someone who lost something, and in each story the one who sought what was lost was an image of God: The father of the prodigal son, the good shepherd, the woman who lost the coin.

There have been some instances in Christian history when the Holy Spirit has been associated with a feminine character.[17] For example, the Syrian *Didascalia* (third century), in speaking of various offices in the church, states: "The deaconess, however, should be honored by you as the image of the Holy Spirit." But in the history of later Christian biblical interpretation nowhere are these images of God, presented here by Luke/Luka, ever used in a Trinitarian manner—that is, thereby giving the Holy Spirit a feminine image. Yet, after the establishment of the doctrine of the Trinity, in the fourth century, this passage would seem to have been particularly apt for Trinitarian interpretation: the prodigal son's father is God the Father (this interpretation has in fact been quite common in Christian history); since Yeshua elsewhere identified himself as the good shepherd, the shepherd seeking the lost sheep is Yeshua, the Son (this standard interpretation is reflected in, among other things, the often seen picture of Yeshua carrying the lost sheep on his shoulders); the woman who sought the lost coin should "logically" be the Holy Spirit, but she has not been so interpreted. Should such lack of "logic" be attributed, as is often suggested, to the Christian abhorrence of pagan goddesses? But then why did Christian abhorrence of pagan gods not also result in a Christian rejection of a male image of God? The only answer can be an underlying widespread Christian deprecatory attitude toward women that blinded most Christian theologians and commentators to the strong feminism of Yeshua in the Gospels.

> The tax collectors and the sinners, meanwhile, were all seeking his company to hear what he had to say, and the Pharisees and the scribes complained. "This man," they said, "welcomes sinners and eats with them." So he spoke this parable to them:
>
> (1) "What person among you with a hundred sheep, losing one, would not leave the ninety-nine in the wilderness and go after the missing one till he found it? . . .
>
> (2) "Or again, what woman with ten drachmas would not, if she lost one, light a lamp and sweep out the house and search thoroughly till she found it? And then, when she had found it, call together her friends and neighbors? 'Rejoice with me,' she would say, 'I have found the drachma I lost.'

In the same way, I tell you, there is rejoicing among the angels of God over one repentant sinner."

(3) He also said, "A man had two sons. The younger said to his father, 'Father, let me have the share of the estate that would come to me.'"[18]

§35 EXTRA-CANONICAL SEXUALLY PARALLEL STORIES OF YESHUA

Whether any of the "new" sayings attributed to Yeshua found in the third-century Gnostic Christian *Gospel of Thomas* can in any demonstrable way be plausibly traced back to Yeshua is debated by scholars. Much of this "Gospel" is a variation of what is found in the four canonical Gospels, but it is nevertheless interesting to find two quite different stories attributed to Yeshua that describe what the Reign of the Father (rather than of God or heaven, as in the canonical Gospels) is like in sexually parallel fashion. It is difficult to be certain exactly what the meaning of the stories is, but that one is directed primarily at women and the other at men is clear, indicating a continuation of the pattern of sexually parallel stories, if not by Yeshua himself, then at least by some of his followers who must have thought it was "in keeping" with his style. After *Logion* ("Saying") number 96, which relates how the Reign of the Father is like a woman who mixed leaven in some dough, *Logia* 97 and 98 are as follows:

(*Logion* 97) Yeshua said: "The Kingdom of the [Father] is like a woman who was carrying a jar full of meal. While she was walking (on a) distant road, the handle of the jar broke. The meal streamed out behind her on the road. She did not know (it); she had noticed no accident. When she came into her house, she put down her jar, she found it empty."

(*Logion* 98) Yeshua said: "The Kingdom of the Father is like a man who wished to kill a powerful man. He drew the sword in his house, he stuck it into the wall, in order to know whether his hand would carry through; then he slew the powerful man."[19]

§36 YESHUA IN A FEMALE IMAGE

Yeshua did not shrink from applying a female image to himself either; he likened himself to a hen gathering her chicks under her wings. Such an image is interesting because throughout the Hebrew Bible the image of protecting wings is often used in connection with God (e.g., Ps 17:8, 36:7, 57:1, 61:4, 63:7, 91:4; Ru 2:12; Is 31:5; Dt 32:11). But in all these images there is never any intimation of the feminine. It is usually a prayer asking for shelter under God's wings. There is one reference to birds hovering in protection[20] and one to an eagle "hovering over its young,"[21] but nowhere to a female bird. The use of that image in the Jewish tradition was left to Yeshua: "Jerusalem, Jerusalem, you that kill the prophets and stone those who are sent to you! How often have I longed to gather your children, as a hen gathers her brood under her wings, and you refused!"[22]

Again, when Yeshua was in the temple on the last day of the Feast of Succoth, at which there was a procession bringing "living" water from the fountain of Shiloh to the temple as a sign of the future messianic salvation, he uttered a saying that cast him in a female image. He said, "If anyone is thirsty, let him come to me and drink!" The image of drinking from a human being can only be that of a mother.[23]

Yeshua went on to apply a Scripture paraphrase to himself: "From his *koilia* shall flow fountains of living water." *Koilia* basically means a hollow place and is used to refer to the whole or part of the abdomen. In the context of feeding from within, the reference would be to the upper part of the body cavity, and the word *koilia* could properly be translated "breast." But modern translations generally are fearful of doing the obvious and projecting Yeshua in a maternal image although Yeshua was not.

> On the last and greatest day of the festival, Yeshua stood there and cried out: "if anyone is thirsty, let him come to me! Let him come and drink who believes in me! As scripture says, 'From his breast (*koilia*)shall flow fountains of living water.'" He was speaking of the Spirit which those who believed in him were to receive; for there was no Spirit as yet because Yeshua had not yet been glorified.[24]

NOTES

1. Mt 13:31–33 and Lk 18–21.

2. Mt 24: 39–41. For further discussion of sexually parallel stories in the New Testament, see Leonard Swidler, *Biblical Affirmations of Woman* (Philadelphia: Westminster Press, 1979), 164ff.

3. Lk 8:10.

4. Lk 8:4–8, 16–17. Cf. Mk 4:1–9, 21–22; Mt 13:4–9, 5:15; and Lk 11:33–36.

5. Lk 11:5–9.

6. Cf. 2 John, which is addressed to the chosen mistress, *eklekta kyria*. See §273.

7. Lk 18:1–8.

8. Lk 4:24–27.

9. Mt 24:39–41.

10. Though the great majority of the best ancient Greek manuscripts do *not* contain v. 36 about the two men in the field, some do; but this is most likely due to scribes transferring that verse from the parallel in Mt 24:40, quoted just above.

11. Lk 17:34–36.

12. Mt 12:38–42 and Lk 11:29–32.

13. Mt 24: 45–51. Cf. Lk 12:42–46 and Lk 12:45, which says, female servants as well.

14. Mt 25:1–13.

15. Cf. Lk 12:35–40 and Mk 13:34–37.

16. Mt 13:31–33. Cf. Lk 13:18–21.

17. See §84.

18. Lk 15:1–5, 8–12.

19. *Gospel of Thomas, New Testament Apocrypha*, 1:289–90.

20. Is 31:5.

21. Dt 32:11.

22. Lk 13:34. Cf. Mt 23:37.

23. The fourteenth-century English mystic, Dame Julian of Norwich, did have a scriptural basis for her vision of Yeshua as mother: "And thus is Jesus our true Mother in kind [nature] of our first making; and he is our true Mother in grace by his taking of our made kind. All the fair working and all the sweet kindly offices of most dear Motherhood are appropriated to the second Person." Dame Julian of Norwich, *The Revelations of Divine Love of Julian of Norwich*, trans. James Walsh (London: Burns & Oates, 1961), chap. 59.

24. Jn 7:37–39.

• *4* •

§37 Women in Yeshua's Teaching

§38 MARRIAGE AND THE DIGNITY OF WOMEN

*N*ote has already been taken of Yeshua's setting women on a par with men on the question of divorce (see §14). But there is still more to be said about this topic. Special note should be taken of the version of Yeshua's words recorded by Mark, judged by many scholars as most likely the closest to Yeshua's original words and certainly faithful to the early tradition that here Yeshua set forth a new teaching, clearly in favor of putting women on the same level as men in the crucial matter of marriage fidelity. In Jewish law, adultery could be committed *only* against a husband, that is, sex between a husband and an unmarried woman was *not* adultery against his wife, but sex between a wife and any man other than her husband was adultery against her husband (deserving the death penalty!). But here in Mark's Gospel Yeshua speaks of a husband "being guilty of adultery against *her* [his wife]," in that culture a revolutionary egalitarianism. It is clear that the parallel accounts in Matthew and Luke also describe the husband as capable of adultery. But to underscore the newness of this teaching Mark's version includes "against her" (*ep' autēn*). "He said to them, 'The man who divorces his wife and marries another is guilty of adultery against her. And if a woman divorces her husband and marries another she is guilty of adultery, too.'"[1]

Yeshua clearly saw women as having equal rights and responsibilities within marriage. This was because he did not see a woman's existence as totally defined by her relationship to a man, that is, as someone's daughter, wife, mother, widow, or harlot; her total being was not caught up in marriage. Rather, Yeshua saw women as being, first of all, individual persons, a view expressed in his response to the Sadducees that, at the fulfillment of human history, each human being will be simply an individual person, that "men and women do not marry; no, they are like the angels in heaven." The Sadducees' question about who the woman would belong to was rejected as containing a false assumption.

> That day some Sadducees—who deny that there is a resurrection—approached him and they put this question to him, "Master, Moses said that if a man dies childless, his brother is to marry the widow, his sister-in-law, to raise children for his brother. Now we had a case involving seven brothers; the first married and then died without children, leaving his wife to his brother; the same thing happened with the second and the third and so on to the seventh, and then last of all the woman herself died. Now at the resurrection to which of those seven will she be wife, since she had been married to them all?" Yeshua answered them, "You are wrong, because you understand neither the scriptures nor the power of God. For at the resurrection men and women do not marry; no, they are like the angels in heaven. And as for the resurrection of the dead, have you never read what God said to you: I am the God of Abraham, the God of Isaac and the God of Jacob? God is God, not of the dead, but of the living."[2]

§39 MARRIAGE AND THE DIGNITY OF WOMEN—AGAIN

It is interesting to note here the remarks of a modern Jewish scholar commenting on the theme of divorce in Matthew 5:31–32:

> In these verses the originality of Jesus is made manifest. So far, in the Sermon on the Mount, we have found nothing which goes beyond Rabbinic religion and Rabbinic morality, or which greatly differs from them. Here we do. The attitude of Jesus towards women is very striking. He breaks through oriental limitations in more directions than one. For (1) he associates with, and is much looked after by, women in a manner which was unusual; (2) he is more strict about divorce; (3) he is also more merciful and compassionate. He is a great champion of womanhood, and in this combination of freedom and pity, as well as in his strict attitude to divorce, he makes a new departure of enormous significance and importance. If he had done no more than this, he might justly be regarded as one of the great teachers of the world.[3]

§40 YESHUA AT CANA

According to the Fourth Gospel, the first of the public signs of Yeshua was worked by him at the, at least indirect, bidding of a woman, his mother. Also to be noted in this account is Yeshua's coupling his respect for his mother with a distancing of himself from her, part of his attempt to loosen the too-often oppressive bonds of family in that culture. Yeshua addresses his mother as "woman," a polite and proper enough public usage with other women, but, according to contemporary literature, surely not usual with one's mother. This "distancing" move is reinforced by his remark, "How does this concern of yours involve me?"[4]

Yeshua's presence at and support of the wedding at Cana also confirms his affirmation of marriage and rejection of hyper-asceticism. Perhaps the evangelist (a woman evangelist will be discussed passim below) had this particularly in mind when deciding to include this account, as a counterweight to the encratic and Gnostic elements that were springing up at the time of the composition of his Gospel, for those movements tended to be anti-marriage and/or anti-sex.

§41 YESHUA AFFIRMS PARENTS

Yeshua affirmed parenthood. Luke/Luka notes that Yeshua "lived under the authority" of his mother and father.[5] And Yeshua reiterated the traditional affirmation of parenthood in his own words on one occasion when he accused his opponents of avoiding their obligations to their mothers and fathers. However, in this support of parents, Yeshua in no way set the father's prerogatives above those of the mother's.

> Pharisees and scribes from Jerusalem then came to Yeshua and said, "Why do your disciples break away from the tradition of the elders? They do not wash their hands when they eat food." "And why do you," he answered, "break away from the commandment of God for the sake of your tradition? For God said: Do your duty to your father and mother, and: Anyone who curses father or mother must be put to death. But you say, 'If anyone says to his father or mother: Anything I have that I might have used to help you is dedicated to God,' he is rid of his duty to father or mother. In this way you have made God's word null and void by means of your tradition. Hypocrites!"[6]

§42 YESHUA'S PROBLEMS WITH HIS FAMILY

Despite Yeshua's affirmation of marriage and parenthood, he had severe problems with his family. Early in his public life they tried to pack him off because they thought he was insane. More than that, he was rejected by his home community simply because they knew his family. His family not only tried to lock him in, but their very existence also tended to lock the community out.

> He went home again, and once more such a crowd collected that they could not even have a meal. When his family heard of this, they set out to take charge of him, convinced he was out of his mind.[7]

> Going from that district, he went to his home town and his disciples accompanied him. With the coming of the Sabbath he began teaching in the synagogue and most of them were astonished when they heard him. They said, "Where did the man get all this? What is this wisdom that has been granted him, and these miracles that are worked through him? This is the carpenter, surely, the son of Mary, the brother of James and Joset and Jude and Simon? His sisters, too, are they not here with us?" And they would not accept him. And Yeshua said to them, "A prophet is only despised in his own country, among his own relations and in his own house"; and he could work no miracle there, though he cured a few sick people by laying his hands on them. He was amazed at their lack of faith.[8]

§43 SPIRITUAL BONDS ABOVE BLOOD BONDS

In Near Eastern society, despite positive qualities, the demands of the patriarchal family relationships were at times overwhelming, often crushing individual personal growth, and most especially was this so for women. Almost any rule could be bent or broken, but not the obligations to family. Yeshua, having experienced family repression himself, clearly and often fought this social form of oppression, which weighed most often and most heavily on women. He insisted on personal, spiritual bonds as being more important than blood bonds.

> He was still speaking to the crowds when his mother and his brothers appeared; they were standing outside and were anxious to have a word with him. But to the man who told him this Yeshua replied, "Who is my mother? Who are my brothers?" And stretching out his hand towards his disciples he said, "Here are my mother and my brothers. Anyone who does the will of my Father in heaven, he is my brother and sister and mother."[9]

§44 YESHUA DISMANTLES RESTRICTIVE FAMILY BONDS

A number of sayings of Yeshua stress following him as rising above the bonds of family obligations so vigorously as to be clearly hyperbolic in tone at times, as, for example, "hating" one's parents (in Aramaic "hating" really means "loving less"). What is apparent is Yeshua's setting himself the task of dismantling the awesomely powerful restrictive forces of the patriarchal family, whose most obvious victims were women.

(1) Peter took this up. "What about us?" he asked him. "We have left everything and followed you." Yeshua said, "I tell you solemnly, there is no one who has left house, brothers, sisters, father, children or land for my sake and for the sake of the gospel who will not be repaid a hundred times over, houses, brothers, sisters, mothers, children and land—not without persecutions now in this present time, and in the world to come eternal life."[10]

(2) Do not suppose that I have come to bring peace to the earth: it is not peace I have come to bring, but a sword. For I have come to set a man against his father, a daughter against her mother, a daughter-in-law against her mother-in-law. A man's enemies will be those of his household.[11]

(3) Anyone who prefers father or mother to me is not worthy of me. Anyone who prefers son or daughter to me is not worthy of me.[12]

(4) And everyone who has left houses, brothers, sisters, father, mother, children or land for the sake of my name will be repaid a hundred times over, and also inherit eternal life.[13]

(5) Do you suppose that I am here to bring peace on earth? No, I tell you, but rather division. For from now on a household of five will be divided: three against two and two against three; the father divided against the son, son against father, mother against daughter, daughter against mother, mother-in-law against daughter-in-law, daughter-in-law against mother-in-law.[14]

(6) If anyone comes to me without hating his father, mother, wife, children, brothers, sisters, yes and his own life too, he cannot be my disciple.[15]

(7) Then Peter said, "What about us? We left all we had to follow you." He said to them, "I tell you solemnly, there is no one who has left house, wife, brothers, parents or children for the sake of the reign of God who will not be given repayment many times over in this present time and, in the world to come, eternal life."[16]

§45 THE WIDOW'S MITE

One of the essential lessons that Yeshua taught, in words and actions, was that what is important about a human being is the intention (*kavod* in Hebrew), integrity, and inner spirit of the person rather than the outward forms of strength, beauty, wealth, power, piety, and so forth. But because the reverse was most often adhered to, Yeshua clearly took up the cause of the oppressed, insisting: "Blessed are the poor," "The last shall be first," "The humble shall be exalted."

Yeshua combined these lessons into one when he contrasted the giving of money by the rich (*plousioi* masculine!) on the one hand and by a poor widow on the other. Yeshua depicted the extremes by rich men on one side, and the lowest of the oppressed on the other, a poor widow, a woman whose almost sole value in society, being a man's wife, was gone. Yeshua was clearly aware of women's oppressed state in society—and took their side: "I tell you solemnly, this poor widow has put more in than all who have contributed to the treasury."

> He sat down opposite the treasury and watched the people putting money into the treasury, and many of the rich put in a great deal. A poor widow came and put in two small coins, the equivalent of a penny. Then he called his disciples and said to them, "I tell you solemnly, this poor widow has put more in than all who have contributed to the treasury; for they have all put in money they had over, but she from the little she had has put in everything she possessed, all she had to live on."[17]

§46 HEALING OF WOMEN BY YESHUA

Unlike other Jewish rabbis about whom stories of miraculous healing and raising from the dead are recorded, Yeshua does heal women. They are seen by him first as persons with both physical needs and spiritual strengths (faith), the two of which call forth his healing action. Perhaps the reason there is no recorded instance of a Jewish woman ever asking Yeshua for a cure is that Jewish women were conditioned by their culture to assume they would not be recognized by a public religious figure.

It is significant that the first healing by Yeshua recorded by the oldest Gospel, Mark (and followed in this by Lk 4:38–39, but not Mt 8:14–15), at the very beginning of Yeshua's public life, was the healing of a woman, Simon Peter's mother-in-law.

> On leaving the synagogue, he went with James and John straight to the house of Simon and Andrew. Now Simon's mother-in-law had gone to bed with fever, and they told him about her straightaway. He went to her, took her by the hand, and helped her up. And the fever left her and she began to wait on them.[18]

§47 HEALING ON THE SABBATH

Luke/Luka, whose Gospel, as we have seen, exhibits the greatest sympathy for women by the relatively large number of events and stories involving women he includes, reports three healings on the Sabbath—which caused Yeshua difficulties. Two were healings of men, the other, the healing of a woman. The Fourth Gospel also records the healing of two men on the Sabbath,[19] whereas both Mark[20] and Matthew[21] report only the healing of one man; none of the three report the healing of any women on the Sabbath. Perhaps Luke's Hellenistic background and intended audience encouraged his taking Luka as a basis of his Gospel, thereby emphasizing Yeshua's feminism, since the Hellenistic world experienced an extended "women's liberation" movement.[22] It should also be noted that in Luke/Luka's story Yeshua not only healed the woman on the Sabbath, but he also spoke to her in public, an unseemly thing for any man in that culture, especially a rabbi. He also referred to her as a "*daughter* of Abraham," an almost unheard-of honorific, although son of Abraham[23] is a standard phrase used throughout Hebrew and Jewish literature as well as by Yeshua (e.g., Lk 19:9) as a way of referring to a member (male) of the chosen people. For Yeshua, women were also clearly full-fledged participants of the people and covenant of God.

> One Sabbath day he was teaching in one of the synagogues, and a woman was there who for eighteen years had been possessed by a spirit that left her enfeebled; she was bent double and quite unable to stand upright. When Yeshua saw her he called her over and said, "Woman, you are rid of your infirmity," and he laid his hands on her. And at once she straightened up, and she glorified God.

> But the synagogue official was indignant because Yeshua had healed on the Sabbath, and he addressed the people present. "There are six days," he said "when work is to be done. Come and be healed on one of those days and not on the Sabbath." But the Lord answered him. "Hypocrites!" he said. "Is there one of you who does not untie his ox or his donkey from the manger on the Sabbath and take it out for watering? And this woman, a *daughter* of Abraham whom Satan has held bound these eighteen years— was it not right to untie her bonds on the Sabbath day?" When he said this, all his adversaries were covered with confusion, and all the people were overjoyed at all the wonders he worked.[24]

§48 THE PAGAN WOMAN AND YESHUA

According to Matthew, Yeshua conceived of his mission as being directed first of all to God's chosen people, the Jews. The first recorded instance of his going beyond the limits of his commission was to heal a female, at the persistent insistence of a woman. It was her human quality, her "faith," that Yeshua perceived and that moved him to extend himself; she was not treated as an inferior category, a woman, but as a "person," who had "great faith." It is also interesting to note that this is the only recorded instance wherein Yeshua is bested in a verbal exchange—and it is by a woman. This is also a unique recorded instance of Yeshua as an adult learning something from another person, and it is a woman.

> Yeshua left that place and withdrew to the region of Tyre and Sidon. Then out came a Canaanite woman from that district and started shouting, "Sir, Son of David, take pity on me. My daughter is tormented by a devil." But he answered her not a word. And his disciples went and pleaded with him. "Give her what she wants," they said, "because she is shouting after us." He said in reply, I was sent only to the lost sheep of the House of Israel." But the woman had come up and was kneeling at his feet. "Lord," she said, "help me." He replied, "It is not fair to take the children's food and throw it to the house-dogs." She retorted, "Ah yes, sir; but even house-dogs can eat the scraps that fall from their master's table." Then Yeshua answered her, "Woman, you have great faith. Let your wish be granted." And from that moment her daughter was well again.[25]

§49 YESHUA'S CONCERN FOR WIDOWS

As already remarked, Yeshua felt himself especially sent to the poor and oppressed, and that clearly included, in a preeminent way, the largest class of that group—women. However, if women were a more oppressed class among the oppressed, the most oppressed of women were widows, for they had almost no means of livelihood or standing before the law, nor anyone to provide them. Yeshua was clearly most concerned about these most oppressed of the most oppressed class of the oppressed, and his concern was translated into action. It should be noted that all the eight following accounts concerning Yeshua and widows, save the final one, are recorded in Luke, again reflecting Luke/Luka's sensitivity to this dimension of Yeshua's mission.

(1) It is recorded by Luke/Luka that, almost at the beginning of his life, Yeshua was prophesied over by a widow.

> There was a *woman prophet* also, Anna the daughter of Phanuel, of the tribe of Asher. She was well on in years. Her days of girlhood over, she had been married for seven years before becoming a *widow*. She was now eighty-four years old and never left the Temple, serving God night and day with fasting and prayer. She came by just at that moment and began to praise God; and

she spoke of the child to all who looked forward to the deliverance of Jerusalem.[26]

(2) Yeshua set before his disciples the example of a widow's minute contribution as being greater than the largesse of the rich.[27]

(3) Yeshua publicly and vigorously condemned the scribes (part of the male establishment) for their oppression of widows—thereby earning himself many enemies.

> In his teaching he said, "Beware of the scribes who like to walk about in long robes, to be greeted obsequiously in the market squares, to take the front seats in the synagogues and the places of honour at banquets; these are the men who swallow the property of widows, while making a show of lengthy prayers. The more severe will be the sentence they receive."[28]

(4) In his teaching Yeshua used the image of widows when illustrating how a prophet is not accepted in his own country.

> There were many widows in Israel, I can assure you, in Elijah's day, when heaven remained shut for three years and six months and a great famine raged throughout the land, but Elijah was not sent to any one of these: he was sent to a widow at Zarephath, a Sidonian town. And in the prophet Elisha's time there were many lepers in Israel, but none of these was cured, except the Syrian, Naaman.[29]

(5) Also in his teaching Yeshua used the image of a widow as one in the weakest and most hopeless of positions to illustrate the need for perseverance in prayer.[30]

(6) Also recorded is Yeshua's curing of a widow, Simon Peter's mother-in-law. The fact that she was living at Peter's house is a clear indication that she was widowed.[31]

(7) As seen in chapter 2, the most moving action of Yeshua for the sake of a widow was his raising to life the only son of the widow of Nain; she, unlike Peter's mother-in-law, had no one to provide for and protect her. Yeshua was "moved with pity" for her "and said to her, 'Do not cry.'"

> Soon afterward he went to a town called Nain, and his disciples and a large crowd accompanied him. As he approached the gate of the town a dead man was being carried out, the only son of a widowed mother. A considerable crowd of townsfolk were with her. The Lord was moved with pity upon seeing her

and said to her, "Do not cry." Then he stepped forward and touched the litter; at this, the bearers halted. He said, "Young man, I bid you get up." The dead man sat up and began to speak. Then Yeshua gave him back to his mother. Fear seized them all and they began to praise God. "A great prophet has risen among us," they said; and, "God has visited his people." This was the report that spread about him throughout Judea and the surrounding country.[32]

(8) Just as there was a widow (Anna) and his mother at the beginning of his life,[33] so also at the end of Yeshua's life there was a widow and his mother—and the two were one. According to the Fourth Gospel, even in his death agony Yeshua looked to the welfare of his beloved, most-oppressed, widows; he provided for his mother's future home with his "beloved disciple."

> Near the cross of Yeshua stood his mother and his mother's sister Mary the wife of Clopas, and Mary of Magdala. Seeing his mother and the disciple he loved standing near her, Yeshua said to his mother "Woman, this is your son." Then to the disciple he said, "This is your mother." And from that moment the disciple made a place for her in his home.[34]

§50 THE WOMAN TAKEN IN ADULTERY

We treated the story of the woman taken in adultery,[35] but it is sufficiently important that it deserves some further analysis. The story of Yeshua and the woman taken in adultery is found in the Fourth Gospel, although scholars agree that the evangelist did not write the story. It is not found in the earliest Greek manuscripts and comes into the canonical scriptures through the manuscripts of the Western Latin Church, although there is a reference to the story in the third-century *Didascalia*, of Syrian origin. Although the report of Yeshua's encounter with the woman seized in the act of adultery is usually located in the Fourth Gospel,[36] it is the scholarly consensus that the evangelist certainly did not write it, that it has many characteristics akin to the style of the Synoptic Gospels (Matthew, Mark, and Luke), and that there is some manuscript evidence that it originally might well have been located in Luke, after Luke 21:38.[37] Why the long resistance to this story? Probably partly because Yeshua was totally forgiving of adultery and much of early Christianity took an extremely severe stance against sexual offenses. At the same time, while Yeshua's treating of the woman in the story as a person rather than simply as a creature of sex probably drew forth resistance from certain elements in the church, other elements (most probably women) persisted in retaining the story, and ultimately succeeded.

We have in this story the crass use by a group of scribes and Pharisees of a woman, reduced entirely to a sex object, to set a legal trap for Yeshua. In fact, it is difficult to imagine a more callous use of a human person than the way the enemies of Yeshua treated the adulterous woman. First, the woman was surprised in the intimate act of sexual intercourse. According to Deuteronomy 19:15, there had to have been two or more witnesses other than the husband. The witnesses, of course, had to be male. Unless the scribes and the Pharisees were themselves the witnesses, it would seem that the poor woman was dragged before them, and they perhaps in turn, along with the witnesses, dragged her to the Sanhedrin. Since Yeshua was teaching in the area of the temple at the time, the scribes and the Pharisees apparently took the opportunity to use the woman to trap Yeshua.

Most scholars suggest that the trap set up for Yeshua was to present him with the dilemma of a woman caught in the very act of adultery, which according to Mosaic law should have resulted in her being put to death, on the one hand, and the restriction of capital punishment to Roman authorities at that time (the *jus gladii*), on the other. It is also clear that the enemies of Yeshua would not have thought of this case as presenting Yeshua with some kind of trap if Yeshua did not already have a reputation among them as a champion of women. There apparently was no question but that the woman was guilty of the "crime" of adultery, since she was caught *in delicto*, and therefore was subject to the Mosaic punishment of death. The question was, would Yeshua retain his reputation as the great rabbi, the teacher of the Torah, or would he retain his reputation as the champion of women?

Yeshua, of course, avoided the horns of the dilemma by refusing to become involved in legalisms and abstractions. Rather, he dealt with the *persons* involved, both the woman herself and her accusers. He spoke to the latter not as a lawyer, nor as to lawyers, but rather as one who was concerned with their humanness, their mind, spirit, and heart: "Let him who is without sin cast the first stone." He spoke similarly to the woman when he said that he also would not condemn her, but that she should from now on avoid that sin.

> At daybreak he appeared in the Temple again; and as all the people came to him, he sat down and began to teach them. The scribes and Pharisees brought a woman along who had been caught committing adultery; and making her stand there in full view of everybody, they said to Yeshua, "Master, this woman was caught in the very act of committing adultery, and Moses has ordered us in the Law to condemn women like this to death by stoning. What have you to say?" They asked him this as a test, looking for something to use against him. But Yeshua bent down and started writing on the ground with his finger. As they persisted with their question, he

looked up and said, "If there is one of you who has not sinned, let him be the first to throw a stone at her." Then he bent down and wrote on the ground again. When they heard this they went away one by one, beginning with the eldest, until Yeshua was left alone with the woman, who remained standing there. He looked up and said, "Woman, where are they? Has no one condemned you?" "No one, sir," she replied. "Neither do I condemn you," said Yeshua, "Go away, and don't sin any more."[38]

§51 YESHUA AND THE PENITENT WOMAN

Scholars have always found the story of Yeshua and the penitent woman difficult to understand and translate (especially the key portion, v. 47); Joachim Jeremias provides perhaps the most helpful suggestion when he supposes that Yeshua had just delivered a powerful sermon that moved the Pharisee Simon to see Yeshua as a prophet and the sinful woman to confess and repent of her sins and be filled with gratitude for the forgiveness she received in the sermon. Several things should be recalled here in the relationship between the woman and Yeshua. First, in that culture one did not publicly speak even to one's own wife, let alone to a strange woman, indeed a known "sinner," probably a prostitute!

Yeshua not only spoke with her but let her touch him and kiss him. Further, a woman was never to let her hair be uncovered, and to loose it in public was grounds for mandatory divorce; this woman uncovered her hair, loosed it, and wiped Yeshua's feet with it, without thereby scandalizing Yeshua, although Simon was clearly scandalized. And why not. Imagine a scene today with its relatively liberal mores if a strange woman, or indeed any woman, washing your feet with tears and wiping them with her hair! Yeshua rebuked the Pharisee and treated the woman not as a sexual creature but as a person; he spoke of her human and spiritual actions, her love, her unlove (her sins), her being forgiven, and her faith.

> One of the Pharisees invited him to a meal. When he arrived at the Pharisee's house and took his place at table, a woman came in, who had a bad name (*ēn hamartōlos*, was a sinner) in the town. She had heard he was dining with the Pharisee and had brought with her an alabaster jar of ointment. She waited behind him at his feet, weeping, and her tears fell on his feet, and she wiped them away with her hair; then she covered his feet with kisses and anointed them with the ointment.
>
> When the Pharisee who had invited him saw this, he said to himself, "If this man were a prophet, he would know who this woman is that is

touching him and what a bad name she has." Then Yeshua took him up and said to him "Simon, I have something to say to you." "Speak, Master," was the reply. "There was once a creditor who had two men in his debt; one owed him five hundred denarii, the other fifty. They were unable to pay, so he pardoned them both. Which of them will love him more?" "The one who was pardoned more, I suppose," answered Simon. Yeshua said, "You are right."

Then he turned to the woman. "Simon," he said, "you see this woman? I came into your house, and you poured no water over my feet, but she has poured out her tears over my feet and wiped them away with her hair. You gave me no kiss, but she has been covering my feet with kisses ever since I came in. You did not anoint my head with oil, but she has anointed my feet with ointment. For this reason I tell you that her sins, her many sins, must have been forgiven her, or she would not have shown such great love. It is the person who is forgiven little who shows little love." Then he said to her, "Your sins are forgiven." Those who were with him at table began to say to themselves, "Who is this man, that he even forgives sins?" But he said to the woman, "Your faith has saved you; go in peace."[39]

§52 PROSTITUTES AND THE REIGN OF GOD

On at least one other occasion Yeshua reached out in his teaching specifically to the most despised of humans, prostitutes. Yeshua made it clear in both his words and actions that he understood his mission to be to preach in word and deed the "Good News," the coming of the Reign of God, to the poor and oppressed. In a debate with the chief priests and the elders of the people, Yeshua named two of the presumably most unlikely classes of these "oppressed" as entering into the Reign of God ahead of the chief priests and elders, namely, tax collectors and prostitutes, the two most despised groups of that society. A sexual parallelism should be noted here: the male tax collector and the female prostitute. It is difficult to believe that such a sexual balance was not struck deliberately by Yeshua, for the Synoptic Gospels usually connect tax collectors and *sinners*, a much broader term than prostitutes, with Yeshua ten different times and only on this occasion are tax collectors and prostitutes mentioned. In fact (except in the parable of the prodigal son), this is the only time the term "prostitutes" is used in any of the Gospels. The source for the term "prostitutes" in this connection could then, almost certainly, only be Yeshua.

Upon reflection, it is really extraordinary that Yeshua would picture prostitutes as in the reign of God, as being "saved." Clearly for him a woman reduced completely to a sex object is seen as the object, not of disdain, but rather of exploitation, who nevertheless is a *person*, one among those who are "making their way into the Reign of God."

> He had gone into the Temple and was teaching, when the chief priests and the elders of the people came to him. . . . Yeshua said to them, "I tell you solemnly; tax collectors and prostitutes are making their way into the Reign of God before you. For John came to you, a pattern of true righteousness, but you did not believe him, and yet the tax collectors and prostitutes did."[40]

§53 THE SAMARITAN WOMAN

See §13 for a discussion of the very important encounter between Yeshua and the Samaritan woman. In that encounter Yeshua broke two very major barriers. The first barrier to fall was for a Jew to talk with a Samaritan, and the second was for a man to speak publicly with a woman. Thirdly, of course, this woman was not just any ordinary woman, but clearly must have been something of a "scandal," since the man she was living with was her fifth man. She must have had quite some reputation for Yeshua to have known about that and even recognize by sight. Hence, by talking with her in such a public place he was also putting his "reputation" on the line.

Of course, at the same time he was building further his reputation for gathering the marginalized of society. The fact that the woman came to the well alone makes it clear that she was ostracized by the rest of the "reputable" women in the town. We cannot know, but one could imagine a scene wherein Yeshua overheard several of the women of the town who were at the well remark about the scandalous woman who was then approaching and then scurried off, leaving Yeshua with the necessary information with which to speak to the woman "with the scarlet letter."

§54 INTELLECTUAL LIFE FOR WOMEN

See §15 for a discussion of Yeshua's close friends Martha and Mary and how Yeshua supported Mary's choice of the intellectual life. As noted, such a choice and support of it by a rabbi was really unique at that time in that culture.

NOTES

1. Mk 10:11–12. Cf. Mt 19:9 and Lk 16:18.
2. Mt 22:23–30. Cf. Mk 12:18–27 and Lk 20:27–38.

3. Claude G. Montefiore, *Rabbinic Literature and Gospel Teaching* (London, 1930), 217–18.
4. Jn 2: 1–11.
5. Lk 2:51.
6. Mt 15:1–7. Cf. Mk 7:1–13.
7. Mk 3:20–21.
8. Mk 6:1–6. Cf. Mt 13:53–58 and Lk 4:16–30.
9. Mt 12:46–50. Cf. Mk 3:31–35 and Lk 8:19–21, 11:27–28.
10. Mk 10:28–30.
11. Mt 10:34–36.
12. Mt 10:37–38.
13. Mt 19:29.
14. Lk 12:51–53.
15. Lk 14:26.
16. Lk 18:28–30.
17. Mk 12:41–44. Cf. Lk 21:17.
18. Mk 1:29–3. Cf. Mt 8:14–15 and Lk 4:38–39.
19. Jn 5:10, 9:14–17.
20. Mk 3:1–6.
21. Mt 12:9–14.
22. See §3 for further detail.
23. Cf. "sons of the covenant," *bnei brith.*
24. Lk 13:10–17. Cf. Lk 6:6–11, 14:1–6.
25. Mt 15:21–28. Cf. Mk 7:24–30.
26. Lk 2:36–38.
27. Lk 21:1–4.
28. Mk 12:38–40. Cf. Lk 20:45–47.
29. Lk 4:25–27.
30. Lk 18:1–8. See §28.
31. Lk 4:38–39. Cf. Mt 8:14–15 and Mk 1:29–31. See also §46.
32. Lk 7:11–17.
33. Lk 2:36–38.
34. Jn 19:25–27.
35. See §11.
36. Jn 7:53 to 8:11.
37. See §177 for further discussion of this passage.
38. Jn 8:2–11.
39. Lk 7:36–50.
40. Mt 21:23, 31–32.

§55 Women in the Life of Yeshua

§56 THE PROPHET ANNA

$\mathcal{A}$s we have seen, Luke/Luka records at least seven sexually parallel images or stories, one about a man and one about a woman, used by Yeshua. The same sexual parallelism is found in his account of the presentation of the child Yeshua in the temple. The parents are met there by Simeon, "an upright and devout man," who, though he is not called a prophet, nevertheless prophesies concerning Yeshua. They are also met by a woman who is specifically called a prophet (*prophētis*) and who also spoke of Yeshua as the Messiah. "There was a woman prophet also, Anna the daughter of Phanuel, of the tribe of Asher . . . and she spoke of the child to all who looked forward to the deliverance of Jerusalem."[1]

§57 WOMEN DISCIPLES OF YESHUA I

The disciples of Yeshua were those who followed Yeshua about, listening to and living with him. This group of disciples included, in a prominent way, a number of women (some are specifically named), mainly from the more rural area of Galilee where the restrictive rules against women were less stringent than in Jerusalem. Still, they had to leave home and family and travel openly with a "rabbi," an unheard-of breach of custom. What is also astonishing is that these three named women, Magdalene, Joanna, and Susanna, and others unnamed, *paid for* the support of Yeshua and his other followers. The text does not simply say that these women served Yeshua and his followers, but that they provided for them "*out of their own resources*" (*ek tōn hyparchontōn.*) Obviously these women were persons of financial means, and they were willing to spend it to promote Yeshua and his movement. They were not shrinking violets! Further, Yeshua not only condoned but obviously encouraged this flouting of sexist custom. These women disciples were such a prominent part of Yeshua's life that all three of the Synoptic Gospels mention them.

> Now after this he made his way through towns and villages preaching, and proclaiming the Good News of the Reign of God. With him went the Twelve, as well as certain women who had been cured of evil spirits and ailments: Mary surnamed the Magdalene, from whom seven demons had gone out, Joanna the wife of Herod's steward Chuza, Susanna, and several others who ministered (*diēkonoun*) to them *ek tōn hyparchontōn*, out of their own resources.[2]

§58 WOMEN "MINISTER TO" (DIAKONEŌ) YESHUA

All three of the Synoptic Gospels use a form of the verb *diakoneō* (to minister or serve) to describe what these women did in addition to saying that they "followed" Yeshua. It is the same basic word as "deacon"; indeed, apparently the tasks of the deacons in early Christianity were much the same as those these women undertook.

> There were some women watching from a distance. Among them were Mary of Magdala, Mary who was the mother of James the younger and Joset, and Salome. These used to follow him and minister (*diēkonoun*) to him when he was in Galilee. And there were many other women there who had come up to Jerusalem with him.[3]

> And many women were there, watching from a distance, the same women who had followed Yeshua from Galilee and ministered (*diakonousai*) to him. Among them were Mary of Magdala, Mary the mother of James and Joseph, and the mother of Zebedee's sons.[4]

§59 WOMEN DISCIPLES OF YESHUA II

That early Christians thought of and referred to the women who are mentioned by name in the above three citations as "disciples" of Yeshua is attested to by at least three early apocryphal Christian documents. But first a brief explanation of apocryphal documents.

Because it was only late in the fourth century that the canon of the New Testament was finally fixed as we now have it, many of the writings that are now called apocryphal were for centuries widely accepted and used by Christian churches. Hence, it would be anachronistic to exclude all of them from consideration in matters concerning early Christianity. Still, caution must be exercised in their use, for usually, to a much greater extent than most of the canonical New Testament writings, most of the apocryphal New Testament writings have very little historical basis; the childhood stories about Jesus, for example, are largely legendary fiction. However, these apocryphal writings are first-class sources for informing us about what many early Christians thought and believed and how they lived: for example, the extremely anti-sex attitudes of the apocryphal Acts of various apostles which far exceed any sexual asceticism of the canonical New Testament documents.

Much, though by no means all, of the Christian writing of these early centuries came under the influence of the broad cultural movement called Gnosticism. Gnosticism, as its name indicated (*gnōsis*, knowledge), taught that salvation was to be attained by means of a secret knowledge lying below the surface of texts, symbols, and events. Thus, in the third-century Gnostic Gospel of Philip it is written: "People do not perceive what is correct but they perceive what is incorrect, unless they have come to know what is correct."[5]

Further, Gnosticism tended to be strongly dualistic in its conception of reality (all reality is ultimately made up of two elements: matter, which is evil, and spirit, which is good). In line with that conception it also tended to be very ascetical and anti-sex. But that did not ipso facto mean it was totally anti-woman, as will be seen below when the various apocryphal Acts of the Apostles are discussed (see §275). Also, partly because of its dualism, the masculine and feminine elements were sometimes projected into its conceptualizations of the divinity. Of course, there were also other causes of such male-female conceptualizations (e.g., the God and Goddess traditions), and similarly, not every feminine-masculine description of the divinity was necessarily a reflection of Gnosticism. With such cautions in mind we can proceed.

The first apocryphal document to look at here is the *Sophia Jesu Christi*, probably written during the second century; it puts these seven holy women followers of Yeshua terminologically on a par with the twelve men followers. It calls the men not only apostles but also disciples (*mathētēs*), and it says of the women that they had followed him "as disciples" (*mathēteuein*).

> After he had risen from the dead, when they came, the twelve disciples (*mathētēs*) and seven women who had followed him as disciples (*mathēteuein*), into Galilee. . . . there appeared to them the Redeemer.[6]

The second document, the second-century *Gospel of Thomas*, contains a rather obscure exchange between Yeshua and Salome, in the midst of which Salome announces that she is Yeshua's disciple, and he does not contradict her.

> Yeshua said: "Two will rest on a bed: the one will die, the one will live." Salome said: "Who art thou, man, and whose son? Thou didst take thy place upon my bench and eat from my table." Yeshua said to her: "I am He who is from the Same, to me was given from the things of my Father." Salome said: "*I am thy disciple.*" Yeshua said [to her]: "Therefore I say, if he is the Same, he will be filled with light, but if he is divided, he will be filled with darkness."[7]

The third document is the early third-century *Pistis Sophia*, wherein Mary Magdalene is not specifically called a disciple, but Yeshua predicts that she "will surpass all my disciples."

> But Mary Magdalene and John, the maiden (*parthenos*), will surpass all my disciples (*mathētai*) and all men who shall receive mysteries in the Ineffable, they will be on my right hand and on my left, and I am they and they are I.[8]

§60 ANOINTMENT OF YESHUA BY MARY OF BETHANY I

It was customary that women did not eat with men when guests were present, nor, indeed, did they even enter the dining area. Nevertheless, when a woman[9] entered the room where Yeshua was dining and anointed him, he neither resisted nor rebuked her. To be sure, others showed unhappiness at her intrusion, expressed especially at her "wasting" the expensive ointment. But, as in the "Martha and Mary" story of Luke 10:38–42, Yeshua defended Mary's act of special discipleship to him.

> Yeshua was at Bethany in the house of Simon the leper; he was at dinner when a woman came in with an alabaster jar of very costly ointment, pure nard. She broke the jar and poured the ointment on his head. Some who were there said to one another indignantly, "Why this waste of ointment? Ointment like this could have been sold for over three hundred denarii and the money given to the poor"; and they were angry with her. But Yeshua said, "Leave her alone. Why are you upsetting her? What she has done for me is one of the good works. You have the poor with you always, and you can be kind to them whenever you wish, but you will not always have me. She has done what was in her power to do: she has anointed my body beforehand for its burial. I tell you solemnly, wherever throughout all the world the Good News is proclaimed, what she has done will be told also, in remembrance of her."[10]

§61 ANOINTMENT OF YESHUA BY MARY OF BETHANY II

The Fourth Gospel's account of the anointment of Yeshua by Mary confirms the all-male character of the banquet, in accordance with the custom of the day, for it states that Lazarus (brother of Martha and Mary) was at table, and that Martha, as usual, served.[11] Also, as usual, Mary did not serve but related to Yeshua in a very special way, both poignantly personal and "transcendent," apparently oblivious of, or disregarding, her intrusion into a male sanctum, probably because she knew from experience that Yeshua would support her, which he did.

> Six days before the Passover, Yeshua went to Bethany, where Lazarus was, whom he had raised from the dead. They gave a dinner for him there; Martha waited on them and Lazarus was among those at table. Mary brought in a pound of very costly ointment, pure nard, and with it anointed the feet of Yeshua, wiping them with her hair; the house was full of the scent of the ointment. Then Judas Iscariot, one of the disciples, the man who was to betray him, said, "Why wasn't this ointment sold for three hundred denarii, and the money given to the poor?" He said this, not because he cared about the poor, but because he was a thief; he was in charge of the common fund and used to help himself to the contributions. So Yeshua said, "Leave her alone; she had to keep this scent for the day of my burial. You have the poor with you always; you will not always have me."[12]

§62 PILATE'S WIFE

We know nothing of Pilate's wife except that she sent a message to her husband in support of Yeshua during his trial. As the wife of a Roman procurator of Judea, she doubtless was not Jewish but rather a pagan. We have no reason to doubt the historicity of her intervention; in fact, elsewhere in the contemporary world there are recorded instances of similar interventions by women. She apparently was so upset by the attempt to destroy Yeshua that she had a bad dream about him. Bad dreams were taken very seriously by most if not all people then, the vast majority being inclined toward superstition. Such a disturbing dream, bringing her to the point of intervening in a public proceeding of the most serious and formal kind ("as he was seated in the chair of judgment"), and of interrupting a husband who was known for his vicious and brutal temper, tells us something about Pilate's wife and Yeshua.

Yeshua obviously was known to her, and most probably not simply by general, or even detailed, reputation. For her to have become so disturbed as to attempt to interfere in Yeshua's behalf, where such a tumult was being raised, would make it most likely that she had personally been deeply impressed by Yeshua. She would not have been the only woman whom Yeshua deeply affected, nor the only pagan, nor indeed the only "Roman,"[13] nor the only pagan woman.[14]

One wonders, of course, how the writer of Matthew's Gospel came to know about this private conversation. Presumably, Pilate's wife was the ultimate source, though conceivably someone could have overheard it and passed on the information. We can only speculate, but the former seems most likely.

> Now as he was seated in the chair of judgement, his wife sent him a message, "Have nothing to do with that man; I have been upset all day by a dream I had about him."[15]

§63 JERUSALEM WOMEN ON THE VIA DOLOROSA

Luke/Luka, again, is the only Gospel writer who mentions the women of Jerusalem meeting Yeshua as he was carrying his cross to the place of execution. S/he recorded that they mourned and cried for him. The Talmud notes that the noble women used to prepare a soothing drink for the condemned, but that is far different from what is described by Luke/Luka. These women clearly must have been devoted followers of Yeshua who were overwhelmed with grief. They are a group distinct from the "large numbers of people" who followed Yeshua; the Greek makes it clear that only the women were said to mourn and lament for Yeshua. They obviously responded with a profound attachment to this Yeshua who had taught them. Nowhere in any of the Gospels is there a similar report of a group of male followers of Yeshua lamenting for him publicly or risking their limbs and lives by meeting and mourning for him in the open. Yeshua's response was typical in that he showed greater concern for them than for himself. Luke/Luka would have him speak with foreknowledge of the coming destruction of Jerusalem (70 C.E.); hence most scholars hold that these specific words were provided by the evangelist, though with a historical basis.

> As they were leading him away they seized on a man, Simon from Cyrene, who was coming in from the country, and made him shoulder the cross and carry it behind Yeshua. Large numbers of people followed him, and of women too, who mourned and lamented for him. But Yeshua turned to them and said, "Daughters of Jerusalem, do not weep for me; weep rather for yourselves and for your children. For the days will surely come when people will say, 'Happy are those who are barren, the wombs that have never borne, the breasts that have never suckled!' Then they will begin to say to the mountains, 'Fall on us!'; to the hills, 'Cover us!' For if men use

the green wood like this, what will happen when it is dry?" Now with him they were also leading out two other criminals to be executed.[16]

§64 ONLY WOMEN REMAIN BY YESHUA THROUGH HIS DEATH

It should first be noted that there is no record of any women seeking the death of Yeshua; all those in any way involved in promoting Yeshua's death were men. Such noninvolvement of women in the violent death of others was by no means a foregone conclusion in Jewish tradition: Deborah, Jael, Esther, Judith, and Salome, for example, all caused the death of men.

On the positive side, the response of the women disciples to Yeshua was extraordinary. He taught and fought for them, and they responded by following him to his bitter end, even at risk to their own limb and life. All Yeshua's male disciples deserted him: "Then all the disciples deserted him and ran away."[17] "And they all deserted him and ran away."[18] Luke, almost certainly a later Gospel than Mark and Matthew, said that "those who knew" Yeshua stood afar and watched the crucifixion. The Fourth Gospel, which is the latest of all the Gospels, placed "the disciple Yeshua loved," traditionally thought to be John the Apostle,[19] beneath the cross with women. Many scholars believe that both Luke and the Fourth Gospel here contain unhistorical additions to the Mark and Matthew report. If one follows this historical judgment, and Mark and Matthew, one would have to conclude that only the women stayed with Yeshua in his moment of despair and humiliation.

(1) There were some women watching from a distance. Among them were Mary of Magdala, Mary who was the mother of James the younger and Joset, and Salome. These used to follow him and minister to him when he was in Galilee. And there were many other women there who had come up to Jerusalem with him.[20]

(2) And many women were there, watching from a distance, the same women who had followed Yeshua from Galilee and ministered to him. Among them were Mary of Magdala, Mary the mother of James and Joseph, and the mother of Zebedee's sons.[21]

(3) All those who knew him stood at a distance; so also did the women who had accompanied him from Galilee, and they saw all this happen.[22]

(4) Near the cross of Yeshua stood his mother and his mother's sister, Mary the wife of Clopas, and Mary of Magdala. Seeing his mother and the disciple he loved standing near her, Yeshua said to his mother, "Woman, this is your son." Then to the disciple he said, "This is your mother." And from that moment the disciple made a place for her in his home.[23]

§65 WOMEN WITNESS THE BURIAL OF YESHUA

The women disciples of Yeshua remained by him through his death and his burial when all was despair. All three of the Synoptic Gospels report the presence of the women at the burial of Yeshua. Joseph of Arimathaea and, probably, Nicodemus were members of the council which participated in the trial of Yeshua. Hence, they had the political weight to obtain Yeshua's body. Except for them, apparently only the women disciples were present for the burial, faithful to the end.

(1) It was now evening, and since it was Preparation Day (that is, the vigil of the Sabbath), there came Joseph of Arimathaea, a prominent member of the Council, who himself lived in the hope of seeing the Reign of God, and he boldly went to Pilate and asked for the body of Yeshua. Pilate, astonished that he should have died so soon, summoned the centurion and enquired if he was already dead. Having been assured of this by the centurion, he granted the corpse to Joseph who bought a shroud, took Yeshua down from the cross, wrapped him in the shroud and laid him in a tomb which had been hewn out of the rock. He then rolled a stone against the entrance to the tomb. Mary of Magdala and Mary the mother of Joset were watching and took note of where he was laid.[24]

(2) When it was evening, there came a rich man of Arimathaea, called Joseph, who had himself become a disciple of Yeshua. This man went to Pilate and asked for the body of Yeshua. Pilate thereupon ordered it to be handed over. So Joseph took the body, wrapped it in a clean shroud and put it in his own new tomb which he had hewn out of the rock. He then rolled a large stone across the entrance of the tomb and went away. Now Mary of Magdala and the other Mary were there, sitting opposite the sepulchre.[25]

(3) Then a member of the council arrived, an upright and virtuous man named Joseph. He had not consented to what the others had planned and carried out. He came from Arimathaea, a Jewish town, and he lived in the hope of seeing the Reign of God. This man went to Pilate and asked for the body of Yeshua. He then took it down, wrapped it in a shroud and put him in a tomb which was hewn in stone in which no one had yet been laid. It was Preparation Day and the Sabbath was imminent. Meanwhile the women who had come from Galilee with Yeshua were following behind. . . . They returned and prepared spices and ointments. And on the Sabbath day they rested, as the Law required.[26]

§66 EMPTY TOMB

Perhaps because the women disciples followed Yeshua to his bitter end on the cross and his burial and came back to his grave after the Sabbath, they were privileged to be the first witnesses to the empty tomb and first appearances of the "resurrected one." This last element doubtless helps explain the prominent place women held in the early Christian community. Though their testimony was then rejected by the male disciples (according to the Jewish custom of the time, which did not allow women to bear witness), all four evangelists recorded the women's witness to the risen Yeshua and/or the empty tomb as primary, obviously reflecting the consensuses of the different primitive Christian communities in the midst of which they wrote their Gospels. But because these traditions differed in the details of how the witnessing of the women took place, it will be helpful to look at each one.

(1) The account by Mark is probably the earliest, but somehow the original ending of the Gospel after Mark 16:8 probably has been lost and the story is incomplete, for example, the women were silent after witnessing the empty tomb.[27]

> When the Sabbath was over, Mary of Magdala, Mary the mother of James, and Salome, bought spices with which to go and anoint him. And very early in the morning on the first day of the week they went to the tomb, just as the sun was rising. They had been saying to one another, "Who will roll away the stone for us from the entrance to the tomb?" But when they looked they could see that the stone which was very big had already been rolled back. On entering the tomb they saw a young man in a white robe seated on the right-hand side, and they were struck with amazement. But he said to them, "There is no need for alarm. You are looking for Yeshua of Nazareth, who was crucified: he has risen, he is not here. See, here is the place where they laid him. But you must go and tell his disciples and Peter, 'He is going before you to Galilee; it is there you will see him, just as he told you.'" And the women came out and ran away from the tomb because they were frightened out of their wits; and they said nothing to a soul, for they were afraid.[28]

(2) In Matthew's account, perhaps the second oldest Gospel, the women were commissioned by an angel to give witness to the male disciples that Yeshua had risen. Thus in a basic sense they were "apostles," ones sent (*apostoloi*) to bear witness to the resurrection.

> After the Sabbath, and towards dawn on the first day of the week, Mary of Magdala and the other Mary went to visit the sepulchre. And all at once there was a violent earthquake, for the angel of the Lord, descending from heaven, came and rolled away the stone and sat on it. His face was like lightning, his robe white as snow. The guards were so shaken, so frightened of him, that

they were like dead men. But the angel spoke; and said to the women, "There is no need for you to be afraid. I know you are looking for Yeshua, who was crucified. He is not here, for he has risen, as he said he would. Come and see the place where he lay, then *go quickly and tell his disciples, 'He has risen from the dead* and now he is going before you to Galilee; it is there you will see him.' Now I have told you." Filled with awe and great joy the women came quickly away from the tomb and ran to tell the disciples.[29]

(3) The third account, by Luke, not only describes the women reporting what they had seen and heard to the male disciples, but, in customary fashion, being disbelieved by them.

On the first day of the week, at the first sign of dawn, they went to the tomb with the spices they had prepared. They found that the stone had been rolled away from the tomb, but on entering discovered that the body of the Lord Yeshua was not there. As they stood there not knowing what to think, two men in brilliant clothes suddenly appeared at their side. Terrified, the women lowered their eyes. But the two men said to them, "Why look among the dead for someone who is alive? He is not here; he has risen. Remember what he told you when he was still in Galilee: that the Son of Man had to be handed over into the power of sinful men and be crucified, and rise again on the third day?" And they remembered his words.

When the women returned from the tomb they told all this to the Eleven and to all the others. The women were Mary of Magdala, Joanna, and Mary the mother of James. The other women with them also told the apostles, but this story of theirs seemed pure nonsense, and they did not believe them.

Peter, however, went running to the tomb. He bent down and saw the binding cloths but nothing else; he then went back home, amazed at what had happened.[30]

(4) The Fourth Gospel, written considerably later than the other three Gospels, describes only Mary Magdalene's visit to the tomb and her report to the male disciples. Though the evangelist does not say explicitly, as does Luke, that they disbelieved her, their actions would fit within that assumption.

It was very early on the first day of the week and still dark, when Mary of Magdala came to the tomb. She saw that the stone had been moved away from the tomb and came running to Simon Peter and the other disciple, the one Yeshua loved. "They have taken the Lord out of the tomb," she said, "and we don't know where they have put him."

So Peter set out with the other disciple to go to the tomb. They ran together, but the other disciple, running faster than Peter, reached the tomb first; he bent down and saw the linen cloths lying on the ground, but did not go in. Simon Peter, who was following, now came up, went right into the tomb, saw the linen cloths on the ground, and also the cloth that had been over his head; this was not with the linen cloths but rolled up in a place by itself. Then the other disciple who had reached the tomb first also went in; he saw and he believed. Till this moment they had failed to understand the teaching of scripture, that he must rise from the dead. The disciples then went home again.[31]

§67 THE RISEN YESHUA AND WOMEN I

Three of the four Gospels report that the first appearance of the risen Yeshua was to Mary Magdalene, or to a group of women disciples, in addition to the women being the first witnesses of the empty tomb and the speech and commission by an angel or angels to witness to the resurrection. Writing before any of the evangelists, Paul in 1 Corinthians 15:5–8 describes five of the appearances of the risen Yeshua, "that he appeared *first* to Cephas (Peter) and secondly to the Twelve." Nowhere did Paul refer to Yeshua's appearance to Mary Magdalene or the other women disciples. Could this be a reflection of the Jewish custom of disallowing the testimony of women, manifested by the Pharisee Paul and not yet counteracted by the women disciples through the oral traditions that fed the Gospel writers?

§68 THE RISEN YESHUA AND WOMEN II

In any case, it is "the gospel truth" that the risen Yeshua appeared first to a woman. The earliest Gospel, Mark, recorded the appearance of Yeshua to Mary Magdalene, but that whole final section[32] is universally held by scholars not to have been written by the author of the Gospel of Mark, but rather added later, perhaps in the second century. As it stands, the Gospel of Mark reports simply that Yeshua appeared to Mary Magdalene and also that the male disciples refused to believe her, which a woman might have expected.

Having risen in the morning on the first day of the week, he appeared first to Mary of Magdala from whom he had cast out seven devils. She then went to those who had been his companions, and who were mourning and in tears, and told them. But they did not believe her when they heard her say that he was alive and that she had seen him.[33]

§69 THE RISEN YESHUA AND WOMEN III

According to Matthew, Yeshua appeared first to Mary Magdalene and "the other Mary." He gave more concrete details and a commission by Yeshua to "go and tell my brothers" about the resurrection; they, women, were being "sent" (*apostellein*) by Yeshua to men, to the male disciples, to bear witness (despite women's inability in Jewish law) to the resurrection, in a word, women were made "apostles" by Yeshua.

> Filled with awe and great joy the women came quickly away from the tomb and ran to tell the disciples.
>
> And there, coming to meet them, was Yeshua. "Greetings," he said. And the women came up to him and, falling down before him, clasped his feet. Then Yeshua said to them, "Do not be afraid; *go and tell my brothers* that they must leave for Galilee; they will see me there."[34]

§70 THE RISEN YESHUA AND WOMEN IV

The Fourth Gospel, the last written, is the most detailed, and touching, in its description of Yeshua's appearance to Mary Magdalene. She obviously had a deep affection for Yeshua: he had cured her and she followed him throughout Galilee and down to Jerusalem, "ministering" (*diēkonoun*) to him; she stayed by him through his bitter death (which, according to most Gospel accounts, the male disciples did not do), attended his burial, returned to his tomb to mourn, "weeping"; when she recognized him she threw her arms around his feet and called him "rabbi," teacher. Yeshua reciprocated by appearing to her first of all; after addressing her as "woman," a frequent form of address, he called her by her proper name, Mary; he commissioned her "to go to the brothers and tell them" of his resurrection, commissioning her as an "apostle to the apostles," in that sense, the "first of the apostles!"

> Meanwhile Mary stayed outside near the tomb, weeping. Then, still weeping, she stooped to look inside, and saw two angels in white sitting where the body of Yeshua had been, one at the head, the other at the feet. They said, "Woman, why are you weeping?" "They have taken my Lord away," she replied, "and I don't know where they have put him." As she said this

she turned round and saw Yeshua standing there, though she did not recognize him. Yeshua said, "Woman, why are you weeping? Who are you
looking for?" Supposing him to be the gardener, she said, "Sir, if you have
taken him away, tell me where you have put him, and I will go and remove
him." Yeshua said, "Mary!" She knew him then and said to him in Hebrew,
"*Rabbuni*," which means Teacher. Yeshua said to her, "Do not cling to me,
because I have not yet ascended to the Father. But *go to the brothers, and tell
them*: I am ascending to my Father and your Father, to my God and your
God." So Mary of Magdala went and told the disciples that she had seen
the Lord and that he had said these things to her.[35]

§71 THE RISEN YESHUA AND WOMEN V

In the several evangelists' accounts Yeshua is depicted as one learned in the
law, and therefore obviously aware of the stricture against women serving as
witnesses. Hence, their describing his first appearing to and commissioning
of women to bear witness to the most important event of his career cannot be
understood as anything but deliberate; it was a dramatic linking of a very clear
rejection of the second-class status of women with the center of Yeshua's
Gospel, his resurrection. The portrayal of Yeshua's effort to connect centrally
these two points is so obvious that it is an overwhelming tribute to *man's* intellectual myopia not to have discerned it effectively in two thousand years.

§72 THE RISEN YESHUA AND WOMEN VI

As mentioned in §57, apocryphal New Testament writings, especially the earlier ones, may well be the vehicles of certain historical traditions, though it
may be difficult at times to discern the historically based element amid the
legendary accretions. Further, they tell us something historical about what
and how some Christians believed and lived at the time they were written.
Hence, it is very interesting to find several apocryphal writings (running from
perhaps the time of the writing of the canonical Gospels in the latter part of
the first century to the third or fourth centuries), which continue both the traditions concerning the women followers of Yeshua, still always including
Mary Magdalene: that it was they who first found the empty tomb and they
to whom Yeshua first appeared, commissioning them to witness to the male
disciples, to no avail, of course.

(1) The earliest of these apocryphal writings is the *Gospel of Peter*, composed anywhere from the latter part of the first century to the middle

of the second century. It is strikingly like the three Synoptic Gospels, especially Mark's first "ending," where the women "fearfully fled the tomb,"[36] suggesting that the apocryphal *Gospel of Peter* was written before the "long ending" of Mark[37] was composed probably early in the second century. It should be noted that Mary Magdalene is especially named here as a woman *disciple* of the Lord.

> Early in the morning of the Lord's day Mary Magdalene, a woman *disciple* of the Lord, for fear of the Jews, since (they) were inflamed with wrath, she had not done at the sepulchre of the Lord what women are wont to do for those beloved of them who die, took with her women friends and came to the sepulchre where he was laid. And they feared lest the Jews should see them, and said, "Although we could not weep and lament on that day when he was crucified, yet let us now do so at his sepulchre. But who will roll away for us the stone also that is set on the entrance to the sepulchre, that we may go in and sit beside him and do what is due? For the stone was great and we fear lest any one see us. And if we cannot do so, let us at least put down at the entrance what we bring for a memorial of him and let us weep and lament until we have again gone home." So they went and found the sepulchre opened. And they came near, stooped down and saw there a young man sitting in the midst of the sepulchre, comely and clothed with a brightly shining robe, who said to them, "Wherefore are ye come? Whom seek ye? Not him that was crucified? He is risen and gone. But if ye believe not, stoop this way and see the place where he lay, for he is not here. For he is risen and is gone thither whence he was sent." Then the women fled affrighted.[38]

(2) In the second apocryphal writing, the *Letter of the Apostles*, or *Epistula Apostolorum*, also written early in the second century, the women, including Mary Magdalene, were not only the first to go and find the empty tomb but also the first to see Yeshua. Moreover, here at this very early period, stress is placed not only on the women being the first to see the risen Yeshua, but also very heavily on the fact that they were sent to witness to the male disciples, who were so recalcitrant that Yeshua sent a second woman, and finally went along with all of them to convince the male disciples of the resurrection. Was the expansion on this theme here both a reflection of the growing restrictions that women were experiencing in the church at that time and also a rebuke of those male leaders responsible for those restrictions?

He, of whom we are witnesses, we know as the one crucified in the days of Pontius Pilate and of the prince Archelaus, who was crucified between two thieves and was taken down from the wood of the cross together with them, and was buried in the place of the skull, to which three women came, Sarah, Martha, and Mary Magdalene. They carried ointment to pour out upon his body, weeping and mourning over what had happened. And they approached the tomb and found the stone where it had been rolled away from the tomb, and they opened the door and did not find his body. And as they were mourning and weeping, the Lord appeared to them and said to them, "Do not weep; I am he whom you seek. But let one of you go to your brothers and say 'Come, our Master has risen from the dead.'"

And Mary came to us and told us. And we said to her, "What have we to do with you, O woman? He that is dead and buried, can he then live?" And we did not believe her, that our Saviour had risen from the dead.

Then she went back to our Lord and said to him, "None of them believed me concerning your resurrection." And he said to her, "Let another one of you go to them." And Sarah came and gave us the same news, and we accused her of lying. And she returned to our Lord and spoke to him as Mary had.

Then the Lord said to Mary and to her sisters, "Let us go to them." And he came and found us inside. . . . And . . . he said to us, "Come, and do not be afraid. I am your teacher whom you, Peter, denied three times; and now do you deny again?"[39]

(3) The third document was written significantly later and was the product of a definitely Gnostic Christian group, the followers of Mani (Manicheans); it was probably written in the third or fourth century. Only fragments are still extant, and the only portion of them dealing with the resurrection concerns Yeshua's appearance to Mary Magdalene, apparently a development of the story at the end of the canonical Fourth Gospel. There are several points of special interest in it. For one thing, Mary Magdalene is specifically made "a messenger (*angelos*) for me to these wandering orphans (*orphannos*)," meaning the eleven male disciples. Further, she is asked to do this as a service, a *leitourgia* to Yeshua. Could there be a deliberate support here for women's involvement in leadership roles in liturgy and an implicit rebuke for those church leaders who did not allow it?

Something similar may perhaps also be the case with the reference to Mary Magdalene's being made a "messenger," as far as women having a leadership role over men is concerned. The male disciples, spoken of as "wandering orphans," are really put down as badly in need of the guidance of this woman. For the women, however, it is noted that they no doubt will meet stiff resistance from the men and that consequently they must develop all their "skill (*technē*) and advice until thou hast brought the sheep to the shepherd," again placing the woman in a much superior, indeed, "pastoral," position vis-à-vis the male disciples, who are suspected by Yeshua of "having their wits gone." Even Peter is placed under Mary Magdalene's evangelistic (*euangelios*) tutelage.

> "Mariam, Mariam, know me: do not touch me. Stem the tears of thy eyes and know me that I am thy master. Only touch me not, for I have not yet seen the face of my Father. Thy God was not stolen away, according to the thoughts of thy littleness; thy God did not die, rather he mastered death. I am not the gardener. . . . Cast this sadness away from thee and do this service (*leitourgia*): be a messenger (*angelos*) for me to these wandering orphans (*orphanos*). Make haste rejoicing, and go unto the Eleven. Thou shalt find them gathered together on the bank of the Jordan. The traitor persuaded them to be fishermen, as they were at first, and to lay down their nets with which they caught men unto life. Say to them: 'Arise, let us go, it is your brother that calls you.' If they scorn my brotherhood, say to them: 'It is your Master! If they disregard my mastership, say to them: 'it is your Lord.' Use all skill (*technē*) and advice until thou hast brought the sheep to the shepherd. If thou seest that their wits are gone, draw Simon Peter unto thee; say to him, 'Remember what I uttered between thee and me . . . in the Mount of Olives: I have something to say, I have none to whom to say it.'"[40]

§73 MARY MAGDALENE

It should be noted that Mary Magdalene, that is, Mary from the town of Magdala, is named in all four of the canonical Gospels. (There is no solid reason to identify her with the sinful woman of Lk 7:37–50 or Mary of Bethany.) In every instance (there are a total of twelve in the four Gospels) except Luke 8:2, the reference is in connection either with her being at the crucifixion and observing Yeshua's burial, or with her seeing the empty tomb and the risen Yeshua, the former being mentioned as a preparation to recording the latter. Each time, Mary Magdalene is either named alone or is at the head of the list (with the exception of the special situation of Jn 19:25, where the focus is specifically on Yeshua's mother, Mary). Moreover, all of the lists vary from evangelist to evangelist, no two lists ever being the same; however, Mary Magdalene is always listed. Scholars conclude that there was a strong and widespread tradition that Yeshua appeared first of all to Mary Magdalene and that she therefore held a place of honor in the early Christian community, thereby explaining her appearance on all the lists of women in the Gospels, and her being first on all save one.

> (1) And many women were there, watching from a distance, the same women who had followed Yeshua from Galilee and ministered to him. Among them were Mary of Magdala, Mary the mother of James and Joseph, and the mother of Zebedee's sons.[41]

> (2) So Joseph took the body, wrapped it in a clean shroud, and put it in his own new tomb which he had hewn out of the rock. He then rolled a stone across the entrance of the tomb and went away. Now Mary of Magdalena and the other Mary were there, sitting opposite the sepulchre.[42]

> (3) After the Sabbath, and towards dawn on the first day of the week, Mary of Magdala and the other Mary went to visit the sepulchre.[43]

> (4) There were some women watching from a distance. Among them were Mary of Magdala, Mary who was the mother of James the younger and Joset, and Salome. These used to follow him and minister to him when he was in Galilee.[44]

> (5) He granted the corpse to Joseph who bought a shroud, took Yeshua down from the cross, wrapped him in the shroud, and laid him in a tomb which had been hewn out of the rock. He then rolled a stone against the entrance to the tomb. Mary of Magdala and Mary the mother of Joset were watching and took note of where he was laid.[45]

> (6) When the Sabbath was over, Mary of Magdala, Mary the mother of James, and Salome, bought spices with which to go and anoint him. And very early in the morning on the first day of the week they went to the tomb, just as the sun was rising.[46]

> (7) Having risen in the morning on the first day of the week, he appeared first to Mary of Magdala from whom he had cast out seven devils.[47]

> (8) With him went the Twelve, as well as certain women who had been cured of evil spirits and ailments: Mary surnamed the Magdalene, from whom seven demons had gone out, Joanna the wife of Herod's steward Chuza, Susanna, and several others who ministered to them out of their own resources.[48]

> (9) When the women returned from the tomb they told all this to the Eleven and to all the others. The women were Mary of Magdala, Joanna, and Mary the mother of James. The other women with them also told the

apostles, but this story of theirs seemed pure nonsense, and they did not believe them.[49]

(10) Near the cross of Yeshua stood his mother and his mother's sister, Mary the wife of Clopas, and Mary of Magdala. Seeing his mother and the disciple he loved standing near her, Yeshua said to his mother, "Woman, this is your son." Then to the disciple he said, "This is your mother." And from that moment the disciple made a place for her in his home.[50]

(11) It was very early on the first day of the week and still dark, when Mary of Magdala came to the tomb. She . . . saw Yeshua standing there. . . . Yeshua said to her. . . . "Go to the brothers, and tell them. . . ." So Mary of Magdala went and told the disciples that she had seen the Lord and that he had said these things to her.[51]

§74 THE APOSTLE TO THE APOSTLES

As a result of Mary Magdalene's role as one sent (*apostellein*) by Yeshua to witness to the male apostles, as recorded in the canonical Fourth Gospel, John 20:17, she was the only woman besides Yeshua's mother on whose feast the creed was recited in the Western Church.[52] The term "apostle," in reference to Magdalene, occurs often in the well-known ninth-century life of her by Rabanus Maurus: Yeshua commissioned her an apostle to the apostles (*apostola apostolorum*);[53] she did not delay in carrying out the office of the apostolate to which she was commissioned;[54] her fellow apostles were evangelized with the news of the resurrection of the Messiah;[55] she was raised to the honor of the apostolate and was commissioned an evangelist (*evangelisto*) of the resurrection.[56] Even the acerbic Bernard of Clairvaux (twelfth century) referred to her as the "apostle to the apostles."[57]

Rabanus Maurus really simply carried on a tradition attested to many centuries earlier. Around the end of the second century or the beginning of the third, Hippolytus of Rome also commented on Yeshua's appearing first to Mary Magdalene, and the other women, and spoke of Mary Magdalene, and the other women and, symbolically Eve, as *apostles* and *evangelists* (proclaimers of the Gospel, *evangelium*). The extant text is in a Slavonic translation, with variations in an Armenian translation:

> Christ himself sent [Mary Magdalene], so that even women become the apostles of Christ and the deficiency of the first Eve's disobedience was made evident by this justifying obedience. O wondrous adviser, Eve becomes an apostle! Already recognizing the cunning of the serpent, henceforth the tree of knowledge did not seduce her, but having accepted the

tree of promise, she partook of being judged worthy to be a part of Christ. . . . Now Eve is a helpmate through the Gospel! Therefore, too, the women proclaimed the Gospel [from here on the Armenian translation has a few differences; see below]. But the basic fact was this—that Eve's custom was to proclaim lies and not truth. What's this? For us the women proclaim the resurrection as the Gospel. Then Christ appeared to them and said, "Peace be with you. I have appeared to the women and have sent them to you as apostles."

[The differences in the Armenian translation are as follows:]

Therefore women, too, proclaimed the Gospel to the disciples. Therefore, however, they believed them mistaken. . . . What kind of a new thing is it for you, o women, to tell of the resurrection? But that they might not be judged mistaken again, but as speaking in truth, Christ appeared to them and said: Peace be with you. Wherewith he showed it as true: As I appeared to the women, sending them to you, I have desired to send them as apostles.[58]

§75 MARY MAGDALENE IN GNOSTIC CHRISTIAN LITERATURE

Besides the strong, positive tradition about Mary Magdalene in the canonical Gospels and the orthodox Christian writers quoted above, and others, there is a similarly strong tradition about her among Gnostic Christians, already amply displayed earlier (§72) in the third- or fourth-century Manichean document wherein Mary Magdalene is sent by Yeshua as a messenger (*angelos*) to "evangelize" (*euangelizein*) the male disciples with all possible skill.

§76 Mary Magdalene, Teacher of the Apostles

This tradition of Mary Magdalene's superiority to the male disciples begins even earlier in the apocryphal Gospel named after her, the *Gospel of Mary*, probably a second-century Gnostic Christian document. In it, after Yeshua commanded the disciples to go and preach the Gospel and then left them, the men played the stereotypical female role, not knowing what to do and crying; whereas Mary played the stereotypical male role, confidently knowing what to do and encouraging the men. At first she succeeded admirably, but then, as she expounded her specialized knowledge from Yeshua, jealousy was engendered among the male disciples, particularly Andrew and Peter, who attacked her for thinking that she, a woman, might have better access to the truths of

Christ than they, the men, did. Mary responded bluntly and was supported by another apostle, Levi, who rebuked Peter for being so hot-tempered and attacking Mary Magdalene. In the end they all went off to preach the Gospel, so that Mary Magdalene prevailed.

> But they were grieved and wept sore, saying: "How shall we go to the heathen and preach the Gospel of the Kingdom of the Son of man? If he was not spared at all, how shall we be spared?"

> Then arose Mary, saluted them all, and spake to her brethren: "Weep not, be not sorrowful, neither be ye undecided, for his grace will be with you and will protect you. Let us rather raise his greatness, for he hath made us ready, and made us to be men."

> When Mary said this, she turned their mind to good, and they began to discuss the words of the [Saviour].

Peter now says to Mary, "We know that the Saviour loved you above all other women." He asks her to recount the revelations that she has received from the Savior, which he and the others have not heard. Mary tells how she saw the Lord in a vision and spoke with him. There follows a lengthy, complicated Gnostic conversation between Yeshua and Mary.

> When Mary had said this, she was silent, so that (thus) the Saviour had spoken with her up to this point. But Andrew answered and said to the brethren. "Tell me, what think ye with regard to what she says? I, at least, do not believe that the Saviour said this. For certainly these doctrines have other meanings." Peter in answer spoke with reference to things of this kind, and asked them about the Saviour: "Did he then speak privily with a woman rather than with us, and not openly? Shall we turn about and all hearken unto her? Has he preferred her over against us?"

> Then Mary wept and said to Peter: "My brother Peter, what dost thou then believe? Dost thou believe that I imagined this myself in my heart, or that I would lie about the Saviour?" Levi answered (and) said to Peter: "Peter, thou hast ever been of a hasty temper. Now I see how thou dost exercise thyself against the woman like the adversaries. But if the Saviour hath made her worthy, who then art thou, that thou reject her? Certainly the Saviour knows her surely enough. Therefore did he love her more than us. Let us rather be ashamed, put on the perfect Man, [form ourselves (?)] as he charged us, and proclaim the Gospel, without requiring any further command or any further law beyond that which the Saviour said (Gr.: neither limiting nor legislating, as the Saviour said)."

But [when Levi had said this,] they set about going to preach and to proclaim (Gr.: When he had thus spoken, Levi went away and began to preach).[59]

§77 Mary Magdalene, Most Beloved Disciple

In the above citation Peter admits that "the Saviour loved [Mary Magdalene] above all other women." He could not bring himself to say that Yeshua loved Mary Magdalene more than him, but a little later Levi does make such an admission: "But if the Saviour hath made her worthy, who then art thou, that thou reject her? Certainly the Saviour knows her surely enough. Therefore did he love her more than us." Earlier it was noted (see §59) that in the early third-century Gnostic Christian document *Pistis Sophia*, Yeshua said, "But Mary Magdalene and John, the maiden (*parthenos*), will surpass all my disciples and all men who shall receive mysteries." Beyond these there is a further Gnostic Christian apocryphal Gospel, the third-century *Gospel of Philip*, in which Mary Magdalene is said to be called the "companion" of Yeshua and loved by "Christ" "more than all the disciples." There is also a startling passage in which "Christ" is said to "kiss her often on the mouth." In this Gnostic Christian document this action obviously has a spiritualized significance, but still, Mary Magdalene is the recipient of the most intimate favors (graces) of "Christ."

> There were three who always walked with the Lord: Mary his mother and her sister and Magdalene, the one who was called his companion. His sister and his mother and his companion were each a Mary. . . . And the companion of the [Savior is] Mary Magdalene. [But Christ loved her] more than [all] the disciples [and used to] kiss her [often] on her [mouth]. The rest of the [disciples were offended] by it and [expressed disapproval]. They said to him, *"Why do you love her more than all of us?"* The Savior answered and said to them, *"Why do I not love you like her?"* When a blind man and one who sees are both together in darkness, they are no different from one another. When the light comes, then he who sees will see the light, and he who is blind will remain in darkness.[60]

§78 Peter's Jealousy of Mary Magdalene

In the canonical Fourth Gospel, Mary Magdalene, rather than Peter, is the one to whom the risen Christ first appears, just as it was Martha, rather than Peter, who declared Yeshua to be the Son of God, giving in the Fourth Gospel community a certain priority of Mary Magdalene and other women over Peter. This does not reflect anything negative toward Peter in the Fourth Gospel community, but it does indicate a conscious stress on the importance of women, especially Mary Magdalene, over Peter, whose importance in the other Gospels was clearly known to the final Redactor of the Fourth Gospel. As will be discussed further below, it should also be recalled that there are several lengthy and important passages in the Fourth Gospel which focus on women, including Mary Magdalene's first discovery of the empty tomb, her reporting of it to Peter and the others, and Yeshua's appearing to her alone, and commissioning her to "go to the brothers, and tell them." It may have been the next sentence (or the tradition behind the sentence), which said, "So Mary of Magdala went and told the disciples that she had seen the Lord and that he had said these things to her,"[61] that gave rise to the expanded report in the apocryphal *Gospel of Mary* about Mary Magdalene reporting her conversation with Yeshua to Peter and the other disciples. Further, the Fourth Gospel would have been found very attractive by Gnostic Christians, for, like them, it stressed light and life and a very "spiritual" kind of theology with many long and complicated discourses placed in the mouth of Yeshua. Hence, it is not surprising to find Gnostic Christians, like the Fourth Gospel, giving prominence to Mary Magdalene and also speaking of Peter's fits of jealousy toward her.

Besides the male disciples, in general, taking offense at Mary Magdalene's favored position with Yeshua recorded in the *Gospel of Philip*, cited just above, and the specific resentment voiced by Andrew and Peter in the above-cited *Gospel of Mary*, there is also the extremely vicious attack on women prophets attributed to Peter in the apocryphal *Kerygmata Petrou* (see §239). Further, Peter's hostility toward women, in general, and Mary Magdalene in particular was referred to twice (chap. 36 and 72) in the early third-century Gnostic Christian *Pistis Sophia*, and reached a kind of climax in the statement attributed to him in the third-century Gnostic Christian *Gospel of Thomas*, wherein Peter wanted to excommunicate Mary Magdalene, *because she is a woman*, but Yeshua defended her (in a way peculiar to that later ascetic time). Again the question naturally arises: was this a protest on the part of some Christian women, and their male sympathizers, against what they saw to be the rising restriction of women and even misogynism exercised by church leaders, who prided themselves on their rootage in the apostles, the chief of whom was Peter, as over against the feminism of Yeshua? The solution for many non-Gnostic as well as Gnostic Christian women was in becoming a man, a male (*vir*) that is, celibate.[62] However, the celibate Gnostic Christian women were less willing to accept subordination to the male hierarch than were the orthodox Catholic women.

Simon Peter said to them: Let Mary go forth from among us, for women are not worthy of the life. Yeshua said: Behold, I shall lead her, that I may make her male, in order that she also may become a living spirit like you males. For every woman who makes herself male shall enter into the kingdom of heaven.[63]

§79 RESURRECTION AND JAIRUS' DAUGHTER

The intimate connection of women with resurrection from the dead was not limited in the Gospels to the resurrection of Yeshua. There are accounts of three other resurrections in the Gospels, each closely involving a woman.[64] In one, Yeshua raised a young girl from the dead; in the other two, he raised persons from the dead largely because of women.

The most obvious connection of a woman with a resurrection account is that of the raising of the daughter of Jairus. In this story, which is contained in all three Synoptic Gospels, the daughter was initially said only to be extremely ill; but Yeshua is delayed, and she is reported dead. Yeshua had already agreed to come to her; he was not deterred by the death report. He raised her to life. Thus, Yeshua made clear that the resurrection was for women as well as for men.

A small detail is of particular interest here. Only in the case of Jairus' daughter did Yeshua touch the corpse, which made him ritually unclean. In the cases of the two men, Yeshua did not touch them, but merely said, "young man, I say to you, arise," or, "Lazarus, come out." One must at least wonder why Yeshua chose to violate the laws for ritual purity in order to help a woman, but not a man. That this point was intended by Yeshua, or at least so understood by all the early Christian communities, was corroborated by the fact that in the middle of the account of the raising of Jairus' daughter, in all three of the Synoptic Gospels, was placed the story of the curing of the woman with the twelve-year flow of blood, which carried a similar message: that as far as Yeshua was concerned, touching, or being touched, by a woman with a flow of blood did not make one unclean before God.

> When Yeshua had crossed again in the boat to the other side, a large crowd gathered round him and he stayed by the lakeside. Then one of the synagogue officials came up, Jairus by name, and seeing him, fell at his feet and pleaded with him earnestly, saying, "My little daughter is desperately sick. Do come and lay your hands on her to make her better and save her life." Yeshua went with him and a large crowd followed him. . . . [here is inserted the account of the curing of the woman with the twelve-year flow of blood].
>
> While he [Jairus] was still speaking some people arrived from the house of the synagogue official to say, "Your daughter is dead: why put the Master

to any further trouble?" But Yeshua had overheard this remark of theirs and he said to the official, "Do not be afraid; only have faith." And he allowed no one to go with him except Peter and James and John the brother of James. So they came to the official's house and Yeshua noticed all the commotion, with people weeping and wailing unrestrainedly. He went in and said to them, "Why all this commotion and crying? The child is not dead, but asleep." But they laughed at him. So he turned them all out and, taking with him the child's father and mother and his own companions he went into the place where the child lay. And taking the child by the hand he said to her, "Talitha, kum!" which means "Little girl, I tell you to get up." The little girl got up at once and began to walk about, for she was twelve years old. At this they were overcome with astonishment, and he ordered them strictly not to let anyone know about it, and told them to give her something to eat.[65]

§80 THE WIDOW OF NAIN

Again Luke/Luka alone recorded an event dealing with Yeshua and a woman, the raising from the dead of the son of the widow of Nain. The plight of this woman should be recalled: she was now alone in the world; she had no male to provide for her or to protect her with legal guardianship, which were almost absolute necessities in that society. For this reason, widows were considered the poorest of the poor. Further, despite the large crowd in the funeral procession who would be there to perform a good deed, a *mitzvah*, she was by custom thought to have caused the early death of her child (he is called "young man," *neaniskē*, by Yeshua) by her sins, and this on top of the loss of her husband. Yeshua saw all this and is touchingly described by Luke as being moved with pity for her and asking her not to cry. When Yeshua raised the young man, he *gave him back to his mother*; she was clearly the center of concern. Scholars note that this story is very similar to the raising of the only son of a widow by the prophet Elijah,[66] even to the use of the phrase "gave him to his mother." Those who reject the miraculous suggest here is the source of the story, especially since resurrections were also attributed to Tannaitic rabbis (rabbis of Yeshua's time) in remembrance of Elijah and Elisha. Those who don't reject the miraculous out of hand would see the Elijah story as a source of some of the *form* of Luke's description. Even the former would often grant a historical kernel of Yeshua's great concern for the welfare of sonless widows, and doubtless some particular instance. Luke, of course, affirms the resurrection.

> Soon afterward he went to a town called Nain, and his disciples and a large crowd accompanied him. As he approached the gate of the town, a dead

man was being carried out, the only son of a widowed mother. A considerable crowd of townsfolk were with her. The Lord was moved with pity upon seeing her and said to her, "Do not cry." Then he stepped forward and touched the litter; at this, the bearers halted. He said, "Young man, I bid you get up." The dead man sat up and began to speak. Then Yeshua gave him back to his mother. Fear seized them all and they began to praise God. "A great prophet has risen among us," they said; and, "God has visited his people." This was the report that spread about him throughout Judea and the surrounding country.[67]

§81 THE RESURRECTION OF LAZARUS

The third, and in some ways most important, account of a resurrection by Yeshua is that of Lazarus, at the request of his sisters, Martha and Mary. From the first, it was Martha and Mary who sent for Yeshua because of Lazarus' illness. But when Yeshua finally came, Lazarus was four days dead. Martha met Yeshua and pleaded for his resurrection: "Lord, if you had been here, my brother would not have died. And, even now, I know that whatever you ask from God, God will give you." Mary, who had been *sitting*, in mourning, hastened to Yeshua and fell *at his feet*[68] in supplication and said much the same. It is interesting that Yeshua sent a special call to Mary. The Fourth Gospel then records how Yeshua is deeply moved by a woman's, Mary's, suffering and weeping, as with the widow of Nain. Yeshua is so moved that he also cries, and then proceeds to raise Lazarus to life.

A further important point to be observed in this account is in Yeshua's conversation with Martha after she pleads for the resurrection of Lazarus. Yeshua declares himself to be the resurrection ("I am the resurrection and the life"), the only time he does so that is recorded in the Gospels. According to the Fourth Gospel, Yeshua here reveals the central event, the central message, in the Gospel—the resurrection, his resurrection, his being the resurrection—to a woman! And, thereafter, performs a resurrection at least partially, at her request.

It should be further noted that Martha here also made the same public profession of Yeshua being the Messiah and the Son of God (*su ei ho christos ho huios tou theou*)[69] as Peter is recorded to have made (*su ei ho christos ho huios tou theou*).[70] It is especially impressive that exactly the same words are used in Greek, since there normally is very little relationship or similarity between the Fourth Gospel and any of the three Synoptic Gospels. This striking identity is further underlined by the fact that in the passages parallel to Matthew 16:16, found in Mark[71] and Luke,[72] the confession by Peter was considerably less in magnitude, that is, Peter confessed Yeshua to be the

Messiah, but not the Son of God. (Luke, however, did record that evil spirits driven out of sick persons by Yeshua proclaimed, "'You are the Son of God' . . . because they knew that he was the Messiah."[73]) According to Matthew, several of the disciples together had earlier proclaimed Yeshua "a son of God" (*theou huios ei*),[74] but since no definite article was used (*ho huios theou*), as in both Matthew 16:16 by Peter and in John 11:27 by Martha, this declaration has a lesser significance.

Raymond E. Brown, after noting that according to the Fourth Gospel, Yeshua first appears to Mary Magdalene, rather than to Peter, as Luke[75] and his missionary colleague Paul[76] report, states: "Giving to a woman a role traditionally associated with Peter may well be a deliberate emphasis on John's part, for substitution is also exemplified in the story of Lazarus, Mary, and Martha. . . . Thus, if other Christian communities thought of Peter as the one who made a supreme confession of Jesus as the Son of God and the one to whom the risen Jesus first appeared, the Johannine community associated such memories with heroines like Martha and Mary Magdalene."[77]

There was a man named Lazarus who lived in the village of Bethany with the two sisters, Mary and Martha, and he was ill. It was the same Mary, the sisters of the sick man Lazarus, who anointed the Lord with ointment and wiped his feet with her hair. The sisters sent this message to Yeshua, "Lord, the man you love is ill." On receiving the message, Yeshua said, 'This sickness will end, not in death but in God's glory, and through it the Son of God will be glorified."

Yeshua loved Martha and her sister and Lazarus, yet when he heard that Lazarus was ill he stayed where he was for two more days before saying to the disciples, "Let us go to Judaea." The disciples said, "Rabbi, it is not long since the Jews wanted to stone you; are you going back again?" Yeshua replied: "Are there not twelve hours in the day? A man can walk in the daytime without stumbling because he has the light of this world to see by; but if he walks at night he stumbles, because there is no light to guide him."

He said that and then added, "Our friend Lazarus is resting, I am going to wake him." The disciples said to him, "Lord, if he is able to rest he is sure to get better." The phrase Yeshua used referred to the death of Lazarus, but they thought that by "rest" he meant "sleep," so Yeshua put it plainly, "Lazarus is dead; and for your sake I am glad I was not there because now you will believe. But let us go to him." Then Thomas, known as the Twin, said to the other disciples, "Let us go, too, and die with him."

On arriving, Yeshua found that Lazarus had been in the tomb for four days already. Bethany is only about two miles from Jerusalem, and many Jews had come to Martha and Mary to sympathize with them over their brother. When Martha heard that Yeshua had come she went to meet him.

Mary remained sitting in the house. Martha said to Yeshua, "If you had been here, my brother would not have died, but I know that, even now, whatever you ask of God, he will grant you." "Your brother," said Yeshua to her, "will rise again." Martha said, "I know he will rise again at the resurrection on the last day." Yeshua said: "I am the resurrection. If anyone believes in me, even though he dies he will live, and whoever lives and believes in me will never die. Do you believe this?" "Yes, Lord," she said, "I believe that you are the Christ, the Son of God, the one who was to come into this world."

When she had said this, she went and called her sister Mary, saying in a low voice, "The Master is here and wants to see you." Hearing this, Mary got up quickly and went to him. Yeshua had not yet come into the village; he was still at the place where Martha had met him. When the Jews, who were in the house sympathizing with Mary, saw her get up so quickly and go out, they followed her, thinking that she was going to the tomb to weep there.

Mary went to Yeshua, and as soon as she saw him she threw herself at this feet, saying, "Lord, if you had been here, my brother would not have died." At the sight of her tears, and those of the Jews who followed her, Yeshua said in great distress, with a sigh that came straight from the heart, "Where have you put him?" They said, "Lord, come and see." Yeshua wept; and the Jews said, "See how much he loved him!" But there were some who remarked, "He opened the eyes of the blind man, could he not have prevented this man's death?" Still sighing, Yeshua reached the tomb: it was a cave with a stone to close the opening. Yeshua said, "Take the stone away." Martha said to him, "Lord, by now he will smell; this is the fourth day." Yeshua replied, "Have I not told you that if you believe you will see the glory of God?" So they took away the stone. Then Yeshua lifted up his eyes and said: "Father, I thank you for hearing my prayer. I knew indeed that you always hear me, but I speak for the sake of all these who stand round me, so that they may believe it was you who sent me."

When he had said this, he cried in a loud voice, "Lazarus, here! Come out!" The dead man came out, his feet and hands bound with bands of stuff and a cloth round his face. Yeshua said to them, "Unbind him, let him go free."[78]

NOTES

1. Lk 2:36–38.
2. Lk 8:1–3. Cf. Mk 15:40–41 and Mt 27:55–56.
3. Mk 15:40–41.
4. Mt 27:55–56.
5. *Nag Hammadi Library*, 133.

6. *Sophia Jesu Christi, New Testament Apocrypha*, 1:246.
7. *Gospel of Thomas, New Testament Apocrypha*, 1:298.
8. *Pistis Sophia, New Testament Apocrypha*, 1:256–57.
9. Mary of Bethany, according to Jn 12:3.
10. Mk 14:3–9. Cf. Mt 26:6–13 and Jn 12:1–8.
11. See §58 for an analysis of the significance of the word "served," *diēkonei*, used here.
12. Jn 12:1–8. Cf. Mk 14:3–97 and Mt 26:6, 13.
13. Cf. the centurion from Capernaum, Mt 8:5 and the centurion under the cross, Mt 27:54.
14. Cf. the Phoenician woman, Mt 15:21–28.
15. Mt 27:19.
16. Lk 23: 26–32.
17. Mt 26:56.
18. Mk 14:49.
19. See the arguments in §198, that the Beloved Disciple was in fact a women, most likely Mary Magdalene.
20. Mk 15:40–41.
21. Mt 27:55–56.
22. Lk 23:49.
23. Jn 19:25–27.
24. Mk 15:42–47.
25. Mt 27:57–61.
26. Lk 23:50–56.
27. See §194 for a discussion of this problem.
28. Mk 16:1–8.
29. Mt 28:1–8.
30. Lk 24:1–12.
31. Jn 20:1–10.
32. Mk 16:9–20.
33. Mk 16:9–11.
34. Mt 28:8–10.
35. Jn 20:11–18.
36. Mk 16:8.
37. Mk 16:9–20.
38. *Gospel of Peter, New Testament Apocrypha*, 1:186–87.
39. *Epistula Apostolorum, New Testament Apocrypha*, 1:195–96.
40. *Gospel of Mani, New Testament Apocrypha*, 1:353–54.
41. Mt 27:55–56.
42. Mt 27:57–58.
43. Mt 28:1.
44. Mk 15:40–41.
45. Mk 15:45–47.
46. Mk 16:1–2.
47. Mk 16:9.
48. Lk 8:1–3.
49. Lk 24:9–11.
50. Jn 19:25–27.
51. Jn 20:1, 15, 17, 18.
52. Josef Andreas Jungmann, *The Mass of the Roman Rite* (Benziger Brothers, 1951), 470, no. 55.
53. Cf. Migne, *Patrologia Latina*, vol. 112, col. 1474B.

54. Col 1475A.

55. Col 1475B.

56. Col 1479C.

57. Migne, *Patrologia Latina*, vol. 183, col. 1148.

58. Hippolytus, in *Die griechischen christlichen Schriftsteller der ersten drei Jahrhunderte*, vol. 1 (Berlin: 1897), 354–55.

59. *Gospel of Mary, New Testament Apocrypha*, 1:342–44.

60. *Gospel of Philip, Nag Hammadi Library*, 135–36, 138. Italics added.

61. Jn 20:18.

62. This is discussed further in §270 and §306.

63. *Gospel of Thomas, New Testament Apocrypha*, 1:522.

64. Also the resurrection of Tabitha by Peter, Acts 9:36–42.

65. Mk 5:21–24, 35–43. Cf. Mt 9:18–26 and Lk 8:40–56.

66. 1 Kgs 17:17–24.

67. Lk 7:11–17.

68. Both italicized elements reminiscent of Mary's posture in the Lk 10:38–42 story of Martha and Mary.

69. Jn 11: 27.

70. Mt 16:16.

71. Mk 8:27–30.

72. Lk 9:18–21.

73. Lk 4:41.

74. Mt 14:33.

75. Lk 24:34.

76. 1 Cor 15:5.

77. Raymond E. Brown, "Roles of Women in the Fourth Gospel," *Theological Studies* (December 1975): 692–3.

78. Jn 11:1–44.

II

THE GOSPELS
CRITICALLY ANALYZED

· 6 ·

§82 The Attitude Toward Women Reflected by the Gospel Writers and Their Sources

$\mathcal{A}$s outlined earlier, one of the contributions of modern scriptural scholarship is the idea that the Gospels are not simple accounts of the words and actions of Yeshua as related by several different eyewitnesses. The fact that they are many-layered faith statements brought together from several sources, written and oral, and put into their present four forms by at least four different Gospel writers means that they tell us something not only of the attitude of Yeshua toward women but also of the attitudes of the evangelists and their sources. At times, in certain accounts, it is difficult to determine whether it is Yeshua's or the evangelists' or their sources' attitudes that are reflected, but for the most part, those passages, which rather clearly reveal Yeshua's own attitude, have been treated in earlier chapters. However, many passages, which in some way deal with women, still remain to be treated. They are listed below by Gospel, and are analyzed where pertinent for any additional light they cast on the attitude toward women expressed by the Gospel writer and his sources. Often this will be traced in some form ultimately back to Yeshua.

By presenting the material systematically according to each Gospel, I anticipate that a picture of the attitude toward women of each evangelist and his/her sources will emerge. The attitude of each can be compared to that of the others, and to that of Yeshua, insofar as his attitude can be distilled out and seen separately from those of the evangelists and their sources.

The first Gospel presented is Mark's since it is thought by most scholars to be the oldest of the Gospels. Then comes Matthew's Gospel because it is second in number of women passages, and most likely also the second Gospel to be written, followed by Luke with the highest number of women passages and most probably the third written. These three Gospels are referred to as the Synoptic (*syn-optic*, which in Greek means "seen together") Gospels because they treat many of the same events and teachings of Yeshua. The Fourth

Gospel is treated last because it was the last to be written, and because it has by far the smallest number of accounts that deal with women, and they are almost totally unrelated to the material in the three Synoptic Gospels, outside of the final section of all the Gospels which treat the passion and resurrection of Yeshua.

§83 THE GOSPEL ACCORDING TO MARK

Mark, as said, is thought by most scholars to be the earliest of the four Gospels we have. It is also the shortest, being about 62 percent of the length of Luke. (Matthew is about 92 percent of Luke's length, and the Fourth Gospel 75 percent.) Of the three Synoptic Gospels, Mark has by far the least to say about women. In Mark, there are 20 passages for a total of 114 verses that deal with one or more women, or with the feminine.

§84 Holy Spirit Shares Symbol with the Goddess of Love

Mark began his Gospel telling of John the Baptist by whom Yeshua was baptized in the Jordan river. As Yeshua came out of the water, Mark reports that a voice from heaven said, "You are my beloved son in whom I am well pleased," and the Spirit descended on him in the form of a dove. From that Markan report, and those of the other three Gospels, the dove has, for two thousand years, been the most frequent symbol of the Holy Spirit, after the fourth century, also known as the third person of the Blessed Trinity. Most Christians, however, do not realize that for centuries before, and after, the dove was the universal symbol of the goddess of love, under many names, including the *Mater Magna*, the "Great Mother"!

However, the connection of the Goddess of Love with the Holy Spirit is, in many ways, quite apt. To begin with, the very idea and language of the Holy Spirit, as somehow a manifestation of God, came from the Hebrew Bible, and therefore in the Hebrew language. And in Hebrew, the Spirit (*Ruach*) is feminine in gender and hence in poetic imagery.

> However, since the most ancient times the dove is the holy animal not only of the Cyprian Aphrodite, but also of almost all the Goddesses of Fertility and Love of the Near East. Already in neolithic times the "Great Mother" who was venerated in Crete was represented with dove and lily. The Greek word for dove, *peristera*, means "bird of Istar," the Assyrian-Babylonian Goddess of Love, but also of the Underworld and Death. Istar had many names: Astarte (Ashtoreth) and Hathor, Inanna and Nut, Cybele and Isis,

and many others. However, as also with the Greek Aphrodite and the Roman Venus, the dove was always holy to them. Often they themselves appeared winged, like a great dove brooding over the world, as in Knossos and Mycenae, in Sicily and Carthage, on the Euphrates and on Cyprus, and even in India. Doves were cultically protected; great towers were built for them in which they could nest; they were called *columbaria* (*columba* is the Latin word for dove). *Columbaria*, dove houses, were also known in ancient Rome, however, as grave chambers with niches for urns.

The dove is the only symbol for the Holy Spirit that is permitted by the Church. Thus the figure of the dove in the cupolas or over the high altars of Diessen, Dietramszell, Ettal, Ottobeuren, Vierzehnheiligen, Weingarten, and the Wieskirche also point to the "Great Mother" just as much as does the fact that the cathedrals of Hagia Sophia in Constantinople, Kiev, and many other Orthodox cities are consecrated to heavenly Wisdom, which is presented in feminine form.[1]

§85 Woman Holy Spirit in Christian Art

Following the Hebrew tradition of the Holy Spirit (*Ruach ha kadosh*) being feminine, some Christian artists have depicted the Holy Spirit as a woman. I offer two striking examples which I saw in Bavaria. Both are from the first half of the fifteenth century, that is, in the late Middle Ages. In one, a three-dimensional figure, the Trinity, crowns Mary as Queen of Heaven. The third person of the Trinity is clearly a woman. The second image is a fresco in a vault in a small gothic church; the painting also is from the first half of the fifteenth century, before the Protestant Reformation, and in it the Trinity is depicted as having one body in the lower half and three torsos and heads above. Again, there is a male with a white beard, God the Father, then a second male with a dark beard, God the Son, and finally a clean-faced woman, God the Holy Spirit.

§86 Yeshua's First Cures: Men and Women

See §48 for an analysis of the account of the cure of Peter's mother-in-law, and §100 for a discussion of how Matthew made use of this account. In Mark's Gospel the cure of Peter's mother-in-law was paired with the cure of a man with an "unclean spirit." These two cures were the first signs of Yeshua's power, as recorded by Mark. It does not seem possible that it could have been an accident that here at the opening of Yeshua's public life stood the cures of a man and a woman. Clearly Mark, or his source here, took this opportunity to show Yeshua's equal commitment to both women and men in his mission.

Luke followed exactly Mark's structure in this matter by recording these two cures at the beginning of Yeshua's public life.

a. Yeshua Teaches in Capernaum and Cures a Demoniac

They went as far as Capernaum, and as soon as the Sabbath came Yeshua went to the synagogue and began to teach. And his teaching made a deep impression on them because, unlike the scribes, he taught them with authority.

In their synagogue, just then there was a man possessed by an unclean spirit, and it shouted, "What do you want with us, Yeshua of Nazareth? Have you come to destroy us? I know who you are: the Holy One of God." But Yeshua said sharply, "Be quiet! Come out of him!" And the unclean spirit threw the man into convulsions and with a loud cry went out of him. The people were so astonished that they started asking each other what it all meant. "Here is a teaching that is new," they said, "and with authority behind it: he gives orders even to unclean spirits and they obey him." And his reputation rapidly spread everywhere through all the surrounding Galilean countryside.

b. Cure of Simon's Mother-in-Law

On leaving the synagogue, Yeshua went with James and John straight to the house of Simon and Andrew. Now Simon's mother-in-law had gone to bed with fever, and they told Yeshua about her straightaway. He went to her, took her by the hand and helped her up. And the fever left her and she began to wait on them.[2]

§87 Yeshua's Mother, Brothers, and Sisters

See §§41–44, 109, 110, 115, and 122 for a discussion of Yeshua's attitude toward his family. Here it should be simply noted that Mark, and Matthew following him, refer to sisters as well as mother and brothers. Luke, for some reason, does not.

His mother and brothers now arrived and, standing outside, sent in a message asking for him. A crowd was sitting round him at the time the message was passed to him, "Your mother and brothers and sisters are outside asking for you." He replied, "Who are my mother and my brothers?" And looking round at those sitting in a circle about him, he said, "Here are my mother and my brothers. Anyone who does the will of God, that person is my brother and sister and mother."[3]

§88 Lamp on a Lamp Stand

See §27 for a discussion. The story of a person placing a lamp on a lamp stand rather than under a tub or bed is in a household context and more likely to be familiar to women than men, and in Luke it makes a clearly sexually parallel story to match the preceding outdoors story of the sower in the field, which is in a context more likely to be familiar to men. In Mark, however, these two stories are not an isolated pair as in Luke. Rather, they are the first two of five consecutive stories in Mark. Hence, the quality of the pair being parallel is considerably diluted in Mark as compared with Luke.

> He taught them many things in parables, and in the course of his teaching he said to them, "Listen! Imagine a sower going out to sow . . ." [after relating the parable Yeshua explained it, and the text continues].

> He also said to them, "Would you bring in a lamp to put it under a tub or under the bed? Surely you will put it on the lampstand? For there is nothing hidden but it must be disclosed, nothing kept secret except to be brought to light."[4]

§89 Jairus' Daughter and the Woman with a Flow of Blood

See §12 for an analysis of these two spliced accounts of cures of women—one from death! Here we should simply focus on the fact that Mark has juxtaposed this spliced account of the cures of women next to the account of a cure of a man, the cleansing of a man of an "unclean spirit." These are the only cures recorded by Mark in this portion of his Gospel; both preceding and following them are other kinds of matters: a series of parables by Yeshua, accounts of Yeshua's traveling, and the beheading of John the Baptist. Though we cannot be certain, it seems likely that Mark, placed these accounts of cures side by side because they showed Yeshua curing both women and men. Or, perhaps the arrangement of the materials is as he found them in his written or oral sources. Because this set of accounts so very closely parallels the earlier cures of, first, a man possessed of an "unclean spirit" in Capernaum,[5] and second, Peter's mother-in-law,[6] it again seems most likely that Mark placed these accounts of cures side-by-side because they likewise show Yeshua curing both women and men. It is possible that here, and in the earlier set, Mark found these accounts already so arranged in his written or oral sources. We cannot know that, but if it was so, it would simply be *evidence that an awareness of Yeshua's sexual egalitarianism preceded the composition of the Gospel of Mark*, and that Mark affirmed it and handed it on.

Also, as in the earlier sexually parallel set of cures, Luke here likewise follows Mark's structure, thereby also handing on this evidence of Yeshua's sexual egalitarian attitude and confirming it with his own. Matthew again rearranged Mark's structure here for other purposes:

§90 The Gerasene Demoniac

They reached the country of the Gerasenes on the other side of the lake, and no sooner had he left the boat than a man with an unclean spirit came out from the tombs towards him.

§91 Cure of the Woman with a Hemorrhage: The Daughter of Jairus Raised to Life

When Yeshua had crossed again in the boat to the other side, a large crowd gathered round him and he stayed by the lakeside. Then one of the synagogue officials came up, Jairus by name, and seeing him, fell at his feet and pleaded with him earnestly, saying, "My little daughter is desperately sick. Do come and lay your hands on her to make her better and save her life." Yeshua went with him and a large crowd followed him, they were pressing all round him.

Now there was a woman who had suffered from a hemorrhage for twelve years; after long and painful treatment under various doctors, she had spent all she had without being any the better for it, in fact, she was getting worse. She had heard about Yeshua, and she came up behind him through the crowd and touched his cloak. "If I can touch even his clothes," she had told herself, "I shall be well again." And the source of the bleeding dried up instantly, and she felt in herself that she was cured of her complaint. Immediately aware that power had gone out from him, Yeshua turned round in the crowd and said, "Who touched my clothes?" His disciples said to him, "You see how the crowd is pressing round you and yet you say, 'Who touched me?'" But he continued to look all round to see who had done it. Then the woman came forward, frightened and trembling because she knew what had happened to her, and she fell at his feet and told him the whole truth. "My daughter," he said, "your faith has restored you to health; go in peace and be free from your complaint."

While he was still speaking some people arrived from the house of the synagogue official to say, "Your daughter is dead: why put the Master to any further trouble?" But Yeshua had overheard this remark of theirs and he said to the official, "Do not be afraid; only have faith." And he allowed no one to go with him except Peter and James and John the brother of James. So they came to the official's house and Yeshua noticed all the commotion, with people weeping and wailing unrestrainedly. He went in and said to them, "Why all this commotion and crying? The child is not dead, but asleep." But they laughed at him. So he turned them all out and, taking with him the child's father and mother and his own companions, he went into the place where the child lay. And taking the child by the hand he said to her. "Talitha, kum!" which means, "Little girl, I tell you to get up." The little girl got up at once and began to walk about, for she was twelve years old. At this they were overcome with astonishment, and he ordered them strictly not to let anyone know about it, and told them to give her something to eat.[7]

§92 Yeshua's Problems with His Family

See §§110, 112, 115, and 122 for an analysis of the difficulties Yeshua had with his family, including, as Mark and Matthew record it, his mother and his sisters.[8]

§93 Herodias, Salome, John the Baptist

This is the only story in Mark, which is not in some way about Yeshua; Mark tells it because he saw John the Baptist as the prophet Elijah returning[9] as a precursor to the Messiah, Yeshua. It projects a very evil picture of women: Herodias indirectly asks for the head of John the Baptist, and Salome her daughter asks for it directly. It is from Josephus, the first-century Jewish historian, that we learn Salome's name.[10] Josephus also records a different description of the execution of John the Baptist, ordered by Herod for political reasons.[11] Mark parallels Queen Jezebel, who wishes to kill Elijah[12] with Herodias, who "was furious with him [John the Baptist, 'Elijah returned'] and wanted to kill him."[13] Mark also was influenced by the story of Esther, with the woman called to "perform" before a crowd of tipsy courtiers, the king's promise of half his kingdom,[14] and the woman's beauty leading to the death of her enemy.

Thus, we have projected one of the few negative images of women in all the Gospels, but it is in a story that is not even about Yeshua. The fact, however, that it is recorded in Mark is simply a reflection of the culturally pervasive negative attitude toward women, perhaps indicating that Yeshua's positive attitude was not completely shared by Mark, or perhaps reflecting also the tradition Mark represented.

Matthew summarizes Mark's twenty-seven verse account in twelve verses. He, in fact, often abbreviates Mark's accounts (some scholars speculate that these short Matthean accounts were really the residues of the earlier Aramaic language which Mark later expanded). In doing so, he placed the desire to kill John the Baptist not in Herodias but in Herod, thereby very slightly mollifying the image of women that is projected; perhaps he, too, knew of the tradition of Herod's political motivation for killing John that Josephus mentioned. Luke, however, simply refers to John's criticism of Herod, "for his relations with his brother's wife Herodias,"[15] and later mentions that Herod had John beheaded;[16] no negative image of women whatsoever. It would seem that, in this instance at least, Yeshua's positive attitude toward women was not sufficiently persuasive to convince either Mark or Matthew not to write the story of Herodias and Salome, but it did convince Luke not to include it. Matthew, however, did partly shift the guilt from the women alone and shorten the account by about 40 percent. Apparently, Luke's sensitivity about women led him to find the vicious popular story about Herodias and Salome offensive or at least irrelevant to the Gospel of Yeshua as he understood it.

> Now it was this same Herod who had sent to have John arrested, and had him chained up in prison because of Herodias, his brother Philip's wife, whom he had married. For John had told Herod, "it is against the law for you to have your brother's wife." As for Herodias, she was furious with him and wanted to kill him; but she was not able to, because Herod was afraid of John, knowing him to be a good and holy man, and gave him his protection. When he had heard him speak he was greatly perplexed, and yet he liked to listen to him.
>
> An opportunity came on Herod's birthday when he gave a banquet for the nobles of his court, for his army officers and for the leading figures in Galilee. When the daughter of this same Herodias came in and danced, she delighted Herod and his guests; so the king said to the girl, "Ask me anything you like and I will give it you." And he swore her an oath, "I will give you anything you ask, even half my kingdom." She went out and said to her mother, "What shall I ask for?" She replied, "The head of John the Baptist." The girl hurried straight back to the king and made her request, "I want you to give me John the Baptist's head, here and now, on a dish." The king was deeply distressed but, thinking of the oaths he had sworn and of his guests, he was reluctant to break his word to her. So the king at once sent one of the bodyguards with orders to bring John's head. The man went off and beheaded him in prison; then he brought the head on a dish and gave it to the girl, and the girl gave it to her mother. When John's disciples heard about this, they came and took his body and laid it in a tomb.[17]

§94 Yeshua Affirms Parents

See §41 for a discussion of Yeshua's affirmation of parenthood. There Matthew's version of Yeshua's angry retort to some of his opponents is given. The commentary there applies equally to the Markan version here.

> [Yeshua said to some Pharisees and scribes:] "You put aside the commandment of God to cling to human traditions." And he said to them, "How ingeniously you get around the commandment of God in order to preserve your own tradition! For Moses said: Do your duty to your father and your mother and, Anyone who curses father or mother must be put to death. But you say, 'If a man says to his father or mother: Anything I have

that I might have used to help you is Corban (that is, dedicated to God), then he is forbidden from that moment to do anything for his father or mother.' In this way you make God's word null and void for the sake of your tradition which you have handed down. And you do many other things like this."[18]

§95 Yeshua's Mission to Non-Jews through a Woman

Mark was writing for a Gentile readership, and, according to a number of scholars, wished to develop a section on Yeshua's mission to Gentiles. Mark wrote: "He set out for the [Gentile] territory of Tyre," and then told the story of the cure of the daughter of the Gentile woman.[19] But then immediately Mark recorded Yeshua's trip farther north to Sidon (also a largely Gentile area) and back to the shores of the Sea of Galilee, a Jewish area: "Returning from the district of Tyre, he went by way of Sidon towards the Sea of Galilee, right through the Decapolis region."[20] Thus, the only evidence Mark could find in the tradition for Yeshua's missionary tour of Gentile territory was this trip to Tyre and Sidon and back. The really interesting fact is that this trip produced nothing remembered other than the encounter with the Syro–Phoenician woman, whose daughter Yeshua cured at her insistence. Was it because the status of women in the Roman world, for whom Mark wrote, was much higher than in Jewish society, that Mark chose this story to show Yeshua reaching out to the Gentiles? Or was it that Mark simply found no other story in the tradition he knew which exemplified Yeshua's mission tour of pagan areas? Given Mark's readership, it seems most likely he would have included other such stories from the trip of Yeshua if there were any, and so the second explanation is the more likely. But the first should not be ruled out as at least a contributing motive as well. In the end, however, all we know from the evidence available is that Yeshua's mission to the Gentile world consisted of the healing of a woman at the persistent request of another woman.

> He left that place and set out for the territory of Tyre. There he went into a house and did not want anyone to know he was there, but he could not pass unrecognized. A woman whose little daughter had an unclean spirit heard about him straightaway and came and fell at his feet. Now the woman was a pagan, by birth a Syro–Phoenician, and she begged him to cast the devil out of her daughter. And he said to her "The children should be fed first, because it is not fair to take the children's food and throw it to the house-dogs." But she spoke up: "Ah yes, sir," she replied, "but the house-dogs under the table can eat the children's scraps." And he said to her, "For saying this, you may go home happy; the devil has gone out of your daughter." So she went off to her home and found the child lying on the bed and the devil gone.[21]

In Matthew's version, Yeshua conceived of his mission as being directed first of all to God's chosen people, the Jews, and the first recorded instance of his going beyond the limits of his commission was to heal a female, at the persistent insistence of a woman. It was her human quality, her "faith," that Yeshua perceived and that moved him to extend himself; she was not treated as an inferior category, a woman, but as a "person," who had "great faith." It is also interesting to note that this is the only recorded instance wherein Yeshua is bested in a verbal exchange and it is by a woman.

> Jesus left that place and withdrew to the region of Tyre and Sidon. Then out came a Canaanite woman from that district and started shouting, "Sir, Son of David, take pity on me. My daughter is tormented by a devil." But he answered her not a word. And his disciples went and pleaded with him. "Give her what she wants," they said, "because she is shouting after us." He said in reply, "I was sent only to the lost sheep of the House of Israel." But the woman had come up and was kneeling at his feet. "Lord," she said, "help me." He replied, "It is not fair to take the children's food and throw it to the house-dogs." She retorted, "Ah yes, sir; but even house-dogs can eat the scraps that fall from their master's table." Then Jesus answered her, "Woman, you have great faith. Let your wish be granted." And from that moment her daughter was well again.[22]

§96 Marriage and the Dignity of Women I

See §§38ff. for an analysis of Yeshua's revolutionary egalitarian attitude toward marriage, adultery, and divorce, particularly as expressed in Mark's account. In Mark, Yeshua flatly contradicts the Jewish law and custom of his time by saying that a husband could be "guilty of adultery against her [his wife]." Yeshua also spoke about a woman divorcing her husband, an impossibility in Jewish law, although possible in Hellenistic and Roman law of the time. Of course, such divorcing women were known in Palestine around the time of Yeshua, and he may well have included them in his remarks. Hence, it is not necessary to suggest that Mark, perhaps writing in Rome, is responsible for that phrase; if the Roman Mark, then why not the Hellenistic Luke? In any case, Yeshua's sexual egalitarianism in marriage comes through here very strongly, and correspondingly Mark's corroboration of it.

> Some Pharisees approached him and asked, "Is it against the law for a man to divorce his wife?" They were testing him. He answered them, "What did Moses command you?" "Moses allowed us," they said, "to draw up a writ of dismissal and so to divorce." Then Yeshua said to them "It was because you were so unteachable that he wrote this commandment for you. But from the beginning of creation God made them male and female. This is why a man must leave father and mother, and the two become one body.

They are no longer two, therefore, but one body. So then, what God has united, man must not divide." Back in the house the disciples questioned him again about this, and he said to them, "The man who divorces his wife and marries another is guilty of adultery against her. And if a woman divorces her husband and marries another she is guilty of adultery, too."[23]

§97 Yeshua Dismantles Restrictive Family Bonds

See §44 for a discussion of the extraordinarily powerful restrictions and obligations which extended-family bonds placed on persons in the Near East (which is still largely seen today). By far the most restricted group of persons in the patriarchal family is women. Hence, they have the most to gain in human freedom by a loosening of such restrictions, as Yeshua advocated. (Note that Mark recorded only one such reference, relatively mild; Matthew had two, and Luke three. The significance of this is discussed in §153.)

> Peter took this up. "What about us?" he asked him. "We have left everything and followed you." Yeshua said, "I tell you solemnly, there is no one who has left house, brothers, sisters, father, children or land for my sake and for the sake of the gospel who will not be repaid a hundred times over, houses, brothers, sisters, mothers, children and land, not without persecutions, now in this present time and, in the world to come, eternal life."[24]

§98 Marriage and the Dignity of Women II

See §38 for an analysis of Yeshua's response to the question of some Sadducees about a woman married seven times: to whom would she belong in heaven? Yeshua's answer presumed that she was a person and belonged to no one.

> Then some Sadducees, who deny that there is a resurrection, came to him and they put this question to him, "Master, we have it from Moses in writing, if a man's brother dies leaving a wife but no child, the man must marry the widow to raise up children for his brother. Now there were seven brothers. The first married a wife and died leaving no children. The second married the widow, and he too died leaving no children; with the third it was the same, and none of the seven left any children. Last of all, the woman herself died. Now at the resurrection, when they rise again, whose wife will she be, since she had been married to all seven?"
>
> Yeshua said to them, "Is not the reason why you go wrong, that you understand neither the scriptures nor the power of God? For when they rise from the dead, men and women do not marry; no, they are like the angels in heaven. Now about the dead rising again, have you never read in the Book of Moses, in the passage about the bush, how God spoke to

him and said: I am the God of Abraham, the God of Isaac and the God of Jacob? He is God, not of the dead, but of the living. You are very much mistaken."[25]

§99 The Oppression of Widows

See §49 for a discussion of Yeshua's slashing condemnation of the oppression of the most downtrodden element of the male-dominated society in which he lived—widows.[26]

§100 The Widow's Mite

See §45 for an analysis of Yeshua's holding up a widow as a model to be emulated.[27]

§101 Yeshua's Concern for Women's Welfare

There have been many scholarly suggestions for the real sources of the apocalyptic-sounding predictions of the end of the world that are found in all three of the Synoptic Gospels; these suggestions include solidly represented arguments that a prophetic statement of Yeshua is the source, just as the Gospels represent. There is rather general agreement that there has been some editorial adaptation by the evangelists, but usually disagreement on exactly what. No one, however, denies that the statement, "Alas for those with child, or with babies at the breast, when those days come!" was in the original version. Since there is no reason why Yeshua could not have made the original prophetic statement, however, it may have been differently adapted by the evangelists, and since the documents claim that he did, it is logical to conclude that it is at least probable that he did. In that case Yeshua would be the utterer of the cry of concern for women.

There is a certain sexual parallelism where the references to a man on the housetop and a man in the fields are "balanced" by references to expectant mothers and nursing mothers. The desolation described is so sudden and devastating that only immediate flight offers some chance of safety; hence, relatively immobilized mothers are at a severe disadvantage, and Yeshua expressed great concern for them. About no one else did he so express his concern.

Both Matthew and Luke used basically the same words concerning the women as did Mark.

> When you see the disastrous abomination set up where it ought not to be (let the reader understand), then those in Judaea must escape to the mountains; if a man is on the housetop, he must not come down to go into the house to collect any of his belongings; if a man is in the fields, he must not

turn back to fetch his cloak. Alas for those with child, or with babies at the breast, when those days come! Pray that this may not be in winter. For in those days there will be such distress as, until now, has not been equaled since the beginning when God created the world, nor ever will be again. And if the Lord had not shortened that time, no one would have survived; but he did shorten the time, for the sake of the elect whom he chose.[28]

§102 Anointment of Yeshua at Bethany

See §§60 and 61 for an analysis of the account of Yeshua's anointment by a woman while he is at table and his defense of her against grumbling men.[29]

§103 Women in Yeshua's Passion and Resurrection

See §63ff. for analyses of the extraordinary supportive involvement of women in Yeshua's passion, death, and burial; their presence at the empty tomb; their seeing the risen Yeshua; and their reporting to the rest of the disciples. Almost all of these elements are reported by each of the four Gospels, an extraordinary near-unanimity.

> *Only Women Remain by Yeshua through His Death*[30]
> *Women Witness the Burial of Yeshua*[31]
> *Women First Witnesses to the Empty Tomb*[32]
> *Women Testify about Resurrection to Male Disciples*[33]
> *The Risen Yeshua Appears to Women First*[34]

§104 Conclusion

Mark's Gospel has the least number of passages dealing with women of the three Synoptic Gospels (twenty to Matthew's thirty-six and Luke's forty-two) and the smallest number of verses concerning women of all four Gospels (114 to the Fourth Gospel's 119, Matthew's 180, and Luke's 220). Of course, it is the shortest Gospel in overall size, but proportionately it nevertheless has the least emphasis on women of the three Synoptics, but still more than the Fourth Gospel's in terms of proportionate quantity. Because it is the earliest Gospel, it apparently was available to both Matthew and Luke, and consequently almost all of it reappears in one form or another in either Matthew or Luke or both, and that includes all the passages dealing with women. Hence, in comparison to the other two Synoptics, Mark seems much less pro-woman in the number of accounts dealing with women he records. Still, the extremely important fact that nothing negative about women is recorded (with the exception of the non-Yeshua story of the beheading of John the Baptist discussed in §93) and the significant number of positive accounts about women which Mark does record, lead to the conclusion that Mark's Gospel is pro-woman in its stance, though not nearly as much so as Matthew and Luke, or even the Fourth Gospel.

§105 THE GOSPEL ACCORDING TO MATTHEW

It is true that there are no negative statements, attitudes, or actions concerning women by Yeshua in the Gospel of Mark. That in itself has a great significance. And while there is a relatively smaller amount of positive evidence of Yeshua's attitude toward women provided by Mark, this evidence nevertheless would indeed support a claim that Yeshua was a champion of women, but only modestly so.

However, the situation is quite different when we come to the next two Synoptic Gospels, Matthew and Luke. Not only in neither of them are there any negative attitudes toward women expressed by Yeshua, but also every one of the above accounts in Mark dealing with women is found in either Matthew or Luke, or in both, and sometimes even in the Fourth Gospel as well. Furthermore, Matthew records eighteen additional accounts significantly concerned with women that Mark does not mention, making a total of thirty-six accounts in Matthew dealing with women. Of these non-Markan accounts, ten are peculiar to Matthew; eight of them Luke also records along with Matthew (the Fourth Gospel records none of these eighteen accounts). The ten passages peculiar to Matthew, plus the four he has in common with Mark which Luke does not have, make fourteen accounts concerning women that Matthew records and that Luke does not.

§106 Passages Common to Matthew and Mark

§107 Women Included in the Reign of God

The first matter that reveals something of Matthew's attitude toward women that should be noted here concerns a passage Matthew has in common with both Mark and Luke. Because Matthew was writing for a Hebrew community, he consciously drew attention to Hebrew Scripture parallels. For Matthew the Sermon on the *Mount* is the starting point for the new "assembly" (*qahal, ekklesia*), paralleling the calling out and forming of the first "assembly" by the teaching and laws on *Mount* Sinai. For Matthew, Yeshua formed this new "assembly" by the healings he performed following his preaching; the cures specifically benefited a leper, a pagan, a woman—the three categories excluded from the Hebrew cultic assembly. According to

Matthew, then, these three categories were obviously intended by Yeshua to be included in his new "assembly." To communicate this in his Gospel, Matthew relocated the account of the cure of Peter's mother-in-law from where it apparently was originally situated (in both Mark's and Luke's Gospels), to group it with the cure of the leper and the centurion's servant, immediately after the close of the Sermon on the Mount.

> And going into Peter's house Yeshua found Peter's mother-in-law in bed with fever. He touched her hand and the fever left her, and she got up and began to wait on him.[35]

§108 Jairus' Daughter and the Woman with a Flow of Blood

See §12 for analyses of Yeshua's cures of two women, one with a long-term hemorrhage and one dead. The account is shorter in Matthew than in Mark, as happens in a number of other instances. This fact gave rise to the earlier theory that Matthew was prior in time and that Mark expanded the account; most (but not all) scholars now, however, hold Mark to be prior and that Matthew abbreviated the account. In any case, in Matthew these cures of women are grouped with two others, all of which are immediately followed by the statement, "Yeshua made a tour through all the towns and villages, teaching in their synagogues, proclaiming the Good News of the Reign of God" and its healing effects.[36] This structural message is the same, and is similarly communicated, as in Matthew's placing of the cure of Peter's mother-in-law where he did, as discussed earlier. The highlighting of this sexual egalitarianism in Yeshua's Gospel and in the Reign of God by structural placement of stories and statements could come from Matthew's sources, written and oral, where he found things so arranged, or from Matthew himself, or a combination. Hence, Matthew either further affirmed Yeshua's pro-woman stance by his own editorial arranging, or at least corroborated that affirmation in his sources by transmitting it in his editorial arrangement.

> While he was speaking to them, up came one of the officials, who bowed low in front of him and said, "My daughter has just died, but come and lay your hand on her and her life will be saved." Yeshua rose and, with his disciples, followed him.
>
> Then from behind him came a woman, who had suffered from a hemorrhage for twelve years, and she touched the fringe of his cloak, for she said to herself, "If I can only touch his cloak I shall be well again." Yeshua turned round and saw her; and he said to her, "Courage, my daughter, your faith has restored you to health." And from that moment the woman was well again.

When Yeshua reached the officials' house and saw the flute players, with the crowd making a commotion he said, "Get out of here; the little girl is not dead, she is asleep." And they laughed at him. But when the people had been turned out he went inside and took the little girl by the hand; and she stood up. And the news spread all round the countryside.[37]

§109 Yeshua's Mother, Brothers, and Sisters

See §§43 and 44 for a discussion of Yeshua's spiritualizing of the bonds of kinship, his dismantling of the oppressive restrictions of family ties which were so especially burdensome to women in that society. Note again that Matthew along with Mark mentions sisters, in addition to mother and brothers (though Luke does not), perhaps thereby reflecting quantitatively the special oppression women experienced in family restrictions.[38]

§110 Yeshua's Problems with his Family I

See §42 for a discussion of the problems Yeshua had with his family, and his response that had a freeing effect on women.

When Yeshua had finished these parables he left the district; and, coming to his home town, he taught the people in their synagogue in such a way that they were astonished and said, "Where did the man get this wisdom and these miraculous powers? This is the carpenter's son, surely? Is not his mother the woman called Mary, and his brothers James and Joseph and Simon and Jude? His sisters, too, are they not all here with us? So where did the man get it all?" And they would not accept him. But Yeshua said to them, "A prophet is only despised in his own country and in his own house," and he did not work many miracles there because of their lack of faith.[39]

§111 Herodias, Salome, John the Baptist

See §93 for an analysis of the implications of Matthew's inclusion of this story which projects such an evil image of women.

Now it was Herod who had arrested John, chained him up and put him in prison because of Herodias, his brother Philip's wife. For John had told him, "It is against the Law for you to have her." He had wanted to kill him but was afraid of the people, who regarded John as a prophet. Then during the celebrations for Herod's birthday, the daughter of Herodias danced before the company, and so delighted Herod that he promised on oath to give her anything she asked. Prompted by her mother, she said, "Give me John the Baptist's head, here, on a dish." The king was distressed but, thinking of the oaths he had sworn and of his guests, he ordered it to be given her, and sent and had John beheaded in the prison. The head was brought in on a dish and given to the girl who took it to her mother. John's disciples came and took the body and buried it; then they went off to tell Yeshua.[40]

§112 Yeshua Affirms Parents

See §41 for a discussion of Yeshua's affirmation of parents, mother as well as father. This position, of course, stands in the Hebraic tradition.[41]

§113 Yeshua's Mission to Non-Jews through a Woman

See §95 for an analysis of Yeshua's "mission to the Gentiles" through a woman, and also the special role this account plays in Mark's Gospel.[42]

§114 Marriage and the Dignity of Women I

See §38 for the analysis of Yeshua's revolutionary egalitarian attitude toward women in marriage by eliminating the husband's right to divorce his wife. Matthew alone, of the three Gospels that discuss divorce, includes the exception, "except for immorality." Most scholarship tends to see this exception clause either as (1) an additional interpretative phrase stemming from the Christian communities that served as Matthew's sources; or (2) possibly under later and more complex circumstances than those which prevailed when Mark and Luke were written. Matthew's sources' recollection and preservation of this helpful exception clause of Yeshua's; or (3) as a phrase of Yeshua's which really did not constitute an exception and therefore also did not contradict his absolute prohibition of divorce recorded in the Gospels. This latter interpretation is supported by Paul's report on Yeshua's teaching on divorce. Paul's epistle was written before any of the Gospels: "For the married I have something to say, and this is not from me but from the Lord: a wife must not leave her husband or if she does leave him, she must either remain unmarried or else make it up with her husband nor must a husband send his wife away."[43] (Paul himself, however, went beyond this restriction in the case of a Christian and non-Christian couple when the non-Christian wished a divorce: "If the unbelieving partner does not consent [to live together], they may separate; in these circumstances, the brother or sister is not tied."[44]) It should be noted that Paul reports an equal balance between the woman's and the man's rights here stemming from Yeshua and maintains the balance himself in his extension, the so-called Pauline Privilege.

The fact that the Matthew exception clause refers only to the man divorcing his wife, and not vice versa, also seems out of character with Yeshua's egalitarian attitude as recorded in the Mark and Luke divorce passages and many other places in the Gospels. This factor would also make it likely that the editor of the Greek version of Matthew (see §127 for a discussion of a possible earlier Aramaic version of Matthew) received the recollection or interpretation from his sources and felt a special need in the circumstances of the time and place to insert the clause in the account already at hand which did not contain it, perhaps to address a dispute pressing in Greek Matthew's source communities, but in inserting it did not do so in a sexually balanced manner, as one would have expected from Yeshua and as Matthew (perhaps the earlier Aramaic Matthew?) does elsewhere in his Gospel. However, this entire discussion will be moot if the new position advocated in §41 by Professor Ann Nyland is sustained.

> And I say to you: whoever divorces his wife, except for unchastity, and marries another, commits adultery.[45]

> But I say to you that every one who divorces his wife, except on the ground of unchastity, makes her an adulteress; and whoever marries a divorced woman commits adultery.[46]

§115 Yeshua's Problems with his Family II

See §42 for an analysis of the problems Yeshua had with his family and what bearing this had on his liberating attitude toward women.

> Then Peter spoke. "What about us?" he said to him. "We have left everything and followed you. What are we to have, then?" Yeshua said to him, "I tell you solemnly, when all is made new, and the Son of Man sits on his throne of glory, you will yourselves sit on twelve thrones to judge the twelve tribes of Israel. And everyone who has left houses, brothers, sisters, father, mother, children or land for the sake of my name will be repaid a hundred times over, and also inherit eternal life."[47]

§116 Marriage and the Dignity of Women II

See §38 for an analysis of Yeshua's response to the question of some Sadducees about a woman married seven times: to whom would she belong in heaven? Yeshua's answer presumed that she was a person and belonged to no one.[48]

§117 Yeshua's Concern for Women's Welfare

See §63 for a discussion of the concern for women's welfare at the final crisis that Yeshua expressed.

> So when you see the disastrous abomination, of which the prophet Daniel spoke, set up in the Holy Place (let the reader understand), then those in Judaea must escape to the mountains; if a man is on the housetop, he must not come down to collect his belongings; if a man is in the fields, he must not turn back to fetch his cloak. Alas for those with child, or with babies at the breast, when those days come! Pray that you will not have to escape in winter or on a Sabbath. For then there will be great distress such as, until now, since the world began, there never has been, nor ever will be again. And if that time had not been shortened, no one would have survived; but shortened that time shall be, for the sake of those who are chosen.[49]

§118 Anointment of Yeshua at Bethany

See §§60, 61 for an analysis of the account of Yeshua's anointment by a woman while he was at table, his defense of her against grumbling men, and his promise that she would be remembered wherever the Gospel was proclaimed. It is slightly ironic that in the Matthew and Mark accounts, which are almost identical, the women's name is not remembered, whereas in the Fourth Gospel's account where she is identified as Mary of Bethany, the sister of Martha and Lazarus, there is no mention made about her act "being remembered," though of course it was.

> Yeshua was at Bethany in the house of Simon the leper, when a woman came to him with an alabaster jar of the most expensive ointment, and poured it on his head as he was at table. When they saw this, the disciples were indignant; "Why this waste?" they said. "This could have been sold at a high price and the money given to the poor." Yeshua noticed this. "Why are you upsetting the woman?" he said to them. "What she has done for me is one of the good works indeed! You have the poor with you always, but you will not always have me. When she poured this ointment on my body, she did it to prepare me for burial. I tell you solemnly, wherever in all the world this Good News is proclaimed, what she has done will be told also, in remembrance of her."[50]

§119 Women in Yeshua's Passion and Resurrection

See §62ff. for analyses of the extremely supportive involvement of women in the passion, death, and burial of Yeshua; their presence at the empty tomb; their seeing the risen Yeshua; and their reporting of all this to the male disciples.

§120 Passages Common to Matthew and Luke Alone

§121 The Virginal Conception of Yeshua

Matthew's account of the virginal conception of Yeshua, that is, by the Holy Spirit in the womb of Mary, does perforce focus on the woman Mary. But it focuses still more sharply on the man Joseph. Even though the couple was only betrothed, the legal force of their state was practically as strong as marriage; sexual intercourse by the betrothed woman with any other man would have been considered not fornication but adultery (though not so for the betrothed man if he did the same). Joseph was under obligation to divorce (necessary even though they were only betrothed) his apparently adulterous betrothed. He could have subjected her to the excruciatingly humiliating ordeal of *Sotah*,[51] and possibly have had her executed. However, Joseph, "being a man of honor and wanting to spare her publicity, decided to divorce her informally," a significant sensitivity toward women enacted at the beginning of Yeshua's life. Luke's account of the virginal conception of Yeshua was within a different context from Matthew's, namely, the "annunciation" to Mary,[52] discussed below. It should be noted that whereas in Matthew's account here Joseph is the main focus of attention and the angel appears to him, in Luke's account Mary is the center of attention and the angel appears not to Joseph but to Mary.

> This is how Yeshua Christ came to be born. His mother Mary was betrothed to Joseph; but before they came to live together she was found to be with child through the Holy Spirit. Her husband Joseph, being a man of honour and wanting to spare her publicity, decided to divorce her informally. He had made up his mind to do this when the angel of the Lord appeared to him in a dream and said, "Joseph son of David, do not be afraid to take Mary home as your wife, because she has conceived what is in her by the Holy Spirit. She will give birth to a son and you must name him Yeshua, because he is the one who is to save his people from their sins." Now all this took place to fulfill the words spoken by the Lord through the prophet: The virgin will conceive and give birth to a son and they will call him Emmanuel, a name which means "God-is-with-us." When Joseph woke up he did what the angel of the Lord had told him to do: he took his wife to his home and, though he had not had intercourse with her, she gave birth to a son; and he named him Yeshua.[53]

§122 Yeshua's Problems with His Family III

See §42 for an analysis of the problems Yeshua had with his family and what bearing this had on his liberating attitude toward women.

Do not suppose that I have come to bring peace to the earth: it is not peace I have come to bring, but a sword. For I have come to set a man against his father, a daughter against her mother, a daughter-in-law against her mother-in-law. A man's enemies will be those of his own household. Anyone who prefers father or mother to me is not worthy of me. Anyone who prefers son or daughter to me is not worthy of me.[54]

§123 Female Imagery

Mark records relatively few stories and images used by Yeshua, and of those he does record, none deal with women. Matthew, on the other hand, records a large number of stories and images used by Yeshua. Five of them deal with women or female imagery, four in common with Luke. The four are as follows:

§124 Heaven the Leaven in Dough   See §33 for an analysis of Yeshua's use of the sexually parallel image likening the reign of heaven to leaven in a loaf, an image familiar to and clearly aimed at women listeners.[55]

§125 Yeshua in a Female Image   See §36 for a discussion of Yeshua's use of female imagery to describe himself.

How often have I longed to gather your children, as a hen gathers her chicks under her wings.[56]

§126 Women at the "End of Days"   See §30 for an analysis of the sexually parallel image of the two women at the "end of days."[57]

§127 Queen of Sheba   Perhaps one of the most interesting passages of this group is the one referring to the Queen of the South, the Queen of Sheba. For a general analysis of it, see §31. The discussion here will be limited to a comparative analysis. In the earlier Markan account there is simply a report of a demand for a sign, which Yeshua rejects.[58] Many scholars argue there was an earlier version of Matthew, written in Aramaic (now lost), and that often this earlier layer can be discerned in our present expanded Greek version. An example of the early Aramaic version of Matthew is said to be found in our present Greek version of Matthew 16:1–4, where a sign is asked of Yeshua, which request he rejects, except for the "sign of Jonah." However, in the second version, the Greek version, of Matthew, the story is repeated in an expanded form which includes a reference not only to Jonah but also to the Queen of Sheba. A tradition including additional references to women was obviously known and used by the author of Greek Matthew, and of Luke, that was not known by the earlier authors of Aramaic Matthew and of Mark. This later tradition of Greek Matthew with the reference to the Queen of the South is found in our present Greek version of Matthew 12:38–42.

Then some of the scribes and Pharisees spoke up. "Master," they said, "we should like to see a sign from you." He replied, "It is an evil and unfaithful generation that asks for a sign! The only sign it will be given is the sign of the prophet Jonah. For as Jonah was in the belly of the sea-monster for three days and three nights, so will the Son of Man be in the heart of the earth for three days and three nights. On judgment day, the men of Nineveh will stand up with this generation and condemn it, because when Jonah preached they repented; and there is something greater than Jonah here. On Judgment day the Queen of the South will rise up with this generation and condemn it, because she came from the ends of the earth to hear the wisdom of Solomon; and there is something greater than Solomon here."[59]

§128 The Wedding Feast

The seventh account dealing with women which both Matthew and Luke alone recorded concerned women, albeit somewhat indirectly, only in Matthew's account. It is a story of Yeshua's describing what the Reign of Heaven (Reign of God in Luke, a synonymous expression) was like. Matthew describes it as a wedding feast, whereas Luke describes it simply as a feast. Furthermore, Luke, in the story, makes getting married an excuse for not going to the banquet. In Matthew's account, that is not offered as an excuse. Hence, in comparison to Luke, in this case Matthew is more sympathetic, if not to women at least to marriage, in two points, one positive and one negative.

§129 The Genealogy of Yeshua

The eighth and last account which Matthew and Luke have in common alone is like the seventh in that only Matthew's version deals with women. The account in each Gospel concerns Yeshua's genealogy. At the beginning of Matthew's Gospel is a very interesting genealogy of Yeshua which is supposed to establish him as the Messiah, as a "son of David," and a "son of Abraham." It is clearly intended to be artificial in that there are three sections with fourteen names each (two times the holy number of fullness, seven), though to make the structure symmetrical, some generations listed in the Hebrew Bible are omitted by Matthew. It is, however, of interest here to note that the names of five women are included in the genealogy, an oddity since paternity alone was the source of legal rights. Moreover, each of the women had a "moral flaw" connected with sex: Tamar played a harlot and seduced Judah, her father-in-law; Rahab was a prostitute; Ruth sneaked into Boaz's bed and seduced him to marry her; Bathsheba, Uriah's wife, committed adultery with David; and Mary was found with child before her marriage. The Christians claimed Yeshua's virginal conception, and doubtless therefore detracting stories circulated about his "immoral," extramarital origin, how could such a one be the Messiah? Matthew's response is a messianic genealogy which lists four sexually "immoral" women (other women, such as the very popular "matriarchs" Sarah, Rebecca, and Rachel, are not mentioned) at key points in the Davidic line: Tamar is associated with the founding fathers of the twelve tribes of Israel, namely, "Judah and his brothers"; Rahab plays a role in the gaining of the Promised Land; Ruth is remembered as founding mother of the House of David;[60] and Bathsheba was the wife of David, the first real king of Israel, and the mother of its greatest king, Solomon. Matthew obviously saw this pattern of sexually "irregular" women playing crucial roles at the turning points in the history of the chosen people, reaching its climax in Mary, the mother of the Messiah. It is perhaps an indication of the relatively high status of women among the primitive Christian communities in Palestine, where (probably) and for whom Matthew's Gospel was written, that such a proud claim could be made to such women in Yeshua's ancestry.

A genealogy of Yeshua Christ, son of David, son of Abraham:

Abraham was the father of Isaac,
Isaac the father of Jacob,
Jacob the father of Judah and his brothers,
Judah was the father of Perez and Zerah, *Tamar being their mother*,
Perez was the father of Hezron,
Hezron the father of Ram,
Ram was the father of Amminadab,
Amminadab the father of Nahshon,
Nahshon the father of Salmon,
Salmon was the father of Boaz, *Rahab being his mother*,
Boaz was the father of Obed, *Ruth being his mother*,
Obed was the father of Jesse;
and Jesse was the father of King David.

David was the father of Solomon, *whose mother had been Uriah's wife*,
Solomon was the father of Rehoboam,
Rehoboam the father of Abijah,
Abijah the father of Asa,
Asa was the father of Jehoshaphat,
Jehoshaphat the father of Joram,
Joram the father of Azariah,
Azariah was the father of Jotham,
Jotham the father of Ahaz,
Ahaz the father of Hezekiah,
Hezekiah was the father of Manasseh,
Manasseh the father of Amon,
Amon the father of Josiah;
and Josiah was the father of Jechoniah and his brothers.
Then the deportation to Babylon took place.

After the deportation to Babylon;
Jechoniah was the father of Shealtiel,
Shealtiel the father of Zerubbabel,
Zerubbabel was the father of Abiud,
Abiud the father of Eliakim,
Eliakim the father of Azor,
Azor was the father of Zadok,
Zadok the father of Achim,
Achim the father of Eliud,
Eliud was the father of Eleazar,
Eleazar the father of Matthan,
Matthan the father of Jacob;
and Jacob was the father of Joseph the husband of *Mary*;
of her was born Yeshua who is called Christ.

The sum of generations is therefore: fourteen from Abraham to David; fourteen from David to the Babylonian deportation; and fourteen from the Babylonian deportation to Christ.[61]

§130 Passages Special to Matthew

As noted earlier, there are ten passages which deal with women that are found in Matthew alone. Of these, three really reflect nothing as far as the attitude toward women is concerned.

§131 Infancy Narratives

Three accounts surrounding the infancy of Yeshua that deal with women are peculiar to Matthew. The woman mainly involved is Mary, the mother of Yeshua. The first account is about the coming of the Magi. Matthew recorded that when the Magi found the house, they went in and "they saw the child with his mother Mary."[62] Later Joseph was told by an angel in a dream to "take the child and his mother"[63] into Egypt; he did so.[64] After Herod's death, Joseph was again told by an angel in a dream to "take the child and his mother"[65] back to Israel; and he did so.[66] Following the pattern established in the earlier portion about the virginal conception of Yeshua, Matthew, in contrast to Luke, continued to make Joseph the lead character in the story, with the angel always appearing to him. Mary appears only as "his mother," who was either with Yeshua when the Magi found him or was taken to or from Egypt by her husband. These passages reflect nothing of Yeshua's attitude toward women, and certainly indicate nothing on the part of Matthew.

(1) After Yeshua had been born at Bethlehem in Judaea during the reign of King Herod, some wise men came to Jerusalem from the east. "Where is the infant king of the Jews?" they asked. "We saw his star as it rose and have come to do him homage." The sight of the star filled them with delight, and going into the house they saw the child with his mother Mary, and falling to their knees they did him homage.[67]

(2) After they had left, the angel of the Lord appeared to Joseph in a dream and said, "Get up, take the child and his mother with you, and escape into Egypt, and stay there until I tell you, because Herod intends to search for the child and do away with him." So Joseph got up and, taking the child and his mother with him, left that night for Egypt, where he stayed until Herod was dead.[68]

(3) After Herod's death, the angel of the Lord appeared in a dream to Joseph in Egypt and said, "Get up, take the child and his mother with you and go back to the land of Israel, for those who wanted to kill the child are dead." So Joseph got up and, taking the child and his mother with him, went back to the land of Israel. But when he learnt that Archelaus had succeeded his father Herod as ruler of Judaea he was afraid to go there, and being warned in a dream he left for the region of Galilee. There he settled in a town called Nazareth.[69]

§132 Adultery of the Heart

The saying attributed to Yeshua that the man who lusts after a woman commits adultery with her in his heart does not reflect a great deal about Yeshua's or Matthew's attitudes toward women. The primary point seems to be that moral evil lies in the will, even if the fulfillment of the act was prevented. In this, Yeshua was not teaching something new, even concerning sexual morality. The sixth (or seventh) commandment says, you shall not commit adultery, and the ninth (tenth) goes on to the evil in the heart when it says, you shall not covet your neighbor's wife. Yeshua's teaching was clearly traditional.[70] The absence of any parallel statements in the Decalogue, in Job, in the Testaments of the Twelve Patriarchs, and here in Matthew forbidding the woman to covet the man does reflect patriarchal assumptions. Is this male bias by omission to be attributed to Yeshua or Matthew and/or his sources? We cannot of course be certain, but given the many other sexually parallel statements, stories, and images used by Yeshua, there is a stronger likelihood the imbalance comes from Matthew and/or his sources.

> You have learnt how it was said: You must not commit adultery. But I say this to you: if a man looks at a woman lustfully, he has already committed adultery with her in his heart.[71]

§133 The Mother of the Sons of Zebedee

In Matthew's Gospel, Salome, the wife of Zebedee and the mother of the apostles James and John, asks Yeshua for places of honor for her sons; in Mark's earlier version the brothers ask for themselves.[72] Matthew's account[73] is a bit awkward, for in verses 20 and 21 the exchange is between Yeshua and the mother (the verbs are singular), but in 22 and 23, without any indication of a change in the conversation partners, Yeshua addresses the brothers (the verbs are now plural). Is this because, in changing the Markan account, Matthew neglected to add a phrase, something like, "and turning to the brothers, Yeshua said . . ."?

Why does Matthew's tradition make the mother ask rather than the sons? If it is because it reflects historical fact, it would indicate that at least this woman wielded a strong influence with two apostles and presumably also with Yeshua. She obviously did not approach Yeshua unbeknownst to her sons; they were there and collaborated. It would seem she was the mediator because she was thought to have greater influence with Yeshua than her two apostle sons—all the more extraordinary since these two men were not shy, being nicknamed by Yeshua "sons of thunder," and along with Peter were regularly part of the inner circle of the apostles, being chosen to view the Transfiguration, go apart with Yeshua at the Garden of Gethsemane, and so on. Her standing with Yeshua must have been considerable! In return, she remained by Yeshua to the crushing end and the resurrection: she stood by the cross,[74] and was at the empty tomb.[75]

> Then the mother of Zebedee's sons came with her sons to make a request of him, and bowed low; and he said to her, "What is it you want?" She said to him, "Promise that these two sons of mine may sit one at our right hand and the other at your left in your kingdom." "You do not know what you are asking" Yeshua answered. "Can you drink the cup that I am going to drink?" They replied, "We can." "Very well," he said, "you shall drink my cup, but as for seats at my right hand and my left, these are not mine to grant; they belong to those to whom they have been allotted by my Father."[76]

§134 The Multiplication of Loaves

All four of the Gospels include the account of the multiplication of the loaves and fishes by Yeshua to feed a multitude in the desert. Two of them, Mark and Matthew, recorded two such events; many scholars argue that these are simply two forms of the same account. However that may be, what should be especially noted here about Matthew's account is that it alone speaks of women; all the other Gospel writers spoke of five thousand *men* (*andres*) being fed. Matthew in both his accounts says there were "five [or four] thousand men (*andres*), besides women (*gynaikōn*) and children." From what we know from elsewhere in the Gospels there were many women among Yeshua's listeners. Yet women are not mentioned in any version except Matthew's. All of the evangelists must have known that women would have been present at this teaching and miracle as well as men. But apparently the primitive form of the story of the five thousand, which the earliest Gospel, Mark,[77] refers only to men, was accepted by Luke and John, without their reflecting that certainly women would also have been present, or if they did, without their thinking it important enough to allude to.[78]

With Matthew, either there was additional information available about the presence of women, or there were some insistent voices among his sources which made it seem important to allude to the women and children, or Matthew himself decided it was important enough that they should be explicitly mentioned. Perhaps the desire to enhance the magnitude of the miracle played a role in inducing Matthew to mention the women. But besides the fact that the women and children were doubtless present, and the fact that mentioning them would magnify the miracle, it is also true that having compassion on the women and children fit perfectly with Yeshua's extremely positive attitude toward both groups. This would seem to be a clear indication that Matthew was sensitive to this "feminist" attitude of Yeshua.

> When Yeshua received this news, he withdrew by boat to a lonely place where they could be by themselves. But the people heard of this and, leaving the towns, went after him on foot. So as he stepped ashore he saw a large crowd; and he took pity on them and healed their sick.
>
> When evening came, the disciples went to him and said, "This is a lonely place, and the time has slipped by; so send the people away, and they can go to the villages to buy themselves some food." Yeshua replied, "There is no need for them to go: give them something to eat yourselves." But they answered, "All we have with us is five loaves and two fish." "Bring them here to me," he said. He gave orders that the people were to sit down on the grass; then he took the five loaves and the two fish, raised his eyes to heaven and said the blessing. And breaking the loaves he handed them to his disciples who gave them to the crowds. They all ate as much as they wanted, and they collected the scraps remaining, twelve baskets full. Those who ate numbered about five thousand men, to say nothing of women and children.[79]
>
> Yeshua went on from there and reached the shores of the Sea of Galilee, and he went up into the hills. He sat there, and large crowds came to him

bringing the lame, the crippled, the blind, the dumb and many others; these they put down at his feet, and he cured them. The crowds were astonished to see the dumb speaking, the cripples whole again, the lame walking and the blind with their sight, and they praised the God of Israel.

But Yeshua called his disciples to him and said, "I feel sorry for all these people; they have been with me for three days now and have nothing to eat. I do not want to send them off hungry; they might collapse on the way." The disciples said to him, "Where could we get enough bread in this deserted place to feed such a crowd?" Yeshua said to them, "How many loaves have you?" "Seven," they said, "and a few small fish." Then he instructed the crowd to sit down on the ground, and he took the seven loaves and the fish, and he gave thanks and broke them and handed them to the disciples who gave them to the crowds. They all ate as much as they wanted, and they collected what was left of the scraps, seven baskets full. Now four thousand men had eaten, to say nothing of women and children.[80]

§135 Prostitutes and the Reign of God

As noted in §51, it is very unlikely that Matthew can be credited in 21:31–32 with apparently substituting the term "prostitutes" (*pornai*) for "sinners" as a pair with "tax collectors" (the latter two are connected ten times with Yeshua by the Gospels; this is the only time "prostitute" is mentioned in the Gospels other than in a parable); Yeshua himself must have used the term deliberately, with all its pro-woman implications. Still, either the term and story were retained only in Matthew's special sources, or if they were also known by Mark or Luke, they either were not used by them, or were used and later suppressed. This latter is just possible with Luke, given his general sympathy for women, his sole recording of the story of Yeshua and the sinful woman,[81] and the likelihood that the story of the adulterous woman now placed in John 8:2–11 was really torn loose from after Luke 21:38 (where some manuscripts locate it, and because the Greek language is quite Lucan and certainly not Johannine). However, in view of the lack of any positive manuscript evidence that Luke had used the term in this connection, the most likely conclusion is that this story was known only to Matthew's special source. The fact that Matthew did not leave the story aside, or substitute the word "sinners" for "prostitutes," not only indicates Yeshua as the ultimate source of the story and term but also that here again Matthew's sources, favorable to women, were at work in the tradition peculiar to Matthew which retained this story, and that Matthew himself was also sufficiently influenced by the pro-woman attitude of Yeshua and the tradition that transmitted the evidence for it as to include this story and term here.[82]

§136 Pilate's Wife

Only Matthew records the story about Pilate's wife speaking to Pilate in be-half of Yeshua (see §62 for analysis). This is another example of the pro-woman element active in Matthew's sources and his sympathizing with it sufficiently to put it in his Gospel. Since the story did show at least this presumably Roman woman in a light sympathetic to Yeshua, one might have expected to find it in Mark's Gospel if he knew of it, since he presumably was writing in Rome for Gentiles. Its absence in Mark, then, can only mean that his sources did not contain it, again highlighting the strongly pro-woman element in Matthew's special sources.[83]

§137 Sexually Parallel Stories and Images in the Synoptics

The several sexually parallel stories and images found in the Gospels were individually analyzed above. However, note should be taken here of their relationship to the several Gospel writers and the implications of those relationships.

These are either sets of stories or images in the Gospels which focus on a man and on a woman in parallel fashion. It is especially interesting that with a single possible exception they all are recorded only in either Matthew or Luke or in both; none are to be found in the Fourth Gospel, and perhaps only one in Mark. Both Matthew and Luke record the same three of the parallel sets; one set is peculiar to Matthew; four are peculiar to Luke. Did one simply copy the idea and three common sets from the other and then go on to put together another one or four pairs on his own? But then why did Luke not copy all four of Matthew's sets instead of just three, or, even more, why did Matthew not copy all seven of Luke's sets instead of just three? These omissions, among other evidence elsewhere, would argue against a copying of one from the other in either direction.

Moreover, scholars are not at all agreed on what the relationship in general is between Matthew and Luke. There are 230 verses which Matthew and Luke have in common that are not found in Mark (nor in the Fourth Gospel). Many, probably most, scholars postulate a third document prior to either Matthew or Luke, now lost (usually called Q, for the German *Quelle*, meaning "source"), which both had separately; Matthew and Luke each also had sources completely peculiar to themselves. It is also suggested by some scholars that not only prior common and independent written documents but also prior common and independent oral traditions are necessary to account for all the similarities and dissimilarities in the Gospels. It would seem that this latter combination is the most likely solution of this "synoptic" problem, though precisely what the documents and oral traditions were and their relationships has by no means been satisfactorily explained to date, if indeed it is completely possible at all.

In this matter of the sexually parallel images and stories it is clear that forces were at work in the sources of both Matthew and Luke which discerned a strongly affirming attitude toward women by Yeshua, an attitude that saw them as equal to men. The images and stories about women were there in the sources of Matthew and Luke, whether written or oral. Hence, a "balancing" of images and stories about women as well as men could not be attributed to Matthew and Luke but probably would have to be attributed to Yeshua himself. However, it should be noted that (1) Mark records almost none of these female images or stories individually, let alone in sexually parallel pairs, and (2) all of the female images and stories used by Yeshua (save the one where Yeshua likens himself to a hen) are found only in these parallel sets in Matthew and Luke. This strongly suggests that these particular close pairings would have to be attributed to the sources of Matthew and Luke, written and/or oral. Yeshua himself, however, may well have juxtaposed one or more of our present sets of sexually parallel images or stories. Since Yeshua obviously told the original stories and used the images, at least in some form, if not always exactly as we have them recorded in the Gospels, and hence, must have consciously "balanced" male images and stories with female ones, it seems very likely that he also "paired" some of the stories, though we cannot easily know which ones. In any case, the presence of these eight sexually parallel images and stories in Matthew and Luke is a clear indication that forces sympathetic to women were strongly at work in the sources of both Matthew and Luke.

Further, from evidence elsewhere in both Matthew and Luke it is also clear that this positive attitude toward women not only was in the sources prior to the Gospels of Matthew and Luke, but was also picked up by the Gospel writers themselves. I argue below that when dealing with Luke's Gospel, there was a woman "evangelist" who was responsible for producing a prior document known as Proto-Luke Gospel. How might that document be related to the putative Q?

Nevertheless, since the pro-woman attitude on the part of Yeshua is expressed, both positively and negatively, in all four of the Gospels, and since we have absolutely no evidence of such a "feminist" movement in Palestinian Judaism of the time (in fact, just the opposite occurred with the development of Rabbinic Judaism), this "feminism" would have to be attributed ultimately and powerfully to Yeshua.

In fact, one of the most fundamental criteria that scholars (e.g., Ernst Käsemann and Reginald H. Fuller) use to discover authentic sayings or actions of Yeshua is to discern whether they are distinctive over against his environment. A Jewish scholar put the principle into action when he wrote:

"The relation of Yeshua to women seems unlike what would have been usual for a Rabbi. He seems to have definitely broken with orientalism in this particular. . . . But certainly the relations of Yeshua towards women, and of theirs towards him, seem to strike a new note, and a higher note, and to be off the line of Rabbinic tradition."[84]

The following are the texts involved:

Common to Luke and Perhaps Mark: Luke 8:16–17; Mark 4:21–22
Common to Luke and Matthew: Luke 17:34–37, 11:29–32, 13:20–21;
   Matthew 24:39–41, 12:38–42, 13:33
Special to Luke: Luke 4:24–27, 15:1–3, 18:1–8
Special to Matthew: Matthew 25:1–3

§138 Conclusions

As noted at the beginning of the section, Matthew's Gospel goes far beyond Mark's in its pro-woman attitude. This is true in terms of absolute quantity (thirty-six passages dealing with women of 180 verses in length compared to Mark's twenty passages of 114 verses in length), proportion of "women passages" in comparison to overall length (Mark is 67 percent of the length of Matthew, but has only 55 percent of the number of women passages), and the uniquely positive attitude of a significant number of Matthew's passages.

One important point is the possibility of an intensification of a sensitivity toward women from the perhaps earliest written form of a Gospel, the Aramaic version of Matthew, of which Papias (130 C.E.) spoke when he referred to Matthew's composition of the discourses (*logia*) of Yeshua in Aramaic. (Scholars do, in fact, find something of a flavor of a Greek translation of Aramaic in Yeshua's discourses as recorded in the present Greek version of Matthew, but not in the narrative sections.) Many scholars contend that Mark had this Aramaic Matthew (or a very literal Greek translation of it) at his disposal when composing his Gospel, and that the canonical Greek Matthew Gospel writer in turn had both the Aramaic Matthew, and Mark, among other sources, at his disposal. Thus, the chronological order of composition would have been: Aramaic Matthew; Mark; Greek Matthew.

When it is recalled that the later Greek Matthew[85] strand of the demand of a sign from Yeshua added the sexually parallel sign of the Queen of Sheba, not found in either the earlier Aramaic Matthew strand[86] or Mark,[87] and that Greek Matthew strongly communicated a pro-woman message in his very structuring of the events and discourses of Yeshua, of course not found in the Aramaic Matthew listing of Yeshua's discourses, a movement of an ever-sharper focus on women in Yeshua's life and Gospel becomes at least dimly visible.

Besides the pro-woman accounts that Mark recorded (all but two of which Matthew also recorded) and the additional accounts that Matthew had in common with Luke, which at times were even more sympathetic toward women than Luke's (see §175), Matthew also recorded a number of unique, pro-women elements: The inclusion of women in Yeshua's genealogy, likening the Reign of Heaven to a wedding feast, placing prostitutes in it before priests, listing women among those whom Yeshua fed by the multiplication of loaves and fishes, and mentioning Pontius Pilate's wife among Yeshua's sympathizers. This plethora of positive material on women—and organizing thereof—significantly more in Matthew than Mark strongly suggests an extraordinarily increasing influence of women in the remembering, recording, and organizing of material about Yeshua.

In sum, the present Gospel of Matthew is very strongly pro-woman in the image of Yeshua it projects, considerably more so than either the putative Aramaic Matthew, or Mark, or the Fourth Gospel, and doubtless had a multitude of women sources, and perhaps even "organizers," behind it.

§139 THE GOSPEL ACCORDING TO LUKE

Where the Fourth Gospel has eight passages dealing with women, Mark twenty, and Matthew thirty-six, Luke has forty-two. It should be noted that the number of passages dealing with women is not simply dependent on the overall relative lengths of the four Gospels. It is true that Luke is both the longest Gospel and the one with the most passages and verses dealing with women. However, the relative proportion of the overall lengths of the Gospels and the number of women passages in them and their length are quite irregular. Taking Luke as the standard in both cases, the relationships are seen in table 6.1.

As seen in table 6.1, the Fourth Gospel has by far the smallest number of women passages, though it is the third in overall length (four of the passages are very long, so in total length the Fourth Gospel has more verses of

Table 6.1.   Verses about Women in the Gospels

Gospel	Length	Number of Women Passages	Number of Women Verses
Luke*	100%	42 (100%)	220 (100%)
Matthew	92%	36 (86%)	180 (82%)
Fourth	75%	8 (19%)	119 (54%)
Mark	62%	20 (48%)	114 (52%)

*Luke, as both the longest Gospel and the one with the most passages, is the standard at 100%.

women passages than Mark). Even Mark is 62 percent of the length of Luke to 48 percent of the number of women passages of Luke (52 percent in terms of verses of the same). Matthew and Luke both have a large number of women passages as compared to Mark and especially the Fourth Gospel; on the basis of the number of women passages, the two of them could be called strongly pro-woman; Mark moderately so, and the Fourth Gospel weakly, but the Fourth Gospel would have to be designated moderately strong in view of the number of women verses and the uniquely positive quality of some of his material. In comparing Matthew with Luke on the basis of number of women passages in comparison to overall length it is clear that Luke is ahead of even Matthew in "feminism." Where Matthew is 92 percent of the length of Luke, it has 86 percent in the number of women passages of Luke (82 percent in terms of verses of the same).

Of Luke's forty-two passages dealing with women or the "feminine," as noted above, three are common to all four evangelists and nine more are common to all three Synoptics, Luke, Matthew, and Mark; another five are common to just Luke and Matthew, and two are reported by only Luke and Mark. Luke has far and away the largest number of unique women passages, twenty-three, whereas Matthew has ten special to him, the Fourth Gospel three, and Mark none. Thus both on the basis of sheer quantity and the very large number of women passages special to Luke, it is clear that Luke exhibits the greatest stress on women by far, followed by Matthew, much farther back by Mark, and least of all by the Fourth Gospel.

The relationship of the forty-two women passages in Luke and the other Gospels is as follows:

Special to Luke	23
Common to Luke and Mark alone	2
Common to Luke and Matthew alone	5
Common to Luke, Mark, and Matthew alone	9
Common to Luke, Mark, Matthew, Fourth Gospel	3

§140 Passages Common to Luke and Mark Alone

§141 Oppression of Widows

See §49ff. for a discussion of Yeshua's biting condemnation of the oppression of the most defenseless group in that male-dominated society, widows.

> While all the people were listening he said to the disciples, "Beware of the scribes who like to walk about in long robes and love to be greeted obsequiously in the market squares, to take the front seats in the synagogues

and the places of honour at banquets, who swallow the property of widows, while making a show of lengthy prayers The more severe will be the
sentence they receive."[88]

§142 The Widow's Mite

See §45, for an analysis of Yeshua's lifting up of a widow as a model to be
imitated.

> As he looked up, he saw rich people putting their offerings into the treas-
> ury, then he happened to notice a poverty-stricken widow putting in two
> small coins, and he said, "I tell you truly, this poor widow has put in more
> than any of them; for these have all contributed money they had over, but
> she, from the little she had, has put in all she had to live on."[89]

§143 Passages Common to Luke and Matthew Alone

§144 Sexually Parallel Stories and Images

See §26ff. for an analysis of the several sexually parallel stories and images
used by Yeshua. As noted, neither Mark nor the Fourth Gospel recorded any
stories told by Yeshua dealing with women. In fact, they recorded relatively
few of Yeshua's stories, in general. Hence, the sexually parallel stories and images of Yeshua are all recorded either by Luke or Matthew or both. Three are
recorded by both Luke and Matthew. They are as follows:

§145 The Queen of the South   See §31 for a discussion of Yeshua's reference to the Queen of the South, namely, the Queen of Sheba, playing a judg-
mental role at the Judgment Day, paralleling a similar role filled by Jonah.

> The crowds got even bigger and he addressed them, "This is a wicked gen-
> eration; it is asking for a sign. The only sign it will be given is the sign of
> Jonah. For just as Jonah became a sign to the Ninevites, so will the Son of
> Man be to this generation. On judgement day, the Queen of the South will
> rise up with the men of this generation and condemn them, because she came
> from the ends of the earth to hear the wisdom of Solomon; and there is
> something greater than Solomon here. On judgement day, the men of Nin-
> eveh will stand up with this generation and condemn it, because, when Jonah
> preached, they repented; and there is something greater than Jonah here."[90]

§146 Heaven the Leaven in Dough   See §33 for an analysis of Yeshua's
image of the Reign of Heaven in the form of leaven in dough, an image
clearly familiar to women and directed at them.

Another thing he said, "What shall I compare the reign of God with? It is like the yeast a *woman* took and mixed in with three measures of flour till it was leavened all through."[91]

§147 Women at the "End of Days"   See §30 for an analysis of the sexually parallel image of two women who are treated exactly the same as men at the "end of days."[92]

§148 Yeshua's Dismantling of Restrictive Family Bonds I

See §44 for an analysis of Yeshua's efforts at dismantling the restrictive family bonds that so often stifled people, especially women, in the culture in which he lived.[93]

§149 Yeshua in a Female Image

See §125 for a discussion of Yeshua's using female imagery to describe himself.[94]

§150 Passages Common to Luke, Mark, and Matthew

The nine "women passages" that Luke has in common with both Mark and Matthew, in the opinion of most scholars, stem either from the earliest of the three Gospels, Mark, or the putative source, Q, prior to all of them.

§151 Yeshua's First Cures: Men and Women

See §86 and §102 for discussion on how Mark and Matthew placed accounts of the first two cures Yeshua performed, of a man and a woman, at the beginning of Yeshua's public life. Luke did the same. The man was from Capernaum and had an "unclean spirit."[95] The woman was Simon's (Peter's) mother-in-law. Hereby the earliest and subsequent Gospel traditions made it clear that the preaching and bringing of the Good News of the Reign of God was equally to women and men.

> Leaving the synagogue he went to Simon's house. Now Simon's mother-in-law was suffering from a high fever and they asked him to do something for her. Leaning over her he rebuked the fever and it left her. And she immediately got up and began to wait on them.[96]

§152 Lamp on a Lamp Stand

See §§27 and 88 for an analysis of Luke's treatment of Yeshua's image of placing a lamp on a lamp stand as a sexually parallel story, which neither of the
other two Synoptic Gospels did, though they did record the image of a lamp
on a lamp stand. This is one bit of evidence of a greater sensitivity to the cause
of women's equality on the part of Luke and/or his sources.[97]

§153 Yeshua's Mother and Brothers

See §42 for a discussion of Yeshua's attitude toward his family and how this reflected his concern for the lot of women. Here it should simply be noted that,
although Mark and Matthew refer to Yeshua's sisters as well as to his mother
and brothers, Luke does not. What significance this may have is not clear.

> His mother and his brothers came looking for him, but they could not
> get to him because of the crowd. He was told, "Your mother and broth-
> ers are standing outside and want to see you." But he said in answer, "My
> mother and my brothers are those who hear the word of God and put it
> into practice."[98]

§154 Yeshua's Dismantling of Restrictive Family Bonds II

See §44 for an analysis of Yeshua's problems with his family and his attempt
to dismantle the restrictive forces of the family, which particularly worked
against women. All three of the Synoptics recorded something of this dismantling effort of Yeshua, but there is a gradation in the recording: Mark has
one such account,[99] Matthew two,[100] and Luke three. In miniature, this pro-
portional relationship also reflects the intensity of the three evangelists' emphasizing the concern of Yeshua for women. Luke again turns out to be the
strongest "feminist," after Yeshua.[101]

§155 Jairus' Daughter, the Woman with a Flow of Blood

See §12 for analyses of Yeshua's cures of two women, one with a long-term
hemorrhage and one dead. In all three Synoptic accounts, Yeshua apparently
violated or accepted the violation of two basic regulations of ritual purity in
order to cure women. First, he touched what everyone thought was a ritually
unclean object, a corpse, Jairus' twelve-year-old daughter; and second, he

commended the ritually unclean hemorrhaging woman for having touched him in faith. Yeshua's championing of children (Luke is the only Gospel writer who recorded that Jairus' daughter was a child of twelve) and women within the context of making light of ritual purity is reflected in a variant reading elsewhere in Luke (see §172), where Yeshua is accused of leading astray children and women with the result that the latter do not observe the ritual purifications.[102]

§156 *Marriage and the Dignity of Women I*

See §38 for an analysis of Yeshua's revolutionary egalitarian attitude toward women in marriage by eliminating the husband's, till then, almost unlimited right to divorce his wife.

> Everyone who divorces his wife and marries another is guilty of adultery, and the man who marries a woman divorced by her husband commits adultery.[103]

§157 *Marriage and the Dignity of Women II*

See §38 for an analysis of Yeshua's response to the question of some Sadducees about a woman married seven times: to whom would she belong? Yeshua's answer presumed that she was a person and belonged to no one.

> Some Sadducees, those who say that there is no resurrection, approached him and they put this question to him, "Master, we have it from Moses in writing, that if a man's married brother dies childless, the man must marry the widow to raise up children for his brother. Well then, there were seven brothers. The first, having married a wife, died childless. The second and then the third married the widow. And the same with all seven; they died leaving no children. Finally the woman herself died. Now, at the resurrection, to which of them will she be wife since she had been married to all seven?"
>
> Yeshua replied, "The children of this world take wives and husbands, but those who are judged worthy of a place in the other world and in the resurrection from the dead do not marry because they can no longer die, for they are the same as the angels, and being children of the resurrection they are sons of God. And Moses himself implies that the dead rise again, in the passage about the bush where he calls the Lord the God of Abraham, the God of Isaac, and the God of Jacob. Now he is God, not of the dead, but of the living; all are alive for him."[104]

§158 Yeshua's Concern for Women's Welfare

See §101 for a discussion of the concern for women's welfare that Yeshua expressed. Unlike Mark and Matthew, Luke does not have sexually parallel images here, pairing the men in the field and on the housetop with the women, who are pregnant and nursing children. Rather, he refers to *only* the women. Thus, Luke's version stresses Yeshua's concern for women even more than the versions of Matthew and Mark.

> When you see Jerusalem surrounded by armies, you must realize that she will soon be laid desolate. Then those in Judea must escape to the mountains, those inside the city must leave it, and those in country districts must not take refuge in it. For this is the time of vengeance when all that scripture says, must be fulfilled. Alas for those with child, or with babies at the breast, when those days come.[105]

§159 Women in Yeshua's Passion and Resurrection

See §§63ff. for analyses of the close connection of women with the passion, death, and burial of Yeshua; their witnessing the empty tomb; and reporting of the resurrection to the male disciples, on all of which all four of the evangelists agree, almost unanimously. It is worthy of note here that Luke, unlike the other three evangelists, does not report any appearances of the risen Yeshua to women. For a discussion of this, see §186.

§160 Women Witness the Burial of Yeshua

See §65 for an analysis of the account of the women disciples watching the burial of Yeshua. Luke here refers to them specifically as those who followed Yeshua from Galilee. Mark and Matthew refer to the same group of women as being at the crucifixion and death of Yeshua, and then specify Mary Magdalene and others, by name, as observing the burial. Luke names Mary Magdalene and others only in connection with the later visit of the women to the tomb. It is clear that all three Synoptic Gospels were here dependent on basically the same tradition, that the women in question were Yeshua's Galilean women disciples, including prominently Mary Magdalene.

> Meanwhile the women who had come from Galilee with Yeshua were following behind. They took note of the tomb and of the position of the body.

Then they returned and prepared spices and ointments. And on the Sabbath day they rested, as the Law required.[106]

§161 Passages Special to Luke

§162 A Woman "Evangelist"?

Of the forty-two passages in Luke dealing with women or the feminine, over half, twenty-three, are special to Luke. This compares to ten special to Matthew out of a total of thirty-six, three special to the Fourth Gospel (though all quite long) out of a total of eight, and none special to Mark out of a total of twenty. Here is further indication that Luke was most especially open to women in the writing of his Gospel.

It is interesting to note that of the twenty-three women passages special to Luke, sixteen of them occur within the sections of Luke's Gospel that are made up either totally of material special to Luke[107] or of material special to Luke, plus material common to Luke and Matthew alone.[108] Several scholars point out that, although Luke clearly was not a Jew or a Palestinian or an eyewitness of Yeshua, those sections have both such a strong unity and definitely Palestinian Jewish eyewitness character that they must have been either originally written or told by a Palestinian Jewish follower of Yeshua.[109] Given the strong presence of stories about women in this "Proto-Gospel" within Luke and the strong prejudice against accepting the witness of women ("When the women returned from the tomb they told all this to the Eleven and to all the others. . . . But this story of theirs seemed pure nonsense, and they did not believe them."[110]), the thought suggests itself that this Proto-Gospel was written, or told, by a woman disciple of Yeshua and used by Luke, without referring to her as his source, lest his Gospel be discredited and disbelieved. A woman Proto-Gospel writer would certainly fit well with the central place women (Elizabeth and Mary) hold in Luke's narrative of events before Yeshua's adult life (Lk 1 and 2), and the intimate sensitivity with which the inner feelings and thoughts of the women are dealt.

Vincent Taylor and Burnett Hillman Streeter were the main initiators of the likelihood of the existence of a Proto-Gospel within Luke:

> The theory has already been mentioned that Luke had composed a gospel before he came into possession of a copy of Mark, and that our present gospel is a revised and enlarged edition of his earlier work. This theory, which is particularly associated with the names of the late Dr. Streeter and of Dr. Vincent Taylor, is based on the fact that in large sections of Luke, Mark is not employed as a source, and that it is possible

to reconstruct from Luke, omitting all his borrowings from Mark, a gospel-like document of considerable extent.[111]

Bernard D. Muller went a yet large step further:

> Here, my main conclusion is that "Luke" was a Christian woman from Philippi, addressing a community traditionally led by women. . . . As I postulated earlier, G[ospel] Luke (and "Acts") was written for the Gentile Christians in Philippi. . . . A reconstruction of what happened may be as follows:

> a) At the time (82–93 C.E.), the traditional leadership of women in the Christian community of Philippi was probably undermined by some prominent members. These ones were more prone to accept Jewish Christian doctrines and doubted the teaching & credentials of the late Paul.

> b) A copy of Mark's gospel was obtained by a prominent woman Christian leader. Others knew about the existence of the gospel and its acquisition: they wanted to read it. Consequently, this lady decided to get rid of the missing block, mainly because of the very damaging Syro-Phoenician Greek woman's story.

> c) Afterwards, another prominent Christian lady, from the same copy, wrote Luke's gospel.[112]

What clearly is very easy to sustain as a step toward claiming a woman writer of Luke's Proto-Gospel is that one or more women disciples were responsible for the remembrance and handing on, either in oral or written form, of at least most of those passages which pertain in a special way to women. It is not likely that in a very male-oriented society men would have been particularly aware of the vital significance of many of the things Yeshua said and did relating to women, whereas to sensitive women they would have seemed as loud as thunderclaps. These women then, having experienced or noticed these things, would have been the ones to remember them and pass them on and would have been the ultimate source for the women material in the Proto-Gospel sections of Luke, and the seven other uniquely Lucan women passages. Thus, even if she, or they, might not be proved the proximate "evangelist" of the Proto-Gospel material of Luke, they should certainly, at the very least, be called "proto-evangelists," in the sense of having communicated the Good News of Yeshua.

However, the question naturally arises: Where did Luke come across this Proto-Gospel material, and in what form? If it all was simply told him by women who had remembered it, then why is it largely grouped together? Did Luke simply take it down in dictation, and then go about the business of later writing his Gospel? That does not seem very likely. What seems much more likely is something near to what Bernard Muller suggests, namely, that a woman wrote down the Proto-Gospel, using largely the recollections of the community of women who were inspired by the actions and teachings of Yeshua. Remember, this Proto-Gospel has all the characteristics of coming from a Palestinian eyewitness, including peculiarities of language, none of which the Hellenist Luke had. Therefore, it is most likely that Luke had the Proto-Gospel at his disposal in written form, written by a woman, who perhaps with other women sources, would have been the only ones who would have noticed and remembered all the pro-woman things Yeshua said and did. Hence, it is appropriate to speak of an anonymous woman evangelist of the Proto-Gospel of Luke. (Because she is anonymous, we could continue to refer to her as the Proto-Gospel writer, or as Proto-Luke. However, perhaps it would be more convenient to refer to her simply as "Luka," an anglicized feminine form of Luke.)

This conclusion is further reinforced, perhaps in a slightly backhanded fashion, by the very carefully argued and documented research of Ann Graham Brock. Brock contends that a very significant tension of authority existed between, if not Peter and Mary Magdalene in the flesh, then certainly between their followers, and between men and women followers of Yeshua after Yeshua's death. She writes:

> It is my contention that it is not merely coincidence that the Gospel of Luke, the most pro-Petrine of the canonical gospels, is also the one in which the witness of Mary Magdalene is most diminished. . . . Furthermore, in contrast to the other three canonical gospels, only Luke refuses her a commission to spread the news of the resurrection, and only Luke refers to the resurrected Lord appearing to Peter alone.[113]

It is seen in §208 that a second of the canonical Gospels was also most likely written by a woman (that is, a penultimate version of the Fourth Gospel). Women were obviously inspired by Yeshua, and were eager to remember the things he did and taught, particularly as they pertained to women. They were impelled to gather this material and eventually write it down for the same reasons other writings about Yeshua occurred—they did not want these important "breakthroughs" to be forgotten.

§163 Elizabeth Conceives John the Baptist

Immediately after his brief prologue, Luke began his Gospel (that is, Luka did) with the story of a man and a woman who were married, but childless. This lack of children was thought to be a great humiliation for the wife, not for the man. In fact, a little later the rabbis legislated that "if a man took a wife

and lived with her for ten years and she bore no child, he shall divorce her."[114]
There is an interesting sort of parity between the man and the woman,
Zechariah and Elizabeth, expressed here by Luka's Proto-Gospel source, interesting in the light of the definite inferior social position women held in
that society. But Luka's Proto-Gospel refers to both the woman and the man
together and is careful to point out the purity of priestly lineage of Elizabeth
as well as of Zechariah. Then the focus on Zechariah, which immediately follows,[115] is balanced by the shift to Elizabeth.[116]

It should also be noted that there is a strong resemblance between the
story of Elizabeth's barrenness and her finally bearing a son who was to become a leading figure in Israel on the one hand, and similar events with Sarah,
who bore Isaac,[117] with Samson's mother whose name we are not told,[118] and
with Hannah the mother of Samuel[119] on the other. The similar form of the
Elizabeth-Zechariah story strongly suggests that Luka was familiar with
these earlier stories of the Hebrew Bible, reinforcing the likelihood of the
Jewishness of Luka's Proto-Gospel source.

In the days of King Herod of Judaea there lived a priest called Zechariah
who belonged to the Abijah section of the priesthood, and he had a wife,
Elizabeth by name, who was a descendant of Aaron. Both were worthy in
the sight of God, and scrupulously observed all the commandments and
observances of the Lord. But they were childless: Elizabeth was barren and
they were both getting on in years.

Now it was the turn of Zechariah's section to serve, and he was exercising
his priestly office before God when it fell to him by lot, as the ritual custom was, to enter the Lord's sanctuary and burn incense there. And at the
hour of incense the whole congregation was outside, praying.

Then there appeared to him the angel of the Lord, standing on the right
of the altar of incense. The sight disturbed Zechariah and he was overcome
with fear. But the angel said to him, "Zechariah, do not be afraid, your
prayer has been heard. Your wife Elizabeth is to bear you a son and you
must name him John. He will be your joy and delight and many will re-
joice at his birth, for he will be great in the sight of the Lord; he must drink
no wine, no strong drink. Even from his mother's womb he will be filled
with the Holy Spirit, and he will bring back many of the sons of Israel to
the Lord their God. With the spirit and power of Elijah, he will go before
him to turn the hearts of fathers towards their children and the disobedi-
ent back to the wisdom that the virtuous have, preparing for the Lord a
people fit for him."

Zechariah said to the angel, "How can I be sure of this? I am an old man
and my wife is getting on in years." The angel replied, "I am Gabriel who
stands in God's presence, and I have been sent to speak to you and bring
you this good news. Listen! Since you have not believed my words, which

will come true at their appointed time, you will be silenced and have no power of speech until this has happened." Meanwhile the people were waiting for Zechariah and were surprised that he stayed in the sanctuary so long. When he came out he could not speak to them, and they realized that he had received a vision in the sanctuary. But he could only make signs to them, and remained dumb.

When his time of service came to an end he returned home. Some time later his wife Elizabeth conceived, and for five months she kept to herself "The Lord has done this for me," she said, "now that it has pleased him to take away the humiliation I suffered among people."[120]

§164 The Annunciation

There are striking similarities between the announcement of the coming birth of John the Baptist and his kinsman Yeshua: both sons were to be leading figures in Judaism; their conceptions were to be extraordinary; John, conceived in old age, and "even from his mother's womb he will be filled with the Holy Spirit,"[121] and Yeshua conceived without an earthly father, but "the Holy Spirit will come upon you and the power of the Most High will cover you with its shadow"; their announcements were delivered by angels. There are also at least two significant differences: Zechariah was somewhat resistant to the announcement and was consequently punished with temporary dumbness, whereas Mary was fully open and hence suffered no punishment; most important, in the case of John the angelic announcement was made to the man, in Yeshua's case it was made to the woman. The importance of this latter difference would not be neutralized simply by noting that any angelic announcement made about the virginal conception of Yeshua would have to be made to the prospective mother because there was no prospective father, for, as a matter of fact, Matthew's Gospel does do just about that: in Matthew there is a single angelic announcement of the virginal conception recorded, and it was made to Joseph, Mary's betrothed.[122]

> In the sixth month the angel Gabriel was sent by God to a town in Galilee called Nazareth, to a virgin betrothed to a man named Joseph, of the House of David; and the virgin's name was Mary. He went in and said to her, "Rejoice, so highly favored! The Lord is with you." She was deeply disturbed by these words and asked herself what this greeting could mean, but the angel said to her, "Mary, do not be afraid; you have won Gods favor. Listen! You are to conceive and bear a son, and you must name him Yeshua. He will be great and will be called Son of the Most High. The Lord God will give him the throne of his ancestor David; he will rule over the House of Jacob for ever and his reign will have no end." Mary said to the angel

"But how can this come about since I am virgin." "The Holy Spirit will come upon you," the angel answered, "and the power of the Most High will cover you with its shadow. And so the child will be holy and will be called Son of God. Know this, too: your kinswoman Elizabeth has, in her old her age, herself conceived a son, and she whom people called barren is now in her sixth month, for nothing is impossible to God." "I am the handmaid of the Lord," said Mary, "let what you have said be done to me."[123]

§165 *The Visitation*

In this passage, Luke (Luka) described Mary's visit to her kinswoman Elizabeth. The focus is entirely on the two women, the two expectant mothers of leading figures of Israel. What is especially to be noted here is that, according to Luka, the first person, besides Mary, to whom Yeshua's Messiahship is revealed, is a woman—Elizabeth: "Elizabeth was filled with the Holy Spirit . . . and said . . . 'Why should I be honored with a visit from the mother of my Lord [i.e., of Messiah]?'"[124] Where Zechariah reacted in a resistant fashion in the face of the "divine," and was punished, Elizabeth reacted positively and was rewarded by a visit from the Messiah in utero and by being informed that her son was to be named John.[125]

> Mary set out at that time and went as quickly as she could to a town in the hill country of Judah. She went into Zechariah's house and greeted Elizabeth. Now as soon as Elizabeth heard Mary's greeting, the child leapt in her womb and Elizabeth was filled with the Holy Spirit. She gave a loud cry and said, "Of all women you are the most blessed, and blessed is the fruit of your womb. Why should I be honored with a visit from the mother of my Lord? For the moment your greeting reached my ears, the child in my womb leapt for joy. Yes, blessed is she who believed that the promise made her by the Lord would be fulfilled."[126]

§166 *The "Magnificat"*

The song of joy uttered by Mary when she met Elizabeth starts with the words, "my soul *magnifies* the Lord," in the Western traditional Latin Vulgate, "*Magnificat* anima mea Dominum," hence the customary title.

The great majority of early manuscripts state, in verse 46, that Mary said the "Magnificat," but a few attribute it to Elizabeth. Some scholars, such as John Martin Creed, *The Gospel according to St Luke*,[127] J. B. Phillips in his 1952[128] translation of the Gospels, and John Drury, *Luke*,[129] follow this minority tradition of attributing the "Magnificat" to Elizabeth because they are convinced the text makes more sense in Elizabeth's mouth than in Mary's. If that were the case, then the balancing of the focus between Zechariah and Elizabeth would be still more clearly parallel (the "Magnificat" in Elizabeth's mouth matching the song, the "Benedictus,"[130] in Zechariah's), and even tip in Elizabeth's favor (she believed and was rewarded rather than disbelieving and punished).

Whomever the "Magnificat" is attributed to, it is clear that it very closely resembles the Song of Hannah, the mother of Samuel,[131] mentioned earlier. In both the "Magnificat" and the "Song of Hannah" there is a stress on praising God for lifting up the lowly and the humble, and feeding the hungry. Who were the lowliest of Near Eastern society? Women. Who were the first to go hungry? Widows. There was a clear sense of solidarity, even almost identity, of women with the lowliest and hungriest expressed by placing these two songs in the mouths of women (who were lifted up in the only way possible for women in that society—by bearing a son). Both songs contain cries of joy that the lowly (read: women) were finally raised up. Whoever may have composed the two songs (it is not likely that Mary, or Elizabeth, composed on the spot the "Magnificat" with its extraordinary parallels to the "Song of Hannah") and in whatever context, it is apparent that the editor of 1 Samuel and Luke's source for the "Magnificat" (Luka the proto-evangelist), both realized that women, especially those who had not borne a son, would be recognized by all as lowly and poor. They expressed this realization simply by attributing these songs, whether composed by women or not, to women.

Magnificat

And Mary said:

> "My soul proclaims the greatness of the Lord
> and my spirit exults in God the Saviour;
> because he has looked upon his lowly handmaid.
> Yes, from this day forward all generations will call me blessed,
> for the Almighty has done great things for me.
> Holy is his name,
> and his mercy reaches from age to age for those who fear him.
> He has shown the power of his arm,
> he has routed the proud of heart.
> He has pulled down princes from their thrones and exalted the lowly.
> The hungry he has filled with good things, the rich sent empty away.
> He has come to the help of Israel his servant, mindful of his mercy,
> according to the promise he made to our ancestors.
> of his mercy to Abraham and to his descendants for ever."

Mary stayed with Elizabeth about three months and then went back home.[132]

Song of Hannah

Then Hannah said this prayer:

> "My heart exults in Yahweh
> my horn is exalted in my God,
> my mouth derides my foes,
> for I rejoice in your Power of saving.
> There is none as holy as Yahweh,
> (indeed, there is no one but you)
> no rock like our God.
>
> Do not speak and speak with haughty words,
> let not arrogance come from your mouth.
> For Yahweh is an all-knowing God
> and his is the weighing of deeds.
>
> The bow of the mighty is broken
> but the feeble have girded themselves with strength.
> The sated hire themselves out for bread
> but the famished cease from labor;
> the barren woman bears sevenfold,
> but the mother of many is desolate.
>
> Yahweh gives death and life,
> brings down to Sheol and draws up;
> Yahweh makes poor and rich,
> he humbles and also exalts.
>
> He raises the poor from the dust,
> he lifts the needy from the dunghill
> to give them a place with princes,
> and to assign them a seat of honour;
> for to Yahweh the props of the earth belong,
> on these he has posed the world.
>
> He safeguards the steps of his faithful
> but the wicked vanish in darkness
> (for it is not by strength that man triumphs).
> The enemies of Yahweh are shattered,
> the Most High thunders in the heavens.
>
> Yahweh judges the ends of the earth,
> he endows the king with power,
> he exalts the horn of his Anointed."[133]

§167 Birth and Circumcision of John the Baptist

In Luke's (Luka's) next passage, Elizabeth is the center of focus as the birth of John is briefly related. She is also the center of attention in the first part of Luka's narration of the circumcision and naming of John. It appears that Elizabeth had the name of John revealed to her. In typical Palestinian fashion, she was not even going to be consulted, "they were going to call him Zechariah after his father," but she interposed and insisted on John. In typical fashion her authority counted for nothing and the crowd insisted on going to the "real" authority, the man: "they made signs to his father [who was still struck dumb by the angel] to find out what he wanted him called."[134] But Elizabeth's decision was vindicated by Zechariah and, as was to be expected, "they were all astonished." Thus Zechariah supported his wife in the naming of the child John. There is no indication in the Gospel that the name John came from anyone except through Elizabeth, though it is possible that Zechariah could have written to Elizabeth, that the angel said the boy's name was to be John; however, if that were the case, one would have expected that the Gospel might have recorded that Elizabeth said that Zechariah had told her the boy's name was to be John. Zechariah now receives his power of speech again and praises God with his song, the "Benedictus" (from the first word of the Latin Vulgate translation: "Blessed be the Lord, the God of Israel," "*Benedictus Dominus Deus Israel*").

> Meanwhile the time came for Elizabeth to have her child, and she gave birth to a son; and when her neighbors and relations heard that the Lord had shown her so great a kindness, they shared her joy.
>
> Now on the eighth day they came to circumcise the child; they were going to call him Zechariah after his father, but his mother spoke up. "No," she said, "he is to be called John." They said to her, "But no one in your family has that name," and made signs to his father to find out what he wanted him called. The father asked for a writing tablet and wrote, "His name is John." And they were all astonished. At that instant his power of speech returned and he spoke and praised God.[135]

§168 The Birth of Yeshua

Only Luka recorded the birth of Yeshua in any detail; who else would have known about, been intensely interested in, and bothered to remember and pass on such "womanly" matters other than a woman? Matthew merely says that Yeshua was "born at Bethlehem in Judaea during the reign of King Herod."[136] Luka's is the familiar story of Joseph and Mary going from Nazareth to Bethlehem to register in a Roman census, and of Yeshua's being born there; angels announced the event to shepherds in the area. Of course, nothing here indicates anything of Yeshua's attitude toward women, but there were two small hints of Luka's positive attitude in the references to Mary. When recording that the shepherds came to Bethlehem to find the Messiah, Luka mentions Mary first, not the usual order in a patriarchal society: "So they hurried away and found Mary and Joseph, and the baby lying in the manger." Secondly, Luka then speaks of Mary, not Joseph, keeping and pondering all these things in her heart. This would seem to indicate that Luke, or much more likely, Luka the Proto-Gospel woman evangelist, had access to Mary, or an intimate tradition stemming from Mary. Joseph apparently died before Yeshua's public life, but Mary lived through it and clearly became an important figure in the early Christian community, although not in the circles Paul traveled in, for he *never* referred to her. Proto-Gospel Luka is especially sensitive to Mary; it has twenty references to Mary or Yeshua's mother, as compared to eleven in Matthew, seven in the Fourth Gospel, three in Mark, and none in Paul. This sensitivity in Luka toward Mary parallels this Gospel's sensitivity toward women in general.

> Now when the angels had gone from them into heaven, the shepherds said to one another, "Let us go to Bethlehem and see this thing that has happened which the Lord has made known to us." So they hurried away and found Mary and Joseph, and the baby lying in the manger. When they saw the child they repeated what they had been told about him, and everyone who heard it was astonished at what the shepherds had to say. As for Mary, she treasured all these things and pondered them in her heart. And the shepherds went back glorifying and praising God for all they had heard and seen; it was exactly as they had been told.[137]

§169 Prophecy of Simeon

When Mary and Joseph took the infant Yeshua to the Temple at Jerusalem for the ritual redemption of the firstborn son, they were met by a devout man, Simeon, who prophesied concerning Yeshua as the Messiah. Then Simeon addressed not Joseph or both parents, but rather Mary alone, reinforcing the above-discussed pattern of focusing on Mary. He spoke not only of Yeshua, but also of what would happen to Mary because of him: "A sword will pierce your own soul."

> As the child's father and mother stood there wondering at the things that were being said about him, Simeon blessed them and said to Mary his mother, "You see this child: he is destined for the fall and for the rising of many in Israel, destined to be a sign that is rejected, and a sword will pierce your own soul too, so that the secret thoughts of many may be laid bare."[138]

§170 Prophecy of Anna

As noted in §56, we have here another instance of sexually parallel passages. Normally at least two witnesses are required in Jewish law to authenticate something; Luka recorded both a male and a female witness, indicating again that he (or rather, she) understood Yeshua's Gospel, his Messiahship, to be for both women and men. Both Simeon and the woman, Anna, were prophets. In fact, only she of the two was explicitly named a prophet (*prophētis*). She, too, prophesied and spoke publicly of the Messianic child. Thus in Luka, for every man playing a significant role in the early and "pre" life of Yeshua, there was also an equally or more significant woman: Elizabeth and Zechariah, Mary and Joseph, Anna and Simeon.

> There was a woman prophet also, Anna the daughter of Phanuel, of the tribe of Asher. She was well on in years. Her days of girlhood over, she had been married for seven years before becoming a widow. She was now eighty-four years old and never left the Temple, serving God night and day with fasting and prayer. She came by just at that moment and began to praise God; and she spoke of the child to all who looked forward to the deliverance of Jerusalem.[139]

§171 Yeshua "Lost" in the Temple

In the sole Gospel account of an event of Yeshua's life between his infancy and his public life, Luka reflects two elements which bear on the status of women. The first is indirect and remote. Elsewhere (§44) it has been pointed out how Yeshua made a strenuous effort to dismantle the restrictive bonds of the family and that this dismantling would have, by far, the greatest liberating effects on women. Already here, at the pre-adult age of twelve (Jewish males took on adult responsibility with the rite of bar mitzvah at thirteen), Yeshua began his efforts at loosening family bonds. When his parents chided him for going off on his own, he responded that they need not be so overly concerned about him, that he had other matters beyond their scope to attend to, an intimation of much stronger words ahead, coupled, nevertheless, with his obeying his parents after this twelve-year-old foreshadowing experience.

Secondly, it should also be noted that, again in this story, Luka focuses not on Joseph, but on Mary. It was her exchange with Yeshua that Luka recorded, again pointing to a tradition that went back to the personal recollections of Mary.

> Every year his parents used to go to Jerusalem for the feast of the Passover. When he was twelve years old, they went up for the feast as usual. When they were on their way home after the feast, the boy Yeshua stayed behind in Jerusalem without his parents knowing it. They assumed he was with the caravan, and it was only after a day's journey that they went to look for him among their relations and acquaintances. When they failed to find him they went back to Jerusalem looking for him everywhere.

Three days later, they found him in the Temple, sitting among the doctors, listening to them, and asking them questions; and all those who heard him were astounded at his intelligence and his replies. They were overcome when they saw him, and his mother said to him, "My child, why have you done this to us? See how worried your father and I have been, looking for you." "Why were you looking for me?" he replied. "Did you not know that I must be busy with my Father's affairs?" But they did not understand what he meant.[140]

§172 Mary's Memoirs

Luka closes the introductory part of her Gospel by noting that Yeshua obeyed his parents and matured, and that "his mother stored up all these things in her heart," rather pointedly implying that much of the foregoing was based, at least ultimately, on her remembrances. But one is given the impression that the significance of the events was by no means always so clear at the moment, but became so only in Mary's later reflections: "As the child's father and mother stood there wondering at the things that were being said about him."[141] "But they did not understand what they meant."[142] "As for Mary, she treasured all these things and pondered them in her heart."[143] "His mother stored up all these things in her heart."[144] Thus, as no other New Testament writer, Luka was concerned to gather into her Gospel the tradition of not just Mary's recollections, but her remembrances reflected on Mary's memoirs.

He then went down with them and came to Nazareth and lived under their authority. His mother stored up all these things in her heart. And Yeshua increased in wisdom, in stature, and in favor with God and humanity.[145]

§173 Summary: Luka's Introduction

In Luke's (Luka's) introductory section, just reviewed, scholars often note the close parallelism and, at the same time, tightly interwoven quality of the John the Baptist and Yeshua stories. But it is equally valid to note the sexual parallelism and, at the same time, integrated quality of the female and the male elements all throughout the whole of this introduction. This sexual balance was clearly deliberate on the evangelist's part and reinforces the earlier argued conclusion that this portion of Luke's Gospel, plus Luke 9:51 to 18:14 (the portion named by a number of scholars as Proto-Gospel), originally stemmed from a woman disciple of Yeshua, and was written down by an anonymous woman evangelist, and, who for convenience, I am referring to as "Luka." Add to this, the argument just made, that these are, in effect, Mary's memoirs.

§174 Yeshua's Concern for Widows

Yeshua's special concern for widows is analyzed in §49ff., and each of the events or stories about widows is treated separately. But here it should again be noted that of the eight stories about widows found in the Gospels, seven of them are found in Luke's Gospel, four of them exclusively so. One is the sexually parallel story of the widow Anna, analyzed just above, as part of Luke's introductory section. The second widow story found in Luke alone is the sexually parallel reference to the widow of Zarephath.[146] The third, also sexually paired, is the touching story of the widow of Nain,[147] and the fourth, again sexually paralleled, is Yeshua's story of the widow and the wicked judge.[148] It is apparent that Yeshua was especially concerned about the plight of widows. But it is also clear that of all the evangelists, Luke was by far the most sensitive to Yeshua's concern about the burdens of widows, since he exclusively recorded half the stories about widows, plus three quarters of the rest. Might this suggest that the female evangelist of the Proto-Gospel, Luka, was herself a widow, or at least closely identified with widows? Yeshua's mother, Mary, of course was a widow and obviously the source of much of Luka's material.

§175 Yeshua and the Penitent Woman

See §51 for a discussion of Yeshua's deliberate breach of several social and religious customs in permitting a woman (of ill-repute!), to touch him in public, and in treating her as a full human being, whose primary quality is personhood.[149]

§176 Women Disciples of Yeshua

See §57 for an analysis of the report that women also were openly among Yeshua's followers, most extraordinary for that time and place. Was it from among them that Luke's woman proto-evangelist Luka came? Or the woman mentioned most often by all the Gospel writers and to whom the risen Yeshua first appeared—Mary Magdalene? Or the committed, intellectual disciple of Yeshua who sat at his feet—Mary of Bethany? Possibly. But we have no documentary means of knowing.[150]

§177 The Intellectual Life for Women

See §15 for an analysis of Yeshua's visit to the house of his friends, Martha and Mary, of how Yeshua made it abundantly clear that the supposedly exclusively male role of the intellectual, of the "theologian," was for women as well as for men, and of how he explicitly rejected the housekeeper role as *the* female role. How this story must have buoyed up those Jewish women whose horizons and desires stretched beyond the kitchen threshold. It is, consequently, not at all surprising to find this story in the Proto-Gospel section of Luke[151] that many scholars attribute originally to a Jewish eyewitness follower of Yeshua, who I have argued almost certainly had to have been a woman disciple, "Luka." One might ask: Who would have particularly noticed or have bothered to remember such a small event as the Martha and Mary story except a woman? It would have meant little to a man, but to a woman it would have been a door to a whole new world. Hence, it is quite likely that a woman (or women) was responsible for the preservation of this episode in Yeshua's life. It also is likely that the woman originally responsible for remembering this event was the one who was there and was deeply impressed by it, namely, Mary of Bethany.

Again, the question naturally arises, was this deeply religious intellectual woman disciple of Yeshua the evangelist of Luke's Proto-Gospel, "Luka"? The likelihood appears strong—Mary of Bethany, of course, being the one most likely to have remembered the scene at Yeshua's feet, and as the "authorized intellectual," also then was the one most likely to have collected and recorded the other pro-woman teachings and actions of Yeshua. In addition, Mary of Bethany also was a Palestinian Jew who perforce knew Hebrew and Aramaic, which characterized the writing of Proto-Luke, Luka. She was an avid student of Yeshua which also suggests that she was literate, although we have no documentary evidence of that. Nevertheless, that seems more likely than, for example, Peter or the other fishermen among Yeshua's followers being literate; and yet, it is commonly assumed that Peter was a source of information about Yeshua. In any case, Luka/Luke's sensitivity to women ultimately preserved this Magna Carta for women.[152]

§178 Rejection of the Baby-Machine Image

See §15 for an analysis of the brief passage wherein Yeshua explicitly rejects the sexually reductionist baby-machine image of women in favor of a personal, spiritual one. Again, one wonders why this tiny event was remembered and recorded. And more, who would have even noticed it and striven to preserve it except one to whom it meant a great deal, namely, a woman? This passage, too, is in Luka's Proto-Gospel section of Luke.[153]

§179 Healing of a Woman on the Sabbath

See §47 for a discussion of Yeshua's healing on the Sabbath of a woman, ill for eighteen years, and the uproar it caused. It should be recalled that the Fourth Gospel recorded no healings by Yeshua on the Sabbath; and Matthew and Mark each recorded one healing, of a man; while Luke/Luka recorded three Sabbath healings, two of men and one of a woman. This single recollection of the healing of a woman is recorded in Luka's Proto-Gospel section of Luke, again reinforcing the argument of its originally stemming from a woman. In the passage, Yeshua also referred to the cured woman in unheard-of fashion as a *daughter* of Abraham, a detail a woman was much more likely to notice and preserve, since it would mean so much more to her.[154]

§180 Yeshua's Dismantling of Restrictive Family Bonds III

Several times now (see §43) it has been noted that Yeshua deliberately set about the task of dismantling the restrictive family bonds that often were overwhelmingly stifling in that culture, and most especially for women. It was also noted that Mark recorded one such explicit passage, Matthew two (in common with Luke), and Luke three. It is interesting that two of these passages in Luke occur in the Proto-Gospel section. Though there was a certain sexual asceticism expressed in two of these Lucan passages, or perhaps rather because there was, the fact that two of the three are found in the Proto-Gospel section adds yet another argument for seeing a woman evangelist as Luke's source here.

> Great crowds accompanied him on his way and he turned and spoke to them. "If anyone comes to me without hating his father, mother, wife, children, brothers, sisters, yes and his own life too, he cannot be my disciple."[155]

§181 God in the Image of a Woman

See §34 for a discussion of Yeshua's use of a woman as an image of God, a usage vigorously resisted by the Hebrew prophets and other Hebrew devotees of the one true God, Yahweh.[156] As noted earlier, because of their unique qualities, the three stories about how God is concerned about the "lost" were doubtless told originally by Yeshua. It is also likely that they were told in response to complaints that Yeshua was consorting with sinners; each one made a most apt reply to such a charge. We cannot, however, be sure that they were all told at one time, as they are recorded in Luke. In fact, since each of them was quite effective in itself, it seems more likely that they were related by Yeshua on similar but different occasions. Still, the inclusion of a story of God's concern for the lost which projects God in a female image doubtless must be attributed to Yeshua, along with the rest of the stories and images.

Yeshua clearly was concerned to maintain a sexual balance in this category of parables, as in others. This, of course, makes very special sense since the complaint was that Yeshua welcomed "sinners" (*hamartōlous*),[157] a term that included the sort of women who followed Yeshua (e.g., *hamartōlos*).[158] However, the bringing together of these three stories of Yeshua in one place probably should be attributed to Luke, or perhaps more aptly, Luke's source, Luka, where Luke most probably found the three parables already successively arranged. This is particularly likely since the stories are located in the Proto-Gospel section which is largely unique to Luke and has an especially cohesive quality. The fact that none of the other Gospels recorded the story projecting God in a female image, though Matthew did record one of these three stories of God's concern for the lost,[159] and that nowhere else in the New Testament is God portrayed in a female image, also enhances the argument of a female evangelist for this Proto-Gospel section of Luke. A woman would have been especially keen to recall and record such imagery coming from the lips of the Messiah.[160]

§182 Yeshua and the Adulterous Woman

See §50 for an analysis of the extraordinary story of the woman caught in the act of adultery being used to set a trap for Yeshua, his avoiding it, and his refusal to condemn the woman, an act which was probably responsible for the long resistance in early Christian history to receiving the story as authentic. As noted, scholars generally agree on linguistic grounds that the story surely was not written by the Fourth Evangelist, though it is usually printed there in most Bibles, but rather, as a note in the Jerusalem Bible states: "The adulterous woman passage of Jn 7:53–8:11, for the Lucan authorship of which there are many good arguments, would fit into this context admirably."[161] For example, the strong similarity of the wording of Luke 21: 37–38 to John 8:1–2 suggests that the latter is simply a modification of the former after the story was cut out of Luke:

> In the daytime he would be in the Temple teaching [1. *didaskōn*], but would spend the night on the hill called the Mount of Olives [2. *eis to oros . . . elaiōn*]. And from early morning all the people [3. *kai pas ho laos*] would gather round him in the Temple [4. *en tō hierō*] to listen to him [5. *pros auton*].[162]

And Yeshua went to the Mount of Olives [2. *eis to oros tōn elaiōn*]. At daybreak he appeared in the Temple [4. *eis to hieron*] again; and as all the people [3. *kai pas ho laos*] came to him [5. *pros auton*], he sat down and began to teach [1. *edidasken*] them.[163]

The story depicts Yeshua as taking an extremely sensitive and courageous stand, but one, as noted in the earlier analysis, which apparently scandalized many early Christians, leading to the story's deletion from all early manuscripts. But it did already have a partial precedent in the other Lucan story of Yeshua and the penitent "prostitute."[164] It thus fit well into the strongly pro-woman spirit of Luka/Luke's Proto-Gospel. Because of that general "feminist" kinship, and because of the special kinship of the putatively Lucan story of the adulterous woman with the definitely Lucan story of the penitent "prostitute" (here are represented the amateur and the professional violators of sexual mores), it is quite possible that the wandering story of the adulterous woman also came from the woman evangelist of the Proto-Gospel of Luke, Luka. Again, a woman follower of Yeshua would have been especially impressed with this event and especially eager to preserve it. Was this unknown woman "Luka" among those earliest Christians driven into the Syrian Diaspora ("both men and *women*"[165] and "men or *women*"[166]), where she composed her "Gospel" (*euaggelizomenoi*, "Good-Newsing,"[167])? Indeed, the solely Lucan passages, that is, the Proto-Gospel, where this story might earlier have been located, not only betrays an intimate knowledge of Palestinian Judaism but was also clearly aimed at non-Jewish readers. Further, the earliest documentary evidence of the story of the adulterous woman is the reference in the third-century *Didascalia*, which originated in Syria (and which also refers to women deacons as an image of the Holy Spirit! See §256).

§183 Yeshua "Leads Women Astray"

Not only are the Gospels full of incidents wherein Yeshua champions the cause of women and of children,[168] but his reputation for this behavior was widespread enough that he may well have been denounced to Pilate for having "led women and children astray." There are at least three variant readings in Luke's Gospel, two of which are very early, which witness to this tradition. The oldest one, stemming from Marcion, who lived in the first half of the second century when some of the canonical New Testament documents were still being written, simply said that Yeshua was accused of "leading astray both the women and the children." The second ancient variant reading comes from the fourth-century Palestinian-born Church Father Epiphanius, whose text states that Yeshua's accusers charged: "and he has turned our children and wives away from us for they are not bathed as we are, nor do they purify themselves." (The variants are given below.)

It is not at all surprising that these very early pro-woman traditions turn up in Luke's Gospel, given the strongly pro-woman character of that Gospel. They support the notion that Yeshua was a feminist, was widely known to be a feminist, was despised by many for being a feminist, and was politically denounced as a feminist.

It would appear from the second tradition that Yeshua's lesson of the relative unimportance (vis-à-vis the woman's person) of regular female ritual impurity from the issuance of blood, as taught in the episode of the woman with the twelve-year hemorrhage, was widely learned and applied. To generate the remembrance of this tradition many women followers of Yeshua must have had a high opinion of their experience of a new attitude toward the purity, or impurity, of their own bodies, and the fact that so many men perceived it as "turning their wives away from them." This so infuriated the men that they publicly denounced Yeshua for it to the Roman governor and demanded that he be executed. These extremely early traditions attached to Luke (were they "suppressed" as was the wandering Lucan story of the adulterous woman was?) reflect the notion that Yeshua's feminism was perceived as a capital crime!

> They began their accusation by saying, "We found this man inciting our people to a revolt, opposing payment of the tribute to Caesar, [leading astray the women and the children (*kai apostrephonta tas gynaikas kai ta tekna*)? Marcion], and claiming to be Christ, a king. . . . He is inflaming the people with his teaching all over Judaea; it has come all the way from Galilee, where he started, down to here, [and he has turned our children and wives away from us for they are not bathed as we are, nor do they purify themselves (*et filios nostros et uxores avertit a nobis, non enim baptizantur sicut nos nec se mundant*? Epiphanius)]."[169]

§184 Feminism a Capital Crime!

As just noted, some texts portray a number of opponents of Yeshua as so furious at his "feminism," his leading their women astray, that they wanted to have him executed! This was, in a way, proleptically reminiscent of the "moral" execution that happened to another Jewish feminist, this time a woman, Beruria.

Beruria was the sole woman who made it into the Talmud and earlier rabbinic writings as a superior scholar of *halacha*, rabbinic law. She lived in Palestine a hundred years after Yeshua, just about the time the last of the New Testament writings were being authored (including the above-cited variant readings concerning feminism as a "capital crime").

Over a quarter of a century ago I wrote the following:

What a weight Beruria's reputation must have had in talmudic times for this vitriolic putdown of a rabbi [by Beruria] to be noted, remembered for hundreds of years, and ultimately made permanent in the final redaction of the Talmud. That there was, obviously also, a counter feeling among the early rabbis is reflected only in a shadowy fashion in the last line of the talmudic story about Rabbi Meir's rescue of Beruria's sister from a brothel. There was a backlash to his rescue efforts and "he then arose and ran away and came to Babylon; others say because of the incident about Beruria" (*Talmud* bAboda Zara 182). No further information about the "incident" is given in the Talmud. There is merely this dark reference, sheer innuendo.

A thousand years later, we find a full-blown legend about the incident in the commentary on this passage by the famous Jewish medieval talmudic scholar Rashi:

Beruria once again made fun of the saying of the Sages that women are lighthearted. Then Meir said to her: With your life you will have to take back your words. Then he sent one of his students to test her to see if she would allow herself to be seduced. He sat by her the whole day until she surrendered herself to him. When she realized (what she had done) she strangled herself. Thereupon Rabbi Meir ran away (to Babylonia) on account of the scandal. (Rashi, quoted in Hans Kosmala, "Gedanken zur Kontroverse Farbstein-Hoch," *Judaica*, 1948, pp. 225–227)

There is nothing at all in the intelligence, perceptiveness, and moral character of Beruria to make this in any way credible. Would she not have perceived that her husband had set a trap for her? Is it not incomprehensible that the great Rabbi Meir could have commissioned his rabbinic student to commit one of the three deadly sins in its most serious form: sexual immorality with a married Jewish woman? Finally, why would it take a thousand years for this story, so out of character with all of the previously known documentation, to surface? It clearly was invented simply to morally annihilate Beruria, the one woman of superior stature in the Talmud, Beruria the feminist, for it was exactly on that point that she was attacked. Because she took an overtly feminist stance of rejecting the rabbinic stereotyping of women as intellectually inferior, she was told she would have to give up her life. Feminism was a capital crime![170]

§185 Jerusalem Women on the Via Dolorosa

See §63 for a discussion of the unique Lucan recording of the exchange between the mourning women of Jerusalem and Yeshua on the way to his execution. As noted, these women must have been strongly committed followers of Yeshua to have risked their safety, publicly to mourn and attempt to comfort a condemned prisoner, something the male followers of Yeshua failed to do, and consequently it is to women alone that Yeshua addresses himself on his *Via Dolorosa*. Clearly, Yeshua did what apparently no other rabbi was even concerned to do, he reached out and deeply touched the hearts of many Jewish women, and they responded to him here with reckless abandon. A male disciple of Yeshua might well have recalled this incident with shame, though there is no hint of such shame in the text as we now have it. But how much more likely is it that a woman follower of Yeshua would have had burned in her memory how the women, perhaps she too, rushed out to meet Yeshua on the way to his agonizing and humiliating death, only to have him speak to their need alone, as he reached out to them one last time to show his concern for them in his last hours: "But Yeshua turned to them and said, 'Daughters of Jerusalem, do not weep for me; weep rather for yourselves and for your children.'"

> As they were leading him away . . . large numbers of people followed him, and of women too, who mourned and lamented for him. But Yeshua turned to them and said, "Daughters of Jerusalem, do not weep for me; weep rather for yourselves and for your children. For the days will surely come when people will say, 'Happy are those who are barren, the wombs that have never borne, the breasts that have never suckled!' Then they will begin to say to the mountains, 'Fall on us!'; to the hills, 'Cover us!' For if men use the green wood like this, what will happen when it is dry?"[171]

§186 Was Luke Pro-Woman or Anti-Woman?

Almost everything that has been analyzed up to now reflects a positive attitude toward women on the part of Luke and/or his sources. However, there are some items that can be seen as perhaps reflecting a somewhat negative attitude when compared with similar passages in Matthew and/or Mark. It would be well to list them, analyze them individually, and evaluate their overall implications. Perhaps ten such passages can be discerned.

(1) Luke 3:23–38. Luke here presents an ancestral genealogy of Yeshua, listing only male ancestors, whereas Matthew includes four women in his genealogy of Yeshua.[172] However, it was not at all customary to include women in genealogies, so one would have to say, not that Luke was thereby negative in his attitude toward women, but rather, that Matthew was especially positive in this instance.

(2) Luke 4:22. "They said, 'This is Joseph's son, surely?'" Again, nothing negative toward women here. But the corresponding description of

Yeshua in Mark is as follows: "This is the carpenter, surely, the son of Mary, the brother of James and Joset and Jude and Simon? His sisters, too, are they not here with us?"[173] And in Matthew: "This is the carpenter's son, surely? Is not his mother the one called Mary, and his brothers James and Joseph and Simon and Jude? His sisters, too, are they not all here with us?"[174] There does seem to have been a greater awareness of women relatives in Mark and Matthew here than in Luke.

(3) Luke 8:19 (see §143). Luke recorded that Yeshua's mother and brothers came to see him and Yeshua responded that those who act on the word of God were his mother and his brothers. Matthew[175] and Mark[176] added "sisters" to the account. Again, this indicates nothing of a negative attitude toward women, especially since Luke does include "mother," but it does perhaps indicate a slightly greater awareness of women on Matthew's and Mark's part than Luke's in this instance.

(4) Luke 9:10–17 (see §134). All four evangelists recorded the accounts of the multiplication of the loaves and fishes.[177] Three, including Luke, refer only to thousands of men being fed (or to a crowd of thousands), whereas Matthew added women and children besides. Again, nothing negative on Luke's or Mark's or the Fourth Gospel's part in this account, but rather a greater awareness of women on Matthew's part.

(5) Luke 12:35–37. Luke recorded a saying of Yeshua about men waiting for their master to return from the wedding feast, nothing negative. However, Matthew's version[178] told of ten bridesmaids waiting. Again, a stronger emphasis on women in Matthew than in Luke.

(6) Luke 14:15–24. Luke records a parable in which the realm of God is likened to people invited to a banquet. However, in Matthew's version,[179] it is a wedding banquet, perhaps adding thereby a "feminine" element. Further, in Luke's version, one excuse offered for not accepting the banquet invitation "I have married a wife," suggesting that marriage might be an obstacle to responding to God's call.

(7) Luke 14:26 (see §44). In quoting Yeshua's listing of those relatives who must give way to the demands of discipleship, Luke recorded not only father, mother, brothers, sisters, and children, as does Matthew[180] but also "wife," perhaps again reflecting an attitude that views marriage as an obstacle to the full following of God's call.

(8) Luke 18:29. A similar listing of relatives left for the "sake of the reign of God" included "wife" in Luke's version, but not in either Mark's[181] or Matthew's.[182]

(9) Luke 23:49 (see §64). Luke mentions Yeshua's women disciples as present at the crucifixion; so do Mark[183] and Matthew.[184] However, the latter two mention only the women as being present, but Luke includes in addition "all his [Yeshua's] friends," perhaps slightly diluting the focus on the loyalty of the women.

(10) Luke 24:1–11 (see (3) in §66). In Luke's Gospel, several women are the first witnesses to the empty tomb, but no appearances of Yeshua to women were recorded, whereas in Matthew,[185] the Fourth Gospel,[186] and the later added ending of Mark[187] they were.

It should be noted first that passages 1–5 and 9 above in no way indicate in themselves anything negative in Luke's attitude toward women, but rather evidence a somewhat sharper focus on women on the part of Matthew and/or Mark. Secondly, passages 6–8 indicate an attitude that marriage was a burden in seeking the Reign of God. Moreover, these three statements are written solely from the man's point of view, that is, wives must be given up, or, "I have married a *wife*, and so I cannot come." No mention is made of marrying or giving up *husbands*. This sexually ascetic perspective reflected very well Paul's attitude toward marriage, that is, best to avoid it if at all possible; his attitude was doubtless influenced by his expectation of the second coming of Christ imminently, which made worldly matters like marriage, slavery, and so forth, of relatively little significance, as expressed in his First Letter to the Corinthians.[188] Luke, according to deuteron-Pauline sources,[189] was a long-time companion and fellow worker of Paul. Perhaps a second influence of Paul on Luke here can also be seen in passage 10 above. According to Paul's writings, Yeshua did not appear first to the women, as in the three Gospels other than Luke; indeed, he did not appear to them at all, unless they were among "the five hundred."[190] It appears that Luke followed his teacher Paul in this regard, also.[191]

But perhaps the most interesting, and obvious, point to be noted about all this perhaps vaguely "negative" evidence of Luke's is that it can be construed negatively only on a basis of comparison with other Gospel accounts of the same event, that is, none of these passages comes from sections of Luke that are unique to him. That means their source is not the Proto-Gospel by the woman evangelist, Luka, embedded within Luke. This would indicate that the Proto-Gospel source was more consciously and strongly pro-woman than Luke's other sources, and Luke himself, another fact that points toward the likelihood of a woman evangelist.

§187 Conclusion: A Woman Evangelist—"Luka"

In sum, it can be said that, beyond the evidence that clearly points to the fact that Yeshua himself was a vigorous feminist, Luke's Gospel reflects in many ways this feminism most intensely of all the Gospels. In choosing to record all this pro-woman material, Luke himself also clearly indicates a sympathetic attitude toward women. However, his pro-woman material fell into two categories: that which was recorded in common with other Gospels and that which is unique to Luke. The former is almost as large (nineteen passages, seventeen of them in common with Matthew) as the latter (twenty-three passages). In the commonly recorded passages, sometimes Luke's version highlighted women more than the other versions; sometimes the other way around. It would have to be judged that, in regard to this commonly recorded material, Matthew and Luke exhibit an attitude that is about equally sympathetic toward the cause of women. But in the material special to each Gospel, Luke is giant strides ahead of all the others in pro-woman passages. Simply in terms of numbers of passages dealing with women, Luke had twenty-three (practically all actively pro-woman) special to him; Matthew ten (though half of these did not reflect an attitude toward women); Fourth Gospel three; and Mark none.

Again, it is in that Proto-Gospel section of Luke that the feminism of his Gospel really stands out. Thus, it is clear that a strongly feminist evangelist was the source of the Proto-Gospel, again enhancing the near-certitude that it was a woman evangelist, "Luka" (quite possibly Mary of Bethany), who perforce had to remain anonymous, at least in Luke's judgment, for the sake of the credibility of the Gospel in that male-dominated society, which, as is discussed immediately below, is also the case with the Fourth Gospel.

§188 THE FOURTH GOSPEL

The Fourth Gospel was the last of the four canonical Gospels to be written (probably close to 100 C.E.). Much of its material is different from the other three Gospels, the Synoptics, and it tends to report the teaching of Yeshua in long discourses. It is third in overall length, being about 75 percent of the length of Luke, the longest Gospel. However, the Fourth Gospel contains far fewer accounts that deal with women or the "feminine," only eight. On the other hand, several of these accounts are quite long, are important, and are very sympathetic toward women. In fact, these nine passages are 122 verses in length, compared to Mark's 114 (Matthew has 180 verses and Luke 220 dealing with women).

The critical question of the authorship of the Fourth Gospel is dealt with at length below. However, let it be stated here that there is a scholarly consensus that the author is definitely *not* John, the son of Zebedee, one of the twelve apostles. The strange source of John's name on the Gospel came from Irenaeus in the late second century. He remembered hearing in his childhood from Polycarp (d. 156 C.E.) that John was the author; Polycarp spoke of a certain Presbyter John, whom Irenaeus mixed up with John the son of Zebedee, one of the twelve.[192] Since the real name of the author was deliberately suppressed, the name of John stuck. More on that below.

§189 Wedding at Cana

See §40 for an analysis of Yeshua's attitude toward his mother, his support of marriage, and the Fourth Gospel's probable balancing of that against ascetic elements of his time which denigrated marriage. The Fourth Gospel alone recorded this event.[193]

§190 Samaritan Woman

See §53 for a discussion of this long and important account, which only the Fourth Gospel recorded. Here we find Yeshua going out of his way to enter into a conversation with a strange woman, to reveal himself to her as the Messiah, and to make her an instrument for the preaching of his "Good News," his Gospel.[194]

§191 Yeshua in a Female Image

See §36 for an analysis of the passage in which Yeshua refers to himself with the maternal image of giving drink at the breast.[195]

§192 Woman Taken in Adultery

Although the report of Yeshua's encounter with the woman seized in the act of adultery is usually located in the Fourth Gospel,[196] it is the scholarly consensus that the Fourth Gospel Evangelist certainly did not write it, that it has many characteristics akin to the Synoptics' style, and that there is some manuscript evidence that it originally might have been located in Luke, after Luke 21:38. See §50 for a discussion of this passage.

§193 The Resurrection of Lazarus

See §81, where I analyze the profound involvement of women in the raising of Lazarus by Yeshua, Yeshua's revealing of himself as "the resurrection" to a woman, and his being proclaimed by her to be the Messiah and the Son of God. Only the Fourth Gospel has this account.[197]

§194 The Anointment of Yeshua by Mary of Bethany

See §§60 and 61 for a discussion of Mary's "wasteful" anointing of Yeshua and the defense of her by Yeshua.[198]

§195 Women in Yeshua's Passion and Resurrection

It is apparent that receiving an appearance of the risen Yeshua was seen as the key to authority in the beginning of the Yeshua Movement. How did Paul, who never met Yeshua, claim to have authority to teach the Gospel? Because he claimed to have seen the risen Yeshua while he, Saul, was on the road to Damascus. That is what gave him the right to call himself an "apostle" (*apostellein*, which in Greek means "to send"). Hence, there were also several women, and preeminently Mary Magdalene, who also experienced an appearance of the risen Yeshua, and indeed, also knew him before his death. This certainly was a major source of their importance in the early period of the Yeshua Movement, eventually the church. We will see below how this authority led to a second woman being an evangelist, a writer of a Gospel, the Fourth Gospel.

§196 Women at the Foot of the Cross

See §64 for an initial analysis of the Fourth Gospel's account of the women present at Yeshua's crucifixion and death. Even though many scholars believe that the Fourth Gospel's adding the presence of the one male disciple to the group of women at the crucifixion was unhistorical, it should be noted that, with all the other evangelists, the Fourth Gospel evangelist did locate the women there. The Fourth Gospel, like Mark and Matthew, lists three women's names; they are not exactly the same as those on the other lists, but Mary Magdalene is there, as in all the lists. This is the only list on which Mary Magdalene is not placed first (see §73). In the Fourth Gospel's account, Yeshua's concern to find his widowed mother a home is almost the last thing he spoke of.[199] But more about this important passage is below.

§197 Women First Witnesses to the Empty Tomb

See §73 for analyses of Mary Magdalene's witness to the empty tomb. All the other evangelists also record this event, and, as in the other accounts, Mary Magdalene is named first in the list of women at the empty tomb, only in the Fourth Gospel did the list begin and end with Mary Magdalene.[200]

§198 Women Testify to Male Disciples about Yeshua's Resurrection

See §67 for a discussion of the women's testifying about the resurrection of
Yeshua to the male disciples. The traditions are extremely various on this
matter:

(1) The earliest of the accounts in the New Testament, namely, Paul's
First Letter to the Corinthians,[201] does not even mention the
women in connection with the resurrection.

(2) The earliest Gospel, Mark, said the women were frightened, ran
away, and "said nothing to a soul," though obviously they did eventually say something to someone; how else could the existence of the
Gospel account be explained?

(3) In Matthew, it simply says they "ran to tell the disciples," and on the
way were met by Yeshua and commissioned by him to "go and tell
my brothers." There is no indication of the brothers' reaction.

(4) Luke, written like Matthew, between the time of the writing of
Mark and the Fourth Gospel, recorded that a whole group of
women told the apostles of the empty tomb, "but this story of theirs
seemed pure nonsense, and they did not believe them; Peter, however, went running to the tomb."

(5) In the Fourth Gospel, the latest to be written, Mary Magdalene ran
and told Peter and "the other disciple"; their response was simply to
run and see for themselves, not necessarily implying that they did
not believe her, but it seems likely so.

(6) The ending added to Mark's Gospel,[202] written probably early in the
second century, sounds in some ways much like Luke's account and
in some ways like the Fourth Gospel's. "But they did not believe her
[Mary Magdalene] when they heard her say that he was alive and
that she had seen him."

Furthermore, of the four Gospels' accounts, Mark recorded that an angel in the empty tomb commissioned the women to testify to the male disciples; Matthew did so as well, but also added that Yeshua himself likewise
commissioned the women; Luke mentions two angels in the empty tomb but
recorded no commissioning at all, though in fact the women did testify to the
male disciples; the Fourth Gospel reports the presence of the angels, but
recorded only Yeshua's commissioning of Mary Magdalene. Thus, three of the
four Gospels speak of a commissioning of the women: one (Mark) by an angel, one (the Fourth Gospel) by Yeshua, and one (Matthew) by both; one
(Luke) did not record such a commissioning. In fact, however, according to
Luke, the women did nevertheless testify, and according to Mark, they did

not, despite the commission, though the matter is confused here because of the strong possibility of a lost original ending and because the second-century ending did record a testifying by Mary Magdalene.

It is perhaps not possible to speak of an original version of the account of the women's commissioning and testifying. Rather, perhaps it is best to speak of several traditions that fed into the different Gospel accounts and that may or may not have been significantly adapted by the Gospel writers. What is clear is that all three elements: (1) the commissioning of the women to testify concerning the empty tomb and/or resurrection to the male disciples; (2) their actual testifying; and (3) a disbelieving response to the women by the men, are strongly represented in the Gospel accounts (though not at all in Paul). Mark, without the "lost" or added ending, is the least supportive of the women's role in these matters; the other three are equally, though differently, supportive. One would have to conclude that the tradition concerning this very significant involvement of women in this most essential matter of Christian belief and their put-down by the men grew so much stronger, either in times after, or places other, or both, than when Paul and Mark wrote, that they found a prominent place in the later three Gospels, and in the later ending of Mark.[203]

§199 The Risen Yeshua Appears to Women

See §67ff. for a discussion of the risen Yeshua's appearance first to women (one or more).[204]

Raymond E. Brown notes that,

> essential to the apostolate in the mind of Paul were the two components of having seen the risen Yeshua and having been sent to proclaim him; this is the implicit logic of I Cor 9:1–2; 15:8–11; Gal 1:11–16. A key to Peter's importance in the apostolate was the tradition that he was the first to see the risen Yeshua (I Cor 15:5; Lk 24:34). More than any other Gospel, John revises this tradition about Peter. . . . In John (and in Matthew) Mary Magdalene is sent by the risen Lord. . . . True, this is not a mission to the whole world; but Mary Magdalene comes close to meeting the basic Pauline requirements of an apostle; and it is she, not Peter, who is the first to see the risen Yeshua. . . . The tradition that Yeshua appeared first to Mary Magdalene has a good chance of being historical . . . he remembered first this representative of the women who had not deserted him during the Passion. The priority given to Peter in Paul and Luke is a priority among those who became official witnesses to the Resurrection. The secondary place given to the tradition of an appearance to a woman or women probably reflects the fact that women did not serve at

first as official preachers of the Church, a fact that would make the creation of an appearance to woman unlikely.[205]

§200 Interim Conclusion

Although the Fourth Gospel had the least number of passages about women (the number of verses was slightly more than Mark's, however), it took a strongly pro-woman stance. It contained a large number of events peculiar to it in which women played extremely important roles: According to the Fourth Gospel, Yeshua performed his first miracle at the bidding of a woman (wedding feast at Cana[206]); the first recorded effective woman evangelist was sent out by Yeshua (the Samaritan woman[207]); Yeshua revealed himself uniquely to a woman as "the resurrection" (Martha[208]); and for the first time, in the Fourth Gospel, as the Messiah (the Samaritan woman[209]); Yeshua was proclaimed publicly by a woman (Martha[210]), rather than Peter, to be the Messiah, and also the Son of God. Likewise, rather than appearing first to Peter, the risen Yeshua is reported by the Fourth Gospel as having appeared first to a woman (Mary Magdalene[211]), who then was sent by Yeshua to bear witness to Peter! This latter point, the first appearance of the risen Yeshua to a woman, however, the Fourth Gospel has in common with Matthew, although there the account is not nearly so detailed and moving as that of the Fourth Gospel. Moreover, Yeshua describes himself with a very female, maternal, image.[212]

It is perhaps also worth noting that, although the account about Yeshua and the adulterous woman[213] is clearly not written by the Fourth Gospel Evangelist, it ended up being located there, indicating perhaps that many early Christians felt that the Fourth Gospel was so sensitive toward women as to be thought the most appropriate place to locate that "orphaned" story. The Fourth Gospel contains long accounts about Mary Magdalene and Mary of Bethany, including the accounts of the latter at her own home[214] and as the anointer of Yeshua's feet.[215] Perhaps this fact, coupled with the tradition which (incorrectly) considered Mary Magdalene, Mary of Bethany, and the penitent "harlot" of Luke 7:36–50, who anointed Yeshua's feet to be one and the same person, encouraged the early Christians to locate this story of Yeshua's befriending another female sexual sinner in the Fourth Gospel.

In any case, it is clear that the Fourth Gospel is, not quantitatively, but certainly qualitatively, very strongly pro-woman. "John gives prominence to women disciples to the point that they seem to be on the same level as members of the Twelve."[216]

It is also interesting to note that "in John there is a clear display of female self-confidence: not only in general, but also with regard to female discipleship. John portrays women as speaking far more than Mark, Matthew and Luke. In Mark, only five instances of women speaking are recorded, in

Matthew women speak nine times, and in Luke eleven times, only four of which occur in stories about Jesus as a grown man. In contrast to the Synoptics, John recorded twenty-two instances of women speaking."[217]

§201 Who Was the Beloved Disciple?

The Fourth Gospel is the only one which uses the term the "Beloved Disciple" (*mathetes egapta*). Clearly, the Beloved Disciple is the hero of the community of the Fourth Gospel, the so-called Johannine community, and is the source of the Gospel. The premier scholar on the Johannine community, Raymond Brown, states: "The evangelist was an unknown Christian living at the end of the first century in a community for which the Beloved Disciple, now deceased, had been the great authority."[218] Further, although all the other disciples are named (and the Fourth Gospel never uses the term "apostle"), the Beloved Disciple is always anonymous. If this particular disciple of Yeshua is the "beloved" one of Yeshua (e.g., leaned his head on Yeshua's bosom at the last supper), is the leader of his community of followers, and is the source of the Gospel which probes much deeper than any of the other three Gospels into the profound meaning of Yeshua and his teaching, the question positively screams: why was the Beloved Disciple unnamed?

There have been many answers offered to that question. However, one has come to the fore recently with arguments so persuasive, that it seems to me to be an "idea whose time has come." The Beloved Disciple, and the source of the Fourth Gospel, was a woman, and the most likely candidate is Mary Magdalene.

Why? Because by the time the Fourth Gospel was written, as we have it (probably sometime around 100 C.E.), the apocalyptic period—when the imminent return of Yeshua was expected—was long passed and the followers of Yeshua were setting up more institutionalized structures. Statements had begun to appear which were increasingly pushing women to the background, statements such as: "wives should regard their husbands as they regard the Lord" ;[219] "wives, give way to your husbands";[220] "wives should be obedient to their husbands";[221] "I permit no woman to teach or to have authority over men; she is to keep silent";[222] "the women should keep silence in the churches. For they are not permitted to speak, but should be subordinate, as even the law says."[223]

According to Raymond Brown, there are four phases in the development of the Johannine community. The Beloved Disciple and her (Brown does not argue that the Beloved Disciple was a woman) followers initially had a low Christology, that is, they understood Yeshua to be purely human. With the passage of time, the Beloved Disciple and her followers discerned ever deeper meaning in the teachings of Yeshua, and moved increasingly in the direction of a higher Christology, that is, seeing more and more of the divine in Yeshua. Brown discerns that a crisis developed in the community in the mid-eighties of the first century of the Common Era when the followers of Yeshua were being forced out of the synagogue by the addition of a required blessing which high Christology followers of Yeshua could not, in conscience, confess.

Then, in phase two, a division occurs in the Johannine community, with the majority (eventually called the Secessionists) stressing Yeshua's divinity and downplaying his humanity. It is then that the Gospel, as we have it, was revised, keeping the high Christology, but also maintaining the importance of Yeshua's humanity. The final Redactor, in phase three, clearly wanted to maintain connections with the *Ekklesia Katholika*, the "Great Church," that was emerging, and perhaps added ameliorating phrases such as "*Kai ho logos sarxa egeneto*, and the word became flesh,"[224] to try to avoid sliding into "spiritism."

> This curious history of the Fourth Gospel would become quite intelligible if we posit that the larger part of the Johannine community, the Secessionists, took the Gospel with them in their intellectual itinerary toward docetism, gnosticism, and Montanism, while the author's adherents carried the Gospel with them as they were amalgamated into the Great Church. This would explain why Johannine ideas, but not quotations, appear in the earlier church writings: because a majority of those who claimed the Gospel as their own had become heterodox, there would have been reluctance among the orthodox to cite the Gospel as Scripture.[225]

Thus it also became imperative that the gender of the Beloved Disciple be suppressed, lest the Gospel of the Johannine community be rejected by the Great Church. In fact, it was not until the middle of the fourth century that the Fourth Gospel was generally accepted by the *Ekklesia Katholika*, although it had earlier been widely favored by various docetic (doctrines that claim *only* divinity for Yeshua) and Gnostic (doctrines that focus on the divinity of Yeshua and stress the importance of secret knowledge) communities. Phase four is marked by the definitive split in the Johannine community, with the so-called Secessionists drifting more and more toward Docetism and Gnosticism and the "orthodox" remaining with the Great Church, and eventually saving the Fourth Gospel for the "orthodox" church.

As mentioned earlier, Ann Graham Brock has convincingly shown that a sort of see-saw relationship exists between Mary Magdalene and Peter in all the documents in which they appear together, including the three Synoptics, and most prominently the pro-Peter Gospel of Luke (ironically despite its Proto-Gospel female author "Luka"), but also very dramatically in the Fourth Gospel, which is almost anti-Peter and surely pro-Beloved Disciple and pro-Magdalene. Beyond that, the authority struggle between Peter and Magdalene persists in the early apocryphal writings, that is, those Christian writings which did not make it into the New Testament canon, such as the *Gospel of Mary*, the *Gospel of Philip*, and the *Gospel of Thomas*. I will look at each of the instances where, in the Fourth Gospel, the term the "Beloved Disciple" occurs.

It should be clearly noted that I do not claim that a woman, specifically Mary Magdalene, was the writer of the Fourth Gospel, as we have it, but that the Beloved Disciple was clearly a woman, and most likely Mary Magdalene, and that hence, she surely was the source of the Fourth Gospel, and the writer of a Proto-Fourth Gospel, with our present Gospel coming from the hand of a Redactor working toward the end of the first century after the prior death of Magdalene. The end of the Fourth Gospel states, referring to the Beloved Disciple: "This is the disciple who is a witness to these things, and has *written about them*, and we know that that witness is true."[226] Thus, the Beloved Disciple (Mary Magdalene) wrote the penultimate version of the Fourth Gospel.

§202 First a Disciple of John the Baptist?

The Beloved Disciple is not mentioned specifically in John 1:35–40, but many scholars see a reference to the Beloved Disciple here. The Fourth Gospel wrote of John the Baptist standing with two of his disciples and proclaiming Yeshua to be the Lamb of God, upon which the two disciples followed Yeshua. One of them was named as Andrew, and the other was unnamed—the first anonymous appearance of the anonymous Beloved Disciple. For the reader asks, why is Andrew deliberately named as Peter's brother, but the other disciple was also specifically referred to, but equally deliberately not named? (And this anonymous referring to the Beloved Disciple occurs in the Fourth Gospel eight times!) The answer is that, because it was a woman, and to reveal that the Beloved Disciple, the source of the Fourth Gospel, was a woman would have lost the Gospel to the Great Church. In this case at hand, although it is not absolutely certain, it is highly likely that the Beloved Disciple, Mary Magdalene, was first a disciple of John the Baptist, and then became one of the first disciples of Yeshua.

> The next day again John was standing with two of his disciples; and he looked at Yeshua as he walked, and said, "Behold, the Lamb of God!" The two disciples heard him say this, and they followed Jesus. Yeshua turned, and saw them following, and said to them, "What do you seek?" And they said to him, "Rabbi" (which means Teacher), "where are you staying?" "He said to them, "Come and see." They came and saw where he was staying; and they stayed with him that day, for it was about the

tenth hour. One of the two who heard John speak, and followed him, was Andrew, Simon Peter's brother.[227]

§203 Yeshua's Dinner Companion

In John 13:23–26 for the first time the term "the disciple whom Yeshua loved" (*ton matheton on egapa tou Iesou*) is used, and she is described as leaning on Yeshua's breast at dinner (the "Last Supper"). They are obviously using the practice customary in the Roman Empire of reclining on cushions at meal. In fact, Peter called her attention and asked her to ask Yeshua who was going to betray him, after which the Gospel said that she "fell back on Yeshua's breast and asked him . . ." Clearly, Peter was unwilling to ask Yeshua out loud who the traitor was, but felt that Magdalene was close enough to Yeshua, physically and psychologically, that she could do the asking—and he was right.

It should be noticed that here is another instance of a pairing of Peter and Magdalene, with Peter coming off lower and Magdalene higher. There is no psychological tension expressed here (as there is in the later *Gospel of Mary* and *Gospel of Philip*), but clearly Magdalene has the more authoritative position above that of Peter, measured in closeness to Yeshua. How different from the Gospel of Luke where Peter predominates and Magdalene makes the least showing of all the Gospels, and in Paul, who recognizes the authority of Peter, but does not even mention Magdalene.

Now this description of the closeness of Yeshua and the Beloved Disciple, Mary Magdalene, strikes the reader as an extraordinary, intimate closeness. Obviously, it also similarly struck Magdalene and the subsequent followers of the community that formed around her, for it is clearly and starkly described in the Gospel here. Further, this scene became so important for the "Community of the Beloved Disciple" that it is reiterated at the very end of the Gospel when Magdalene is again anonymously identified as "the disciple whom Yeshua loved who also leaned on his breast at the supper and said . . ."[228]

The "Beloved Disciple leaning on Yeshua's breast" became a kind of "branding" for Magdalene and her subsequent community. But in order for her insights into the meaning of Yeshua and his teaching to become accepted and widespread, like John the Baptist, she "had to decrease so that he might increase." But that period is now passing. Though only a few scholars to date have discerned that Magdalene was the most intimate interpreter of the meaning and teaching of Yeshua, it will, in my judgment, doubtless rather quickly become an accepted realization, and Magdalene and the other women disciples of Yeshua, such as that "intellectual" Mary of Bethany, and "Luka" (who might well be Mary of Bethany) will take their rightful places in the Christian tradition.

One of his disciples, whom Yeshua loved, was lying close to the breast of Jesus; so Simon Peter beckoned to him and said, "Tell us who it is of whom he speaks." So, falling back on Yeshua's breast, he said to him, "Lord, who is it?" Yeshua answered, "It is he to whom I shall give this morsel when I have dipped it."[229]

§204 Friends in High Places

In John 18:15–16, Yeshua has just been taken into custody and the Fourth Gospel has it that Peter "and another disciple" (*kai allos mathetes*) follow Yeshua. Brown and many scholars are convinced that this is the Beloved Disciple, for the Fourth Gospel was always hyper-careful to give names and detailed specifics, except when it pertains to the Beloved Disciple—read: Mary Magdalene. The Fourth Gospel notes that the unnamed disciple knew the High Priest—a very interesting detail, suggesting that Magdalene was a self-confident, outgoing kind of person. She speaks to the woman watching the gate to let Peter in. Shortly thereafter, Peter denies that he ever knew Yeshua, while nothing further is reported about the "other disciple," Magdalene. Once again Magdalene is shown to be superior to Peter—why else is she introduced here in the story?

> Simon Peter followed Yeshua, and so did another disciple. As this disciple was known to the high priest, he entered the court of the high priest along with Yeshua, while Peter stood outside at the door. So the other disciple, who was known to the high priest, went out and spoke to the maid who kept the door, and brought Peter in.[230]

§205 Magdalene, the Beloved Disciple, at the Foot of the Cross

On the one hand, John 19:25–27 is a very confusing and confused text, and on the other, it is one with an unusually deep meaning. To begin with there apparently are three women listed as standing below the cross of Yeshua, and all three of them are named Mary. The confusion begins with the fact that verse 25 states that there are the three women named Mary standing by the cross, and then suddenly verse 26 says that Yeshua saw both his mother and the Beloved Disciple. But *he* wasn't there! How did Yeshua see him? Ramon Jusino argues that the Redactor simply replaced the name of Mary Magdalene with that of the "anonymous Beloved Disciple." Why? Because the words Yeshua was about to utter were far too central to have safely said to a woman, if the "orthodox" of the Fourth Gospel Community could hope to have the Gospel accepted by the Great Church.[231]

Esther A. de Boer argues quite persuasively that, yes, the Beloved Disciple was indeed a woman, Mary Magdalene, but that the Redactor of the final version, the version we have, did not simply arbitrarily bring in the Beloved Disciple and therefore had to put the word "son" in Yeshua's mouth to fit the Disciple's presumed male gender. Rather, she argues that this exchange at the foot of the cross was understood by the head of the Fourth Gospel Community (the Beloved Disciple, Magdalene) as a sort of commission into the deeper meaning of being a follower of Yeshua. De Boer contends that when the Gospel said, "When Yeshua therefore saw his mother and the disciple whom he loved standing there," he was looking at Mary his mother and Mary Magdalene, and he said to his mother, "behold your son," referring first to himself and then to his *alter ego*, the Beloved Disciple, who had been with him from the days of John the Baptist and was the intimate at the Last Supper, and was now to be the first of numberless ones loved by him and his Father. Then Yeshua said to the Beloved Disciple, Magdalene, "Behold your mother. And from that hour the disciple took her onto his [her] own."

De Boer writes: "The ultimate importance of the scene in 19:26–27 lies in Jesus' invitation to his mother to look away from her dying son to find him, alive, in the disciple he loved [Magdalene]. At the same time Jesus' words are a solemn declaration to this disciple [Magdalene]: she may act on Jesus' behalf, as if she were Jesus himself."[232]

This commission is obviously the "launching pad" for Magdalene, when seen in retrospect, for her becoming the center of a community of followers probing the deeper meaning of the life and teaching of Yeshua. But precisely because it was understood as so central to the proclaiming of the Good News, the "orthodox" Redactor felt compelled to suppress the fact that the leader of the "Fourth Gospel Community" was a woman, Mary Magdalene.

§206 A Race to the Tomb

In John 20:1–11 there is clearly confusion as a result of the work of the Redactor, apparently trying to fuse two traditions together. In verse 1, Mary Magdalene goes alone to the tomb (in no other Gospel did she go alone), finds an empty tomb and runs to tell Peter and "the *other* disciple whom Yeshua loved." Then Peter and the other disciple run to the tomb, although the other disciple gets there first, but does not go in. Peter arrives and goes in, followed then by the other disciple, "who saw and believed." This latter is clearly important. Peter does not believe, but the "other disciple whom Yeshua loved" does. They then go home. But where was Magdalene? Somehow she was back at the tomb, weeping, though nothing is said about her returning.

Then follows the famous scene wherein Magdalene meets Yeshua (more about that below). Some scholars believe that "the other disciple" is in fact *the* Beloved Disciple. If so, then, again in the Fourth Gospel the "Beloved Disciple" bests Peter, both in running and in believing. However, some scholars question whether "the other disciple whom Yeshua loved" was the Beloved Disciple. Why was reference made to the "other" disciple Yeshua loved? Was that someone other than the one at the Last Supper and elsewhere? When the Gospel speaks of this "other" disciple whom Yeshua "loved," it here uses the term "*ephilei*" instead of "*egapa*," as elsewhere when speaking of "the" Beloved Disciple. To further the confusion, Yeshua also is said to love Martha and her sister Mary and brother Lazarus of Bethany (once using *egapa* and twice *ephilei*[233]). Was the "other disciple whom Yeshua loved" (*ephilei*) also a woman and was this another instance of the Fourth Gospel having a woman disciple besting Peter, both in running and in believing ("and she believed")?

However, the confusion easily clears up if we assume the basic premise that the Redactor felt it necessary to suppress the prominent presence of women disciples of Yeshua (and he was, of course, proven correct): In the Fourth Gospel an anonymous disciple is always a woman. In this case, "the *other* disciple whom Yeshua loved" is Mary of Bethany, who is with Peter when Mary Magdalene bursts upon them with the report of the empty tomb. Peter and Mary of Bethany then run to the tomb, Mary arriving there first, and also "believing."

§207 Magdalene Again Superior to Peter

In the post-resurrection verse John 21:7, it is the Beloved Disciple, Magdalene, who recognizes Yeshua standing on the lake side speaking to the disciples who had gone fishing, and tells Peter that it is Yeshua speaking. The reader wonders, why the detail about Magdalene telling Peter that it is Yeshua? Oscar Cullmann points out that, "the ambivalent relationship which we have seen in John's Gospel between Peter, the representative of the rest of the original community, and the Beloved Disciple mirrors very precisely the double effort of the Johannine circle: On the one hand, holding on to a conscious independence, and on the other, the conviction of the necessity of a mutual expansion for the sake of the whole."[234] Once again, the Fourth Gospel puts Magdalene up, and Peter down. Most scholars, in fact, consider this entire chapter 21 a later appendix, "the result of a later Redactor's attempt to represent an effort by the Johannine community to unite with the church at large."[235]

§208 The Fourth Gospel: The Gospel of Magdalene

If, as most scholars believe, the entire chapter 21 was written by the later Redactor of the Fourth Gospel, it is important to note that the whole of it is, as Cullmann alluded, a balancing act between Magdalene, now disguised as the Beloved Disciple, and Peter, the perceived leader of the *Ekklesia*

Katholika.[236] The chapter begins by stating that Yeshua showed himself again to several of his disciples, and then called each very carefully by name—except "and two other disciples" (*kai alloi ek ton matheton autou duo*). Puzzle: Why are they unnamed? A little later in the chapter, as we have seen, the Beloved Disciple is present. Remembering that in the Fourth Gospel an anonymous disciple is always a woman, most likely Mary Magdalene is one of the "two other disciples," and the second one is also a woman. Something was about to happen that was very important for the Christian community, the church, namely, an appearance of the Risen Lord, which then made those to whom he appeared "apostles" with the authority and commission to preach the Good News, the Gospel—as happened to Paul (who never knew the earthly Yeshua) on the road to Damascus. But this could not be accepted in the church which issued statements like: I allow no woman to have authority over man. . . . women must keep silence in the church. . . . Hence, both the women disciples were neutered.

There then follows the "put down" of Peter by Magdalene of verse 7. Verses 15–19 are where the Redactor "did obeisance" to Peter, who of course at the time of the Redactor's writing was long dead ("signifying by what death he [Peter] should glorify God"[237]). Then Magdalene comes to the fore once more in the guise of the Beloved Disciple, still with tension toward Peter reflected in the language. Peter turns and sees Magdalene—again identified as "the one who leaned on the breast of Yeshua at supper"—and says to Yeshua in rather abrupt fashion: What about this one? (*outos de ti?*). Yeshua then proceeds to scotch a rumor that the Beloved Disciple, Magdalene, had not died.

Then comes the re-affirmation that Magdalene, without being named, is, in fact, the source of all their information about Yeshua and his meaning: "This is the disciple who bears witness of these things . . ." (*Outos estin ho mathetes ho martyron peri touton . . .*). The Redactor went further and announced that Magdalene wrote a Proto-Gospel, which he, and perhaps others before him, re-edited: "and *wrote* these things" (*kai ho grapsas tauta*). Hence, the Fourth Gospel should, in fact, not be named the Gospel of John, but the Gospel of Magdalene, even though we have it only in a slightly edited form.

§209 Summary Concerning the Fourth Gospel

To summarize: the Community of the Beloved Disciple, as Raymond Brown referred to the community within which the Fourth Gospel, John's Gospel, or more accurately, Magdalene's Gospel, was born, stemmed from one of the first disciples of Yeshua, Mary of Magdala. She was most probably a disciple of John the Baptist and became one of the first followers of Yeshua. That means that she was a strong, self-deciding woman. Judging from her Gospel, she also apparently had friends in high places, and obviously was a very intelligent and sensitive person.

Not only did she, along with many others, find Yeshua a very charismatic, deep, and loving person, but Yeshua clearly also found her very understanding and appealing. Even in all three of the Synoptic Gospels she is mentioned in the list of women following and working with Yeshua, and in all cases save one (the pro-Peter/anti-Magdalene Luke) is mentioned first. But when it comes to her own Gospel, she figures very prominently (along with several other strong women, e.g., the Samaritan woman, Martha, and Mary of Bethany), and was given a "star" role in the extended first encounter with the Risen Lord. As the Beloved Disciple, she is also portrayed as an intimate of Yeshua, "leaning on his breast," not once, but twice. If one looks at the early non-canonical *Gospel of Mary* and *Gospel of Philip*, there she is said to be the one that Yeshua "loved above all else," is said to be his "companion" and whom Yeshua "kisses often on the [mouth]."

Because Magdalene was so intelligent and sensitive she obviously reflected long and deeply after Yeshua's departure, producing thereby the long "soliloquies" of Yeshua so characteristic of her Gospel, but not that of the Synoptics or the Sayings Gospels. She apparently had a good memory and meditated on the deeper meaning of what she recalled of Yeshua's words. This development was reflected also in the *Gospel of Mary* where Magdalene reports that she heard Yeshua say things in a vision, and then is asked by the male disciples to relate them and explain them. Raymond Brown states that, "The evangelist was a remarkably gifted thinker and dramatist."[238]

This went on over several decades, during which a rather straightforward understanding of the words and actions of Yeshua prevailed in the beginning, but with the passage of time and further contemplation, divinity was seen shining through Yeshua more and more, until a very "high Christology" developed and even led to a split in the community, quite probably after the "anchor" of Magdalene had passed on. But before she died, Magdalene wrote a Proto-Gospel, a version of the Fourth Gospel preceding the version we now have.

Then, after Magdalene died and the majority group ("Secessionists") of her community pushed still further in the direction of divinity (Docetism) in Yeshua, the "orthodox" elements strove to be accepted by the Great Church, and hence edited Magdalene's Gospel, eliminating her major role by name and substituted that of the anonymous Beloved Disciple. The Secessionists apparently moved further in the direction of the communities that formed the *Gospel of Mary*, the *Gospel of Philip*, *Pistis Sophia*, and so on, while the Redactor was eventually successful and the Fourth Gospel was accepted by the *Ekklesia Katholika*, though at the price that until almost the twenty-first century it was largely unknown that Mary Magdalene was the Beloved Disciple and the author of the earlier version of the Fourth Gospel. But now it is beginning to be known.

§210 YESHUA: THE "ORIGIN" OF THE CHURCHES

It seems increasingly clear that there was the historical figure of John the Baptist who had a number of followers, and that some of them moved to Yeshua of Nazareth, especially after John's death. Yeshua was obviously an extraordinarily charismatic person who deeply impressed a number of Jews. His person, teaching, and then death and the response, the resurrection event, however understood, engendered a variety of groups of followers. In fact, from the nineteenth century forward "scholars gathered substantial evidence to show that the early Christian church did not exist as a unified body but rather consisted of distinctive, competing groups that associated themselves with different foundational figures and various theologies."[239]

We can today discern several distinct groups:

1. The oldest is the community that generated the "Sayings Gospel," the so-called Q. Scholars have discerned some three phases in the Q community, the first phase starting even during Yeshua's lifetime and the last phase ending by its absorption into the community that produced the Gospel of Matthew in the middle eighties of the first century.[240] Doubtless the Q document was copied many times during the decades of the first century, and even beyond, but after the narrative Gospels were written, and especially after both Matthew and Luke absorbed all of the Q material, people stopped copying the Q document and apparently the existing copies eventually disintegrated. Hence, we have no direct copies of it, but have to reconstruct it from its presence in Matthew and Luke.

2. The next oldest is the Christ-centered group, best represented by Paul and Barnabas. Here salvation was to be found through "the Christ" (*ho Christos*), which was a kind of "salvation from above." It is significant that nowhere in his many letters did Paul quote or try to pass on the teaching of Yeshua. Paul, of course, often talked about ethical issues, but they were *his* teachings (largely then widely current Stoic ethics) or what he said talking about Christ entailed, but nowhere did he write that Yeshua taught such and such. These communities tended to be scattered around the Roman Empire wherever the six and a half million Jews spread around the empire were located.

3. After 1945, we slowly learned that there was also a separate Sayings Gospel, the *Gospel of Thomas*, discovered at Nag Hammadi in Egypt. Presumably there was a community behind it as well, for it is different than the Sayings Gospel as found in Matthew and Luke. This suggests that there could have been yet other early Yeshua communities with their own list of sayings which we have not yet found.

In addition, of course, there are the several different communities that generated our known Gospels:

4. the Gospel of Mark community
5. the Gospel of Matthew community
6. "Luka's" Proto-Luke Gospel community
7. the canonical Gospel of Luke community
8. Magdalene's Proto-Fourth Gospel community
9. the redacted canonical Fourth Gospel community

At least these early communities of followers of Yeshua we know about, and in many ways they are strikingly different, each going off in various directions, depending on what struck them most in their encounter with Yeshua. Even more, some of them sprang from preachers who were not even direct witnesses of Yeshua, such as Paul—and this was reflected in the fact that he was not really interested in Yeshua's teachings, for he seemingly did not even know them; he was interested only in Yeshua's Messiahship of a very special sort, a sort of Cosmic Christ operating from above.

Doubtless, there was one Yeshua behind all these different responses, but the different responses gave rise to various understandings of Yeshua, to various Christologies. Presumably, there was value and validity in all of them, but I personally would argue that it is the person *Yeshua ha Notzri* who is the most inspiring, who is the foundation of what it means to be a follower of Yeshua, which we have rather misnamed a Christian. And one very important thing about trying to be a Christian, a follower of Yeshua, of Jesus, is that he was a feminist. Hence, ought we Christians not also strive to be one?

NOTES

1. Gerd-Klaus Kaltenbrunner, "Ist der Heilige Geist weiblich?" *Una Sancta* (1977), 275ff.
2. Mk 1:21–28, 29–31. Cf. Lk 4:31–37, 38–39 and Mt 8:14–15.
3. Mk 3:31–35; Mt 12:46–50; and Lk 8:19–21.
4. Mk 4:2–4, 21–22. Cf. Lk 8:4–8, 16–17 and Mt 13:1–9, 5:14–15.
5. Mk 1:21–28.

6. Mk 1:29–31.

7. Mk 5:1–2, 21–43. Cf. Mt 8:28–34, 9:18–26 and Lk 8:26–39, 40–56.

8. Mk 6:1–6. Cf. Mt 13:53–58. In the parallel passage in Luke, Yeshua's family is not mentioned.

9. Mk 9:11–13.

10. *Antiquities* 28.136.

11. *Antiquities* 28.5.1–2.

12. 1 Kings 21.

13. Mk 6:19.

14. Est 5:6.

15. Lk 3:19.

16. Lk 9:7–9.

17. Mk 6:17–29. Cf. Mt 14:3–12 and Lk 3:19–20, 9:7–9.

18. Mk 7:8–13. Cf. Mt 15:1–7.

19. Mk 7:24–30.

20. Mk 7:3 1.

21. Mk 7:24–30. Cf. Mt 15:21–28.

22. Mt 15:21–28. Cf. Mk 7:24–30.

23. Mk 10:2–12. Cf. Mt 19:1–97, 5:32 and Lk 16:18.

24. Mk 10:28–30. Cf. Mt 19:27–30 and Lk 18:28–30.

25. Mk 12:18–27. Cf. Mt 22:23–33 and Lk 20:27–40.

26. Mk 12:40. Cf. Lk 20:47.

27. Mk 12:41–44. Cf. Lk 21:1–4.

28. Mk 13:14–20. Cf. Mt 24:15–25 and Lk 21:20–24.

29. Mk 14:3–9. Cf. Mt 26:6–13 and Jn 12:1–8.

30. Mk 15:40–41. Cf. Mt 27:55–56; Lk 23:49; and Jn 19:25.

31. Mk 15:47. Cf. Mt 27:61 and Lk 23:55.

32. Mk 16:1–8. Cf. Mt 28:1–8; Lk 24:1–8; and Jn 20:1–10.

33. Mk 16:7, 11. Cf. Mt 28:8; Lk 24:9–11; and Jn 20:18.

34. Mk 16:9. Cf. Mt 28:9–10 and Jn 20:11–17.

35. Mt 8:14–15. Cf. Mk 1:29–31 and Lk 4:38–39.

36. Mt 9:35.

37. Mt 9:18–26. Cf. Mk 5:21–43 and Lk 8:40–56.

38. Mt 12:46–50. Cf. Mk 3:31–35 and Lk 8:19–21.

39. Mt 13:53–58. Cf. Mk 6:1–6. In the parallel passage in Luke, Yeshua's family is not mentioned.

40. Mt 14:3–12. Cf. Mk 6:17–29 and Lk 3:19–20; 9:7–9.

41. Mt 15:1–7. Cf. Mk 7:1–13.

42. Mt 15:21–38. Cf. Mk 7:24–30.

43. 1 Cor 7:10–11.

44. 1 Cor 7:15.

45. Mt 19:9.

46. Mt 5:32. Cf. Mk 10:1–12 and Lk 16:18.

47. Mt 19:27–29. Cf. Mk 10:28–30 and Lk 18:28–30.

48. Mt 22:23–33. Cf. Mk 12:18–27 and Lk 20:27–40.

49. Mt 24:15–22. Cf. Mk 13:14–20 and Lk 21:20–24.

50. Mt 26:6–13. Cf. Mk 14:3–9 and Jn 12:1–8.

51. For a description of it, the only trial by ordeal in the Bible, see Nm 5:11–31 and the Talmudic tractate *Sotah*.

52. Lk 1:18–26.

53. Mt 1:18–25. Cf. Lk 1:26–38.

54. Mt 10:34–37. Cf. Lk 12:51–53.

55. Mt 13:33. Cf. Lk 13:20–21.

56. Mt 23:37. Cf. Lk 13:34.

57. Mt 24:39–41. Cf. Lk 17:34–37.

58. Mk 8:11–12.

59. Mt 12:38–42. Cf. Mt 16:1–4; Mk 8:11–12; and Lk 11:29–32.

60. See Ru 4:17–22.

61. Mt 1:1–17. Cf. Lk 3:23–38, where the genealogy is almost completely different and no women are mentioned.

62. Mt 2:11.

63. Mt 2:13.

64. Mt 2:14.

65. Mt 2:20.

66. Mt 2:21.

67. Mt 2:1–2, 10–11.

68. Mt 2:13–15.

69. Mt 2:19–23.

70. See also Jb 31:1 and the *Testaments of the Twelve Patriarchs*, written around 106 B.C.E.: "Do ye, therefore, my children, flee evildoing and cleave to goodness. For he that hath it looketh not on a woman with a view to fornication, and he beholdeth no defilement." *Testament of Benjamin* 8:1–2; "I never committed fornication by the uplifting of my eyes." *Testament of Issachar* 7:2; R. H. Charles, ed., *The Apocrypha and Pseudepigrapha of the Old Testament*, 2 vols. (Oxford: Oxford University Press, 1913), vol. 2, 358, 327.

71. Mt 5:27–28.

72. Mk 10:35–40.

73. Mt 20:20–23.

74. Mt 27:56 and Mk 15:40.

75. Mk 16:1.

76. Mt 20:20–23. Cf. Mk 10:35–40.

77. Mk 6:31–44.

78. Mark's other account, of the feeding of four thousand, Mk 8:1–10, refers to the crowd, and not to men or women.

79. Mt 14:13–21. Cf. Mk 6:31–44; Lk 9:10–17; and Jn 6:1–13.

80. Mt 15:29–38. Cf. Mk 8:1–10.

81. Lk 7:38–50. The sinful woman is most likely a prostitute.

82. Mt 21:23, 31–32.

83. Mt 27:19.

84. C. G. Montefiore, *Rabbinic Literature and Gospel Teaching* (London: Macmillan, 1930), 217–18.

85. Mt 16:1–4.

86. Mt 12:38–42.

87. Mk 8:11–12.

88. Lk 20:45–47. Cf. Mk 12:38–40.

89. Lk 21:1–4. Cf. Mk 12:41–44.

90. Lk 11:29–32. Cf. Mt 12:38–42, 16:1–4 and Mk 8:11–12.

91. Lk 13:20–21. Cf. Mt 13:33.

92. Lk 17:34–37. Cf. Mt 24:40–41.

93. Lk 12:51–53. Cf. Mt 10:34–37; Lk 18:28–30; and Mt 19:29.

94. Lk 13:34. Cf. Mt 23:37.

95. Lk 4:33–37.

96. Lk 4:38–39. Cf. Mk 1:29–31 and Mt 8: 14–15.

97. Lk 8:16–18. Cf. Mk 4:21–22; Mt 5:15; and Lk 11:33–36.

98. Lk 8:19–21. Cf. Mk 3:31–35 and Mt 12:46–50.

99. Mk 10:29–30.

100. Mt 10:37–38; 19:29.

101. Lk 18:28–30. Cf. Mk 10:28–30 and Mt 19:27–29. See also Lk 12:51–53, 14:26–27 and Mt 10:35–39.

102. Lk 8:40–56. Cf. Mk 5:21–43 and Mt 9:18–26.

103. Lk 16:18. Cf. Mk 10:1–12 and Mt 5:32; 19:9.

104. Lk 20:27–38. Cf. Mk 12:18–27 and Mt 22:23–33.

105. Lk 21:20–23. Cf. Mk 13:14–20 and Mt 24:15–22.

106. Lk 23:55–56. Cf. Mk 15:47 and Mt 27:61.

107. Lk 1:1 to 2:52.

108. Lk 9:51 to 18:14.

109. Karl Heinrich Rengstorf, et al. *Das Neue Testament Deutsch* (Göttingen, 1968), 1:10.

110. Lk 24:9, 11.

111. Richard Heard, *An Introduction to the New Testament* (New York: Harper & Brothers, 1950).

112. Bernard D. Muller, "The Great Omission in Luke's Gospel," Jesus: A Historical Reconstruction website. www.geocities.com/b_d_muller/appf.html#woman.

113. Ann Graham Brock, *Mary Magdalene, The First Apostle: The Struggle for Authority.* (Cambridge, MA: Harvard University Press, 2003), 40.

114. Talmud bYebamoth 64a. Cf. Mishnah Yebamoth 6, 6.

115. Lk 1:8–22.

116. Lk 1:23–25, 36–45, 57–62.

117. Cf. Gn 17:15ff.

118. Jgs 13:2–7.

119. 1 Sm 1:5–6.

120. Lk 1:5–25.

121. Lk 1:24.

122. Cf. Mt 1:18–25.

123. Lk 1:26–38.

124. Lk 1:41–43.

125. Cf. Lk 1:60: "But his mother spoke up. 'No,' she said, 'he is to be called John.'"

126. Lk 1:39–45.

127. John Martin Creed, *The Gospel according to St Luke* (London: Macmillan, 1930).

128. First edition.

129. John Drury, *Luke* (New York: Macmillan, 1973).

130. Lk 1:68–79.

131. 1 Sm 2:1–10.

132. Lk 1:46–56.

133. 1 Sm 2:1–10.

134. Lk 1:62.

135. Lk 1:57–64.

136. Mt 2:1.

137. Lk 2:15–20.

138. Lk 2:33–35.

139. Lk 2:36–38.

140. Lk 2:41–50.

141. Lk 2:33.
142. Lk 2:50.
143. Lk 2:19.
144. Lk 2:51.
145. Lk 2:51–52.
146. Lk 4:25–27.
147. Lk 7:11–17.
148. Lk 18:1–8.
149. Lk 7:36–50.
150. Lk 8:1–3.
151. Lk 1:1 to 2:52, 9:51 to 18:14.
152. Lk 10:38–42.
153. Lk 11:27–28.
154. Lk 13:10–17.
155. Lk 14:25–26. Cf. Lk 12:51–53, 18:28–30.
156. For example, Jgs 3:7. See Raphael Patai, *The Hebrew Goddess* (New York: KTAV Publishing House, 1967), for details.
157. Lk 15:2.
158. Lk 7:37.
159. Mt 18:12–14.
160. Lk 15:8–10.
161. Lk 21:38.
162. Lk 21:37–38.
163. Jn 8:1–2.
164. Lk 7:36–50.
165. Acts 8:3.
166. Acts 9:2.
167. Acts 8:4.
168. For example, Lk 9:46–48 parallels Mt 18:1–5 and Mk 9:33–37 as well as Lk 18:15–17 and parallels Mt 19:13–15 and Mk 10:13–16, where Yeshua drew children to himself and said that all must become like them.
169. Lk 23:2, 5. For variant texts and references, see Eberhard Nestle, ed. *Novum Testamentum Graece et Latine* (Stuttgart, 1954), 221 and Roger Gryson, *The Ministry of Women in the Early Church* (Collegeville, MN: Liturgical Press, 1976), 126.
170. Leonard Swidler, *Biblical Affirmations of Woman* (Philadelphia: Westminster Press, 1979), 105.
171. Lk 23:26–31.
172. Mt 1:1–17. See §121.
173. Mk 6:3.
174. Mt 13:55.
175. Mt 12:46–50.
176. Even more Mk 3:31–35.
177. Mk 6:31–44, 8:1–10; Mt 14:13–21, 15:29–38; and Jn 6:1–13.
178. Mt 25:1–13. See §125.
179. Mt 22:2–10. See §120.
180. Mt 10:37–38 does not mention siblings, but see Mt 19:29.
181. Mk 10:28–30.
182. Mt 19:29.
183. Mk 15:41.
184. Mt 27:56.

185. Mt 28:9–10.

186. Jn 20:11–18.

187. Mk 16:9–11.

188. Chapter 7.

189. Col 4:14; 2 Tm 4:11; and Phlm 24.

190. 1 Cor 15:3–7.

191. In this connection, see the discussion below within the context of the Fourth Gospel about the tension between Peter, or, at least his later "promoters," and Mary Magdalene or women in general.

192. Pheme Perkins, "The Gospel according to John," in *The New Jerome Biblical Commentary*, Raymond E. Brown et al., eds. (Englewood Cliffs, NJ: Prentice Hall, 1990), 946.

193. Jn 2:1–12.

194. Jn 4:5–42.

195. Jn 7:37–39.

196. Jn 7:53 to 8:11.

197. Jn 11:1–44.

198. Jn 12:1–8. Cf. Mk 14:3–9 and Mt 26:6–13.

199. Jn 19:25–27. Cf. Mk 15:40–41; Mt 27:55–56; and Lk 23:49.

200. Jn 20:1–10. Cf. Mk 16:1–2; Mt 28:1–8; and Lk 24:1–8.

201. 1 Cor 15:5–8.

202. Mk 16:1–9.

203. Jn 20:18; Mk 16:7, 11; Mt 28:16–20; and Lk 24:9–11.

204. Jn 20:11–18. Cf. Mk 16:9 and Mt 28:9–10.

205. Raymond E. Brown, "Roles of Women in the Fourth Gospel," *Theological Studies* (December 1975): 692.

206. Jn 2:1–12.

207. Jn 4:5–42.

208. Jn 11:25.

209. Jn 4:26.

210. Jn 11:27.

211. Jn 20:11–18.

212. Jn 7:37–38.

213. Jn 7:53 to 8:11.

214. Jn 11:1–44.

215. Jn 12:1–8.

216. Raymond Brown, *The Community of the Beloved Disciple* (New York: Paulist Press, 1979), 76.

217. Esther A. de Boer, "Mary Magdalene and the Disciple Jesus Loved," *lectio difficilior*, no 1. (2006). www.lectio.unibe.ch/00_1/m-forum.htm.

218. Brown, *The Community of the Beloved Disciple*, 186.

219. Eph 5:21.

220. Col 3:18.

221. 1 Pt 2:13.

222. 1 Tm 2:9.

223. 1 Cor 14:33.

224. Jn 1:14.

225. Brown, *The Community of the Beloved Disciple*, 149.

226. Jn 21:24.

227. Jn 1:35–40.

228. Jn 21:20.

229. Jn 13:23–26.

230. Jn 18:15–16.

231. Ramon K. Jusino, "Mary Magdalene: Author of the Fourth Gospel?" (author's personal website) (1998). www.BelovedDisciple.org.

232. De Boer, "Mary Magdalene and the Disciple Jesus Loved."

233. Jn 11:3, 5, 36.

234. Oscar Cullmann, *Der johanneische Kreis: Sein Platz im Spätjudentum, in der Jüngerschaft Jesu und im Urchristentum: Zum Ursprung des Johannesevangeliums* (Tübingen: Mohr Siebeck, 1975), 60.

235. De Boer, "Mary Magdalene and the Disciple Jesus Loved."

236. Jn 21:1–2, 20–24.

237. Jn 21:19.

238. Brown, *The Community of the Beloved Disciple*, 101.

239. De Boer, "Mary Magdalene and the Disciple Jesus Loved."

240. Ivan Havener, *Q: The Sayings of Jesus* (Wilmington, DE: Michael Glazier, 1987) and Burton L. Mack, *The Lost Gospel: The Book of Q and Christian Origins* (San Francisco: Harper, 1993).

· 7 ·

§211 Conclusions

$\mathcal{T}$here are three major conclusions that I draw from all this analysis, and a fourth one proleptically after the analyses of the material in the three subsequent appendixes.

However, as a prophylactic against unwarranted Christian hubris and anti-Judaism, it should first of all be noted that Yeshua was not a Christian, he was a Jew, indeed an observant, Torah-true Jew, a rabbi.[1] Yeshua stood very much in the Jewish, Pharisaic, Rabbinic tradition of his day.[2]

However, in matters of attitude toward women, Yeshua was very different from his peers, as the Jewish scholar Claude Montefiore notes: "Certainly the relations of Yeshua towards women, and of theirs towards him, seem to strike a new note, and a higher note, and to be off the line of Rabbinic tradition."[3]

1) Yeshua took an egalitarian, feminist position on women. He was not a social activist organizer like Saul Alinsky; he was not like Betty Friedan, the founder of the National Organization for Women. Yeshua was much more personalist in his approach. It was his disciples who came after him who developed the organization, the *ecclesia*, the church. Hence, it is personal attitudes and actions that can be looked for in Yeshua, regarding the place of women, as well as all other human issues of import, not organized actions, and systematic social implementation of principles. This latter came, to the extent it came, later, with the church, with Christianity.

It was noted that it is very difficult to discern precisely what in the Gospels is to be attributed to Yeshua and what to the first believing communities or the evangelists, our only sources of information about Yeshua. Nevertheless, it was also pointed out that the extraordinarily positive attitude toward women (especially for the Palestinian Jewish context of that time), depicted in the Gospels as that of Yeshua, ultimately must indeed be attributable to him, though the form, exact wording, and so on, of many of the specific statements attributed to Yeshua doubtless were reshaped by the evangelists and their sources.

The fact that the Gospels, whether written by Jews (probably Mark, Matthew, Mary Magdalene, and "Luka") or a Greek (Luke), whether for a Greco-Roman readership (Mark) or a Jewish one (Matthew), all depict Yeshua as egalitarian toward women argues that this feminism was not dictated by either a Greek or a Jewish author or readership. The fact that Matthew's Gospel, the most Jewish of all the Gospels, was quantitatively much more positive toward women than Mark's (in many ways the least Jewish of the Gospels), and almost as much as Luke's Gospel (probably the only one written by a Greek), eliminates the possibility that the Gospel feminism was projected onto Yeshua either by a Greek (Luke) influenced by the relative "feminism" of the contemporary Hellenist world or by an evangelist (Mark) writing to impress favorably a Gentile audience. If either of those assumptions were true, then the Jewish Matthew and his Jewish audience, and indeed his Jewish sources, should never have produced the feminist image of Yeshua that they, in fact, did produce. Further, the fact that most of the strongest pro-woman sections of Luke's Gospel are found in the "most Jewish" section of his Gospel reinforces that argument. In the end, the strongly pro-woman, feminist image of Yeshua, projected in the Gospels, must find its source in Yeshua. And, in this matter, Yeshua profoundly differed from his peers, another, technically persuasive argument that Yeshua, and not the community, was the source of that attitude and action.

Further, Yeshua's positive attitude toward women, his feminism, clearly inspired many women followers who not only show up in the pages of the Gospels, Acts of the Apostles, and letters of Paul, but they also were the source about precisely Yeshua's feminist teachings and actions. Surely no Jewish men would have noticed or been moved to remember and pass on such things. In addition, as I have argued, this group of eager women disciples of Yeshua were also the source of "Proto" versions of, at least, two of our canonical Gospels, namely, the anonymous "Luka" (Mary of Bethany?), who wrote a Proto version of Luke, and Mary Magdalene, the anonymous Beloved Disciple of the Johannine community and writer of the Proto version of the Fourth Gospel. It is also clear that, the version of Matthew's Gospel that we have, also doubtless had a multitude of women sources, and perhaps even "organizers," behind it. In brief:

2) Two of our canonical Gospels were either largely or entirely based on Proto-Gospels written by women, namely, the Gospel of Luke by "Luka" and the Fourth Gospel by Mary Magdalene.

3) Without the women followers of Yeshua and their remembering and recording (and "missionary work") we would be missing half of the Gospels, and **we would not have Christianity today**. Were all the materials on Jesus' teaching and life that were gathered and handed on by women missing—we would not have Christianity today. One could imagine—*per impossibilem*—that if all the other material—not handed on by women—about Jesus' teaching and life were nevertheless gathered together and written down, and the other missionary activities we learn about by Paul, Barnabas, Silas, Timothy, and others (but sans the work of all the women listed by name, and not, in the New Testament), did in fact occur, doubtless some kind of religion around Jesus would have grown up. However, it would have been rather anemic, and doubtless would have faded from all but human memory, like Mithraism and numberless other cults popular for a few centuries.

If one reviews the material of the rest of the New Testament and the early Christian writings (analyzed in the following appendixes), not only is the just-above conclusion reinforced by the ubiquitous evidence of the leading roles women that played in the early expansion of Christianity, the following fourth conclusion draws itself, namely:

4) Yeshua's feminism, though it was practically the indispensable "incubator" for Christianity, **was quickly and largely suppressed by his second/third generation followers,** down largely to today. I offer some reasons why in the proleptic analysis before appendix I.

The total conclusion for Christians is: Yeshua was a feminist! Why aren't we?

NOTES

1. See Hans Küng and Pinchas Lapide, "Is Yeshua a Bond or Barrier? A Jewish-Christian Dialogue," *Journal of Ecumenical Studies* 14 (1977): 466–83.

2. See Robert Aron, *The Jewish Yeshua* (Maryknoll, NY: Orbis Books, 1971) and Eugene Fisher, *Faith without Prejudice* (Mahwah, NJ: Paulist Press, 1977).

3. C. G. Montefiore, *Rabbinic Literature and Gospel Teaching* (London: Macmillan, 1930), 217–18.

III

EARLY CHRISTIANS' VIEWS OF WOMEN

§212 Summary Analysis of the Appendixes of the New Testament Outside of the Gospels and Early Christian Writings

The positive feminist attitude of Yeshua toward women clearly affected the early followers of Yeshua, though patriarchal social structures by no means immediately all fell away. Nevertheless, women did play leading roles in the earliest Christian communities, from Lydia the first European convert, to the various women evangelists, deacons, and rulers, to the apostle Junia.

Paul, who never met Yeshua, had an ambivalent attitude toward women, partly positive and partly on the borderline between positive and negative. The deutero-Pauline materials and the other later New Testament writings became progressively more negative toward women, veering toward the misogynist. The woman deacon (*diakonos*) of Paul's day became the deaconess (*diakonissa*, the diminutive "issa," with all its downgrading implications, having been added) of the fourth-century *Apostolic Constitutions*, a holy order lesser in status than that of the male deacon. As Christianity moved into the age of the Fathers (the earlier and originally more numerous "Desert Mothers" being almost entirely purged from history) the status of Christian women became ever more restricted. The Fathers took a uniformly male superior attitude that often was misogynist. This trend continued into the Middle Ages and up to the most recent times.

What is puzzling here is that, although a strong anti-Jewish and pro-Greek trend quickly developed in Christianity as it spread in the Gentile world, unfortunately leading to a rejection of much of Yeshua's and Christianity's Jewish heritage, on the subject of women it was the Hellenistic stance which was rejected. Why, with such a clear difference in attitude expressed by Yeshua and by some of the Pauline writings, did Christianity's choice go not to Yeshua but to the negative Pauline and deutero-Pauline writings? Apparently the rigid patriarchal system, which Yeshua did his best to dismantle,[1] was so pervasive in the lives of the majority of the early Christians, especially the second/third generation, that they were blind to this choice; they automatically gravitated toward the most restrictive, subordinationist passages of the New Testament. Christianity early became so intent on identifying itself by differentiating itself from the world around it that it often vigorously rejected the pagan world, or at least part of it, and that pagan world included a relatively high status for women.

One additional partial answer to this puzzle is suggested by Johannes Leipoldt: after the destruction of Jerusalem in 70 C.E., many Hellenistic Jews became Christian because they felt repelled by the intensified observation of the rabbinic prescriptions that developed in the attempt to preserve Jewish identity. These Hellenistic Jews, being used to a less rigorous observance, found in Christianity an environment which was familiar and receptive. They, of course, brought with them the strongly subordinating attitudes toward women that were then prevalent in Judaism, even Hellenistic Judaism.[2]

Whether or not, or to whatever degree, that may be true, the receding *eschaton,* the "final days," imminently awaited by Paul and the other early Christians, doubtless played a major role in the early decline in the status of women in Christianity. As long as the *parousia,* the Second Coming of Christ, was expected at any moment, the need to develop organized structures in the community of believers was felt very little. But as that expectation faded, the need for structured patterns of community life was increasingly sensed. In an almost inevitable development, these "second/third generation" Christians naturally turned to the structures of the societies in which they lived for models to apply to the newly forming church structures. In the Greco-Roman society of the Roman Empire, despite the advances women made in family life, economics, law, and so on, women were almost entirely excluded from political life. Hence, in following this Greco-Roman model (e.g., "diocese" and "parish" are originally Roman civil administrative terms) the church set up authority structures that almost entirely excluded women.

To this was added the pervasive Greek notion of dualism (matter and spirit, the former evil, the latter good, personified by woman and man, respectively) and its offshoot, asceticism. Of course, dualism was not exclusively Greek (e.g., Persian Zoroastrianism, Manichaeism), nor was asceticism (e.g., Essenes, Therapeutae), but they became extremely and increasingly widespread throughout the Roman Empire. Paradoxically these aspects of pagan society, far from being rejected by the newly forming church, were embraced by it, again putting women at a serious disadvantage, vis-à-vis men.

Thus, three attitudes characteristic of Yeshua: (1) a service rather than authority orientation; (2) a full life-affirming stance (eating, wine-drinking, wedding-celebrating); and (3) an egalitarian view of women, were all significantly reversed by the early Christian Church.

Furthermore, a restrictive attitude toward women was also fostered in Christianity by the fact that early Christians in the Greco-Roman world faced the worship of the Goddess in strong resurgence, from the worship of the Phrygian Mater Magna or Kybele throughout Asia Minor and even in Rome, to the cult of Isis and her veneration under many other names, Demeter, Athena, Venus, Ceres, Ma Bellona, and so forth. The worship of Mater Magna or Kybele in Asia Minor was not only extremely influential but also often included ecstatic passion, self-mutilation, even self-castration by male devotees so as to attain complete identity with the Goddess.[3] Although, in fact the most pervasive Goddess worship at the beginning of the Christian era, the Isis cult, did not promote sexual excesses of promiscuity,[4] it was widely rumored to do so, and thus the effect of seeing women priests of Isis on the early Christians was just as negative, as if it were true. Edwin O. James notes that "her cultus was the most effective rival to Christianity from the second century onwards, and during the temporary revival of classical paganism in Rome in 394 C.E., it was her festival that was celebrated with great magnificence."[5] He further notes that "the unprecedented victory of the cultus [the cult of Isis] over official opposition and its persistence during the first three centuries of the Christian era are a testimony to the deep and genuine religious emotion aroused in the initiates by the ritual."[6] In fact, her public worship was brought to an end only by Emperor Justinian in 560 C.E.

Thus, the in-group/out-group mechanism that was at work within Judaism, intensifying its restrictions of Jewish women, also was at work in early Christianity with a similar result. With Christian history, however, there is a special irony in that by turning *toward* the subordination of women, Christianity turned *away* from its Jewish founder Yeshua and his feminist attitude. The conclusion for Christians: Yeshua was a feminist. Shouldn't we be as well?

NOTES

1. Cf. Mt 10:37–39 and Lk 14:26.

2. Johannes Leipoldt, *Die Frau in der antiken Welt und im Urchristentum* (Leipzig: Koehler & Amelang, 1954), 127.

3. Edwin O. James, *Cult of the Mother Goddess* (New York: Barnes & Noble, 1961), 21–22.

4. See Sharon K. Heyon, *The Cult of Isis among Women in the Graeco-Roman World* (Leiden: E. J. Brill, 1975), 11ff.

5. James, *Cult of the Mother Goddess*, 180.

6. James, *Cult of the Mother Goddess*, 177.

Appendix I

§213 The New Testament
Other than the Gospels

$\mathcal{B}$esides the four Gospels, the New Testament is made up of a variety of writings, mainly the Acts of the Apostles, the lengthy account of the early missionary years of the spread of the belief in Yeshua as the Messiah or Christ (it is largely about the efforts of Peter and Paul); and letters written to the early Christian communities (these were mostly, but not exclusively, written by Paul and his followers). As noted above, this section of the New Testament is not directly about Yeshua, but about the followers of Yeshua, their beliefs and lives.

Perhaps the first difference between the Gospels and the rest of the New Testament to be noticed in this study is the attitude toward women. There is not only a large amount of evidence of a positive attitude by Yeshua toward women exhibited in the Gospels; there is also a complete lack of any evidence of a negative attitude toward women by Yeshua. The same cannot be said of the followers of Yeshua in the rest of the New Testament. There are a number of negative statements about women in the New Testament outside of the Gospels. These generally are very familiar to hundreds of millions of people, having been read and preached on in churches for millennia, having had thousands of books written on them, and having been incarnated in church laws, structures, and customs. For the sake of completeness they are quoted and briefly commented on elsewhere in this book.

However, the positive attitudes toward women held by the early followers of Yeshua are focused on much less often; in fact, they are often almost totally overlooked. Hence, in an attempt to right that imbalance somewhat, I gather them together here and briefly comment on them.

§214 THEMATIC ANALYSIS

§215 Women Converts to Christianity

Despite the restrictions women experienced in religion in the Semitic world, from the very beginning women were not only followers of Yeshua but also formal adherents of the religion that sprang up in response to his life—Christianity. Women converts everywhere permeated the beginnings of Christianity, apparently riding on the momentum of the liberating experience they underwent during the lifetime of Yeshua.

It should be noticed that all the quotations documenting this initial involvement of women in primitive Christianity come from the Acts of the Apostles, which was written by Luke, whose Gospel was in many ways one of the most sympathetic to women, and incorporated many such elements that stemmed from women, whether in the role of the proto-evangelist "Luka," or otherwise as sources. The influence of women in this second writing of Luke's, the Acts of the Apostles, will be apparent throughout many of the sections that follow.

§216 Women in the Upper Room

After the ascension of Yeshua, Jewish-Christian women were part of the praying community in the upper room in Jerusalem:

> All these joined in continuous prayer, together with several women, including Mary the mother of Yeshua, and with his brothers.[1]

§217 Women Receive the Holy Spirit

The women as well as the men received the Holy Spirit and the gift of tongues:

> When Pentecost day came round, they [the group previously mentioned in Acts 1:14] had all met in one room, when suddenly they heard what sounded like a powerful wind from heaven, the noise of which filled the entire house in which they were sitting; and something appeared to them that seemed like tongues of fire; these separated and came to rest on the head of *each of them*. They were *all* filled with the Holy Spirit, and began to speak foreign languages as the Spirit gave them the gift of speech.[2]

§218 Women among First Converts

Women were among the first converts to "Christianity":

> And the numbers of men and *women* who came to believe in the Lord increased steadily.[3]

§219 Saul Persecutes Women Converts I

That there was a large number of women converts to Christianity in Palestine is reflected in the accounts of their persecution by Saul (Paul). Normally, in that society, women would hardly have been mentioned in religious matters. But they were specifically referred to here:

> Saul then worked for the total destruction of the Church; he went from house to house arresting both men and *women* and sending them to prison.[4]

§220 Saul Persecutes Women Converts II

In two different accounts of Saul's traveling as far as Syria to arrest Christians, women as well as men are again specifically mentioned:

> Meanwhile Saul was still breathing threats to slaughter the Lord's disciples. He had gone to the high priest and asked for letters addressed to the synagogues in Damascus that would authorize him to arrest and take to Jerusalem any followers of the Way, men *or women*, which he could find.[5]

> Paul said . . . "I even persecuted this Way to the death, and sent *women* as well as men to prison in chains, as the high priest and the whole council of elders can testify."[6]

§221 Paul Preaches to Women

Once converted to Christianity, Paul preached the Gospel just as eagerly to women as to men. At the Roman colony of Philippi, he gladly preached to a prayer group made up only of women, probably a combination of born Jews, converts to Judaism (proselytes), and Gentiles who largely followed Jewish belief and practice ("God-fearers"):

> We sat down and preached to the *women* who had come to the meeting.[7]

§222 Women Resist Paul

However, in Antioch in Pisidia (Asia Minor), Paul met with stiff resistance, and here too, women played a key role, so much so that they were mentioned first by the author of the Acts of the Apostles:

> But the Jews worked upon some of the devout women of the upper classes and the leading men of the city and persuaded them to turn against Paul and Barnabas and expel them from their territory.[8]

§223 Lydia, First "European" Christian

The first "European" convert to Christianity was a woman, Lydia (living in Philippi), who, it seems, was also a head of a household, a person of some means and strong initiative:

> One of these women was called Lydia, a God-worshipper, who was from the town of Thyatira and was in the purple-dye trade. She listened to us, and the Lord opened her heart to accept what Paul was saying. After she and her household had been baptized she sent us an invitation: "if you really think me a true believer in the Lord," she said, "come and stay with us"; and she would take no refusal.[9]

§224 Upper-Class Greek Women become Christian

Many important women of Greek society actively joined the Christian Church. So it was in Thessalonika:

> And some of them were persuaded, and joined Paul and Silas; as did a great many of the devout Greeks and *not a few of the leading women.*[10]

So, also, in Beroea (again note that the women's importance is reflected by their being listed first):

> Many of them therefore believed, with *not a few Greek women of high standing* as well as men.[11]

And in Athens:

> But some men joined him and believed, among them Dionysius, the Areopagite, and *a woman* named Damaris and others with them.[12]

§225 Women Co-Workers in the Gospel

Women were not merely converts to Christianity in its earliest phase but also critical workers in the spread and administration of Christianity. Paul, the chief missionary of Christianity to the Jews scattered throughout the Roman Empire and to the Gentiles, referred to many such co-workers in the spread of the Gospel, both in his earlier letters to the Philippians (c. 56 C.E.) and to the Romans (c. 57 C.E.) and in the "latest" letter, the Second Epistle to Timothy (doubtless largely written by a disciple of Paul's late in the first century). The spread of Christianity took place not only because women were accepted into the church but also because they worked to promote it, to spread the Gospel, the *evangelium*, that is, they were "evangelists." The names of some of these women workers in the Gospel have been preserved in the New Testament documents:

(1) Paul is said to have exchanged greetings between two women collaborators, Prisca and Claudia, among others:

> Greetings to Prisca and Aquila. . . . Greetings to you from Eubulus, Pudens, Linus, Claudia and all the brethren.[13]

(2) At the end of his long epistle to the church at Rome, Paul sent greetings to twenty-eight persons, ten of them women, including Julia, Nereus' sister, and Olympas:

> Greetings . . . to Philologus and Julia, Nereus and sister, and Olympas.[14]

(3) One woman Paul called his "mother":

> Greetings . . . to Rufus, a chosen servant of the Lord, and to his mother who has been a mother to me, too.[15]

(4) Prisca was specifically called a co-worker in the Lord:

> My greetings to Prisca and Aquila, my co-workers in Christ Jesus.[16]

(5) Four women worked very hard "for the Lord," obviously in spreading the Gospel and building up the church:

> Greetings to Mary who worked so hard among you. . . . Greet those workers in the Lord, Tryphaena and Tryphosa. Greet the beloved Persis, who has worked hard in the Lord.[17]

(6) John Chrysostom (337–407 C.E.), usually very critical of women as such, wrote a series of homilies commenting on Paul's letter to the Romans. In reference to Paul's greeting of Mary, he said:

> How is this? A woman, again, is honored and proclaimed victorious! Again, are we men put to shame. Or rather, we are not put to shame only, but have even an honor conferred upon us. For an honor we have, in that there are such women among us, but we are put to shame, in that we men are left so far behind by them. . . . For the women of those days were more spirited than lions.[18]

(7) The woman Junia, called a compatriot by Paul, and an outstanding Apostle, apparently also suffered imprisonment for the Gospel:

> Greetings . . . to those outstanding apostles Andronicus and Junia, my compatriots and fellow prisoners who became Christians before me.[19]

(8) Phoebe, deacon and ruler of the church at Cenchreae, is thought by many scholars to be the bearer of Paul's epistle to the Romans, and was commended to their hospitality:

> I commend to you our sister Phoebe, a deacon of the church at Cenchreae. Give her, in union with the Lord, a welcome worthy of saints, and help her with anything she needs: for she has been a ruler over many, indeed over me.[20]

(9) Paul spoke of Euodia and Syntyche "struggling" (*syn-ethlesan*, the same root as in "athletics") along with him and other fellow missionaries in the "Gospel." Clearly, if Paul used such a strong verb, these women did not simply supply material support for Paul and the other men but preached, taught, and spread the Gospel as vigorously as they. In fact, Paul thought Euodia and Syntyche were so important to the life of the church at Philippi that he bade them by name to overcome their differences:

> I plead with Euodia just as I do with Syntyche: come to some mutual understanding in the Lord. Yes, and I ask you, too, my dependable fellow worker, to go to their aid; they have struggled at my side in promoting the gospel, along with Clement and the others who have labored with me, whose names are in the book of life.[21]

§226 Women's House Churches

(1) Not only did many women embrace and work to spread the Gospel; their houses were often the first Christian "churches." Perhaps the earliest such reference was to the house of Mary, the mother of John Mark (traditionally, but not necessarily, the writer of the Gospel of Mark), which was in Jerusalem:

> [Peter, when he had escaped from prison,] went straight to the house of Mary the mother of John Mark, where a number of people had assembled and were praying.[22]

(2) Some scholars see a house church in Paul's reference to the woman Chloe; it is possible, though questionable:

> For it has been reported to me by Chloe's people that there is quarreling among you.[23]

(3) A clearer example is that of Lydia, Paul's convert:

> One of these women was called Lydia. . . . After she and her household had been baptized she sent us an invitation: "If you really think me a true believer in the Lord," she said, "come and stay with us"; and she would take no refusal. . . . From prison they went to Lydia's house where they saw all the brethren and gave them some encouragement.[24]

(4) Not an absolutely certain reference to a house church, but very likely so, is that concerning the woman deacon Phoebe:

> I commend to you our sister Phoebe, a deacon of the church at Cenchreae . . . for she has been a ruler over many, indeed over me.[25]

(5) An unquestionable example of a church at the house of a woman is that of Nympha (though even here, because of an *inferior* Greek manuscript tradition, some try to make the unlikely case that Nympha is a man's name). Paul wrote:

> Please give my greetings to the brethren at Laodicea and to Nympha and the church which meets at her house.[26]

(6) Although one house church at Colossae was in a woman's house (Nympha's), a second was not. Nevertheless, even in that one a

woman, Apphia, is singled out by Paul, apparently as a leader in that house church:

> From Paul, a prisoner of Christ Jesus, and from our brother Timothy; to our dear fellow worker Philemon, our sister Apphia, our fellow soldier Archippus and the church that meets at your [singular] house.[27]

(7) A final example of a church at the house of a woman (Prisca) and her husband is clearly documented twice:

> My greetings to Prisca and Aquila. . . . My greetings also to the church that meets at their house.[28]

> Aquila and Prisca, with the church that meets at their house, send you their warmest wishes, in the Lord.[29]

§227 Priscilla (Prisca)

(1) One of Paul's staunchest supporters and most able collaborators in teaching and spreading the Gospel was Priscilla (Prisca). She, along with her husband Aquila, are mentioned six times in the New Testament. Four of the six times she is named first. Paul met them in Corinth:

> After this Paul left Athens and went to Corinth, where he met a Jew called Aquila whose family came from Pontus. He and his wife Priscilla had recently left Italy because an edict of Claudius had expelled all the Jews from Rome. Paul went to visit them, and when he found they were tentmakers, of the same trade as himself, he lodged with them, and they worked together.[30]

(2) The three then traveled together toward the east:

> After staying on for some time, Paul took leave of the brothers and sailed for Syria, accompanied by Priscilla and Aquila. . . . When they reached Ephesus, he left them.[31]

(3) Paul sent greetings to and from Priscilla by name in three of the "Pauline" epistles, an indication of her prominence in Paul's work and the early Christian church:

> My greetings to Prisca and Aquila . . .[32]

> Aquila and Prisca, with the church that meets at their house, send you their warmest wishes, in the Lord.[33]

> Greetings to Prisca and Aquila . . .[34]

(4) On one occasion, Paul not only acknowledges Priscilla and Aquila's saving of his life, at the risk of their own, he refers to them as co-workers (*syn-ergous*) in Christ and indicates that the whole Gentile Christian church lay within the scope of their work:

> My greetings to Prisca and Aquila, my co-workers in Christ Jesus, who risked death to save my life: I am not the only one to owe them a debt of gratitude, all the churches among the pagans do, as well. My greetings, also, to the church that meets at their house.[35]

(5) Priscilla's teaching the Gospel, along with her husband Aquila, to the brilliant preacher Apollos reveals something of the range of women's involvement in early Christianity. It has even been thought by a number of scholars, for example, Adolf Harnack,[36] that Priscilla was the anonymous author of the Letter to the Hebrews in the New Testament.

> An Alexandrian Jew named Apollos now arrived in Ephesus. He was an eloquent man, with a sound knowledge of the scriptures, and yet, though he had been given instruction in the Way of the Lord and preached with great spiritual earnestness and was accurate in all the details he taught about Jesus, he had only experienced the baptism of John. When Priscilla and Aquila heard him speak boldly in the synagogue, they took him and expounded to him the Way of God more accurately.[37]

(6) John Chrysostom, who often spoke very negatively of women, was clearly very impressed with Priscilla, and the fact that she was greeted by Paul first, before her husband Aquila. He refers to the significance of this fact when preaching on the second letter to Timothy.[38] However, when he wrote his homilies commenting on the text of Paul's letter to the Romans, he was so struck by Priscilla's precedence that he wrote two separate homilies on the topic and delivered them within a few days of each other! A brief excerpt follows:

> It is worth examining Paul's motive, when he greets them, for putting Priscilla before her husband. Indeed, he did not say: "Salute Aquila and Priscilla," but rather, "Salute Priscilla and Aquila" [Rom 16:3]. He did not do so without reason: the wife

must have had, I think, greater piety than her husband. This is not a simple conjecture; its confirmation is evident in the Acts. Apollos was an eloquent man, well versed in Scripture, but he knew only the baptism of John; this woman took him, instructed him in the way of God, and made of him an accomplished teacher.[39]

§228 Woman as a Disciple

In the early Palestinian Church there was a woman called a disciple (*mathētria*, the feminine form of *mathētēs*, the Greek word for "disciple"); could she perhaps have been one of the "seventy-two" sent out by Yeshua in Luke 10:1? Again, a woman is centrally involved in a resurrection story:

> At Jaffa there was a woman *disciple* called Tabitha, or Dorcas in Greek, who never tired of doing good or giving in charity. But the time came when she got ill and died, and they washed her and laid her out in a room upstairs. Lydda is not far from Jaffa, so when the disciples heard that Peter was there, they sent two men with an urgent message for him, "Come and visit us as soon as possible." Peter went back with them straightaway, and on his arrival they took him to the upstairs room, where all the widows stood around him in tears, showing him tunics and other clothes Dorcas had made when she was with them. Peter sent them all out of the room and knelt down and prayed. Then he turned to the dead woman and said, "Tabitha, stand up." She opened her eyes, looked at Peter and sat up. Peter helped her to her feet; then he called in the saints and widows and showed them she was alive. The whole of Jaffa heard about it and many believed in the Lord.[40]

§229 Woman as an Apostle

Paul refers to a woman, Junia, as an "outstanding *apostle*" (*apostolos*). Some scholars, unwarrantedly, argued that Junia was a contraction of a much less common male name; but even the virulently misogynist fourth-century bishop of Constantinople, John Chrysostom, notes: "Oh, how great is the devotion of this woman that she should be counted worthy of the appellation of apostle!"[41] "John Chrysostom was not alone in the ancient church in taking the name [*Jounian*] to be feminine. The earliest commentator on Romans 16:7, Origen of Alexandria (c. 185–253 C.E.), took the name to be feminine (*Junia* or *Julia*, which is a textual variant), as did Jerome (340/50–419/20 C.E.), Hatto of Vercelli (924–961 C.E.), Theophylact (c. 1050–c. 1108 C.E.), and Peter Abelard (1079–1142 C.E.). In fact, to the best of my knowledge, no commentator on the text until Aegidus of Rome (1245–1316 C.E.) took the name to be masculine."[42] It is odd that it is only in more modern times that Christian writers have strained to make Junia into a male name; misogynism apparently still persists:

Greetings . . . to those outstanding *apostles* Andronicus and *Junia,* my compatriots and fellow prisoners who became Christians before me.[43]

§230 Women Prophets

Although women prophets (persons through whom God spoke) were not as prominent as men prophets in the Hebraic tradition, they were clearly there.

§231 Anna the Prophet

This female prophetic tradition also passed over into the Christian tradition, and it is by way of the bridge woman prophet (*prophētis*) Anna who stood in the Hebraic tradition and reached out to Yeshua as Messiah:

> There was a woman prophet (*prophētis*) also, Anna the daughter of Phanuel, of the tribe of Asher. She was well on in years. Her days of girlhood over, she had been married for seven years before becoming a widow. She was now eighty-four years old and never left the Temple, serving God night and day with fasting and prayer. She came by just at that moment and began to praise God; and she spoke of the child to all who looked forward to the deliverance of Jerusalem.[44]

§232 Elizabeth the Prophet

Another Jewish woman who was a bridge figure in the prophetic tradition from the Hebraic to the Christian tradition was Elizabeth, Yeshua's aunt; she stood in the prophetic line because she spoke upon being filled with the Holy Spirit of God, that is, she became God's mouthpiece:

> Elizabeth was filled with the Holy Spirit. She gave a loud cry and said, "Of all women you are the most blessed, and blessed is the fruit of your womb. Why should I be honoured with a visit from the mother of my Lord? The moment your greeting reached my ears, the child in my womb leapt for joy. Yes, blessed is she who believed that the promise made her by the Lord would be fulfilled."[45]

§233 Mary the Prophet

Mary likewise has been seen by Christians as standing in this same prophetic tradition when she responded to her cousin Elizabeth with her "Magnificat," concerning which Pope Paul VI said: "She was a woman who did not hesitate to proclaim that God vindicates the humble and the oppressed and removes the powerful people of this world from their privileged positions."[46]

§234 Women Pentecostal Prophets

"Christian" prophets (persons who were filled with God's Spirit and through whom God spoke) appeared on the first Christian Pentecost, and *women* were among them:

> They went to the upper room. . . . All these joined in continuous prayer, to-gether with several women, including Mary the mother of Yeshua. . . . When Pentecost day came round, they had all met in one room, when suddenly they heard what sounded like a powerful wind from heaven, the noise of which filled the entire house in which they were sitting; and something appeared to them that seemed like tongues of fire; these separated and came to rest on the head of each of them. They were *all* filled with the *Holy Spirit, and began to speak* foreign languages as the *Spirit* gave them the gift of speech.[47]

§235 Joel and Women Prophets

In keeping with the tradition of women prophets in the Hebrew Scriptures (and the Gospels), Peter quotes, on that first Christian Pentecost, from the prophet Joel,[48] who twice speaks of women prophesying:

> But Peter standing with the Eleven, lifted his voice and addressed them. . . . "This is what was spoken by the prophet Joel":
>
> "And in the last days it shall be, God declares, that I will pour out my Spirit upon all flesh, and your sons and daughters shall prophesy, and your young men shall see visions, and your old men shall dream dreams; yea, and on my menservants and my maidservants in those days I will pour out my Spirit; and they shall prophesy."[49]

§236 Philip's Daughters, Prophets I

Not only did the Jewish-Christian women who were gathered in the upper room in Jerusalem at the descent of the Holy Spirit "prophesy," but so also did the Jewish-Christian daughters of the "deacon" Philip:

> The end of our voyage from Tyre came when we landed at Ptolemais, where we greeted the brethren and stayed one day with them. The next day

we left and came to Caesarea. Here we called on Philip the evangelist, one of the Seven, and stayed with him. He had four virgin daughters who were prophets.[50]

§237 Philip's Daughters, Prophets II

The reputation of Philip's daughters as prophets was so significant and long-lasting in its influence that their burial place was used (along with that of the apostles John and Philip, among others; the latter was mistakenly thought to be the same as Philip the evangelist of Acts 21:8–9 by Eusebius, and probably also by Polycrates, whom he quoted) to back the claim of apostolicity of a particular tradition by Bishop Polycrates of Ephesus (present-day Turkey) against Pope Victor I (189–198 C.E). The second document referring to these four women prophets stemmed from Gaius in the years 198–217. Both documents are found only as excerpts in the *Ecclesiastical History* of Eusebius of Caesarea (260–340 C.E.), written before 303:

> The date of John's death has also been roughly fixed: the place where his mortal remains lie can be gathered from a letter of Polycrates, Bishop of Ephesus, to Victor, Bishop of Rome. In it he refers not only to John but to Philip the apostle and Philip's daughters as well: "In Asia great luminaries sleep who shall rise again on the last day, the day of the Lord's advent, when He is coming with glory from heaven and shall search out all His saints, such as Philip, one of the twelve apostles, who sleeps in Hierapolis with one of his daughters, who remained unmarried to the end of their days, while his other daughter lived in the Holy Spirit and rests in Ephesus." So much Polycrates tells us about their deaths. And in the *Dialogue* of Gaius of whom I spoke a little while ago, Proclus, with whom he was disputing, speaks thus about the deaths of Philip and his daughters, in agreement with the foregoing account: "After him there were four women prophets at Hierapolis in Asia, daughters of Philip. Their grave is there, as is their father's." That is Gaius's account. Luke in the Acts of the Apostles refers to Philip's daughters as then living with their father at Caesarea in Judaea and endowed with the prophetic gift.[51]

§238 Veiled Women Prophets

In a "left-handed" way Paul documents the spread of prophecy among Greek-Christian women:

> For a woman, however, it is a sign of disrespect to her head if she prays or prophesies unveiled.[52]

§239 A Woman Prophet Leader of a Church

In the latter part of the first century, John the author of the Apocalypse wrote in a prophetic fashion to the church in Thyatira (present-day Turkey) complaining about a "Jezebel" of a woman prophet, apparently the leader of a whole group of Christians who advocated a coexistence with pagan culture that permitted them the "immorality" of eating food offered to idols; John insisted on a radical break. Obviously this "woman prophet" exercised her gifts of prophecy and teaching (*didaskein*) within the Christian Church, for she was "encouraged" (*apheis*) by the local church and "given time to reform" even by her apocalyptic opponent John. She clearly had many followers, as the reference to her so-called children (*tekna*) and John's great concern indicate. Whether she was too lax or John too rigoristic is not at issue here; her exercising "prophecy" and wide influence within the Christian Church is substantiated by the text. It should also be noted that Thyatira became the center of the Montanist movement, in which women prophets played a prominent role, in the middle of the next (the second) century. The influence of our woman prophet apparently was long-lasting. It is unfortunate that the burgeoning anti-feminism of the Christian Church forced Montanism, and women prophets, into sectarianism:

> Nevertheless, I have a complaint to make: you are encouraging the woman Jezebel who claims to be a prophet, and by her teaching she is luring my servants away to commit the immorality of eating food which has been sacrificed to idols. I have given her time to reform but she is not willing to change her immoral life. Now I am consigning her to bed, and all her partners in immorality to troubles that will test them severely, unless they repent of their practices; and I will see that her children die.[53]

§240 Women Prophets Attacked by Apocryphal Peter

Leadership roles exercised by women in Christianity, including that of prophecy, were frequently attacked by many Church Fathers and in other writings. Here is partially cited one early, second-century, apocryphal document, the *Kerygmata Petrou*, in which Peter was made to say extremely vicious things about women prophets. They were seen as aping men prophets, as having tendencies toward polytheism and seeing the female element in the divine. The latter was doubtless a reference to the echoes of the Goddess worship that could be heard in the Hebraic-Judaic feminine Wisdom tradition that entered into the Christian, both Orthodox Catholic and Gnostic, tradition. Apocryphal Peter's protest here is a continuation of the patriarchal Yahwist protest against women leaders and the Goddess; it was quite alien to the Jewish and Christian Wisdom and the Yeshua traditions.

> Along with the true prophet there has been created as a companion a female being who is as far inferior to him as *metousia* is to *ousida*, as the moon is to the sun, as fire is to light. . . .
>
> There are two kinds of prophecy, the one is male . . . the other is found amongst those who are born of women. Proclaiming what pertains to the present world, female prophecy desires to be considered male. On this account she steals the seed of the male, envelops them with her own seed of the flesh and lets them, that is, her words, come forth as her own creations. She promises to give earthly riches gratuitously in the present world and wishes to exchange (the slow) for the swift, the small for the greater. She not only ventures to speak and hear of many gods, but also believes that she herself will be deified; and because she hopes to become something that contradicts her nature, she destroys what she has. Pretending to make sacrifice, she stains herself with blood at the time of her menses and thus pollutes those who touch her.[54]

§241 Women as Teachers

Although in the later New Testament documents women are told to remain silent in the church, not to have authority over men, are to ask their husbands the meaning of something they don't understand, it was not so at the beginning of the Yeshua movement. All through the lifetime of Paul (d. 67 C.E.?) women served as teachers.

§242 Priscilla the Teacher

The author of the Pauline epistle to Timothy did "not permit a woman to teach or exercise supreme authority over a man." But Priscilla taught the great Apollos the Gospel:

> But when Priscilla and Aquila heard him, they took him and *expounded* (*exethento*) to him the Way of God *more accurately*.[55]

§243 "Gray Panther" Women Teachers

Even the author of the Pauline epistle to Titus also bade the older women (*presbytidas*) to teach what is good:

> Bid the older women . . . to teach (*kalodidaskalous*) what is good.[56]

§244 The Ecclesial Order of Widows

In the Christian tradition, widowhood was not only the object of charity, but also one of the earliest "orders" of women in the church, analogous to that of priests and bishops.

§245 The Widow Anna

A bridge person, a Hebrew widow who spent her life in a search for holiness and who is connected to Yeshua as Messiah, is Anna.[57]

§246 Widows Follow Yeshua and a Woman Disciple

Later, many other Hebrew women followed Yeshua. Often scholars suggest that many of the women who "ministered" (*diēkonoun*)[58] were of necessity widows, devoting their lives to a search for holiness. That these women formed a society or "order" after the time of Yeshua can be seen by the distinction Peter made between ordinary Christians ("saints") and widows, who apparently were banded together around their leader Tabitha; she also obviously enjoyed a great prominence in the Palestinian Christian Church. See §228 for the complete text:

> At Jaffa there was a woman disciple called Tabitha. . . . Peter went back with them straightaway, and on his arrival they took him to the upstairs room, where *all the widows* stood round him in tears. . . . Peter helped her to her feet then he called in the *saints and widows* and showed them she was alive.[59]

§247 Widows Ministered to I

The widows, who ministered (*diēkonoun*) to Yeshua and his disciples, in turn became the objects of special physical service (*diakonia*) instituted by the twelve, the beginning of the special "office" of the diaconate. Since all church "members who might be in need"[60] received whatever food and shelter they needed, the reference to distributions to widows indicated their special quality. This "order of widows" was provided such "logistical support" already in the Jerusalem Church in both Hebrew- and Greek-speaking cultural forms:

> About this time, when the number of disciples was increasing, the Hellenists made a complaint against the Hebrews: in the daily distribution their own widows were being overlooked. So the Twelve called a full meet-

ing of the disciples and addressed them, "It would not be right for us to neglect the word of God so as to give out food; you, brethren, must select from among yourselves seven men of good reputation, filled with the Spirit and with wisdom; we will hand over this duty to them."[61]

§248 Widows Ministered to II

But it was clear that these "deacons" were to supply more than material goods, for we know from elsewhere that at least two of them, Stephen and Philip, were also teachers of the Good News:

> You, brethren, must select from among yourselves seven men of good reputation, filled with the Spirit and with wisdom; we will hand over this duty to them. . . . The whole community approved of this proposal and elected Stephen, a man full of faith and of the Holy Spirit, together with Phillip. . . . They presented these to the apostles, who prayed and laid their hands on them.[62]

§249 Widows Ministering and Ministered to

The author of the Pauline epistle to Timothy distinguishes between widows who were simply women whose husbands had died and those who belonged to the "order" of widows who devoted their lives to the service of the Christian community and who in turn were supported by it:

> Enrolment as a widow is permissible only for a woman at least sixty years old who has had only one husband. She must be a woman known for her good works and for the way in which she has brought up her children, shown hospitality to strangers and washed the saints' feet, helped people who are in trouble and been active in all kinds of good work.[63]

§250 The Several "Orders" of Widows

The "orders" of widows took several forms in both Eastern and Western Christianity and lasted several centuries. They are briefly listed below.

§251 "Virginal" Widows in the East   At the end of the first century or at the beginning of the second, we find a reference to Christian widows that clearly must be meant as a church "order," for they are referred to as virgins! Ignatius of Antioch (35–107 C.E.) wrote to the Smyrnians:

> Greetings to the families of my brethren including their wives and children, and to the virgins who are enrolled among the widows.[64]

§252 "Virginal" Widows in the West   In the West, Tertullian (160–225 C.E.) confirmed Christian widowhood as an "order" that had virgins as members. Even the Pauline age requirement of sixty years was no longer observed, for Tertullian spoke of teenage members!

> I know for sure, places where virgins not yet twenty years of age are established in the state of widowhood.[65]

§253 Wise Widows   Ignatius of Antioch was taught by the apostles, and it was his disciple Polycarp (d. 155 C.E.) who wrote that this Christian teaching was to be passed on in its fullness to the order of widows:

> Let us teach the widows to be wise, intelligent about the faith of the Lord.[66]

§254 Widows Teach Women

The fifth-century *Statuta ecclesiae antiqua* (from southern France) indicates that this instruction in the Gospel was given so that the widows could further teach, albeit just other women:

> Widows, or virgins, who are chosen for the ministry of the baptism of women . . . should be instructed for this office, so that they can teach ignorant and backward women with apt and sound words, so that at the time of baptism they can answer the questions of the baptizer and about how they should live once they are baptized.[67]

§255 "Pastoral" Widows are Ordained

In another fifth-century document, this one from Syria, the *Testamentum Domini Nostri Jesu Christi*, the order of widows attained their highest status. This document, originally written in Greek, unfortunately is extant only in various ancient translations, preeminently the Syriac, which was critically edited and published with a Latin translation by I. E. Rahmani, Mainz, 1899. The widows in this document are distinguished from ordinary widows by the designation, "widows who sit in front" (*viduae habentes praecedentiam sessionis*), a term used six times. Once, in a litany chanted by the deacon, she is referred to as a "female priest" (*pro presbyteris [feminis] supplicemus*, after similar petitions for the *episcopo, presbyteris, diaconis*). Unlike all other documents, which speak of "appointing" widows, the *Testamentum Domini* speaks of "ordaining" (*ordinetur*) them. They are instructed to receive communion with the rest of the clergy, after the deacons and before the readers and subdeacons. Moreover, they are placed within the veil around the altar during the Eucharist (much like the iconostasis in later Orthodox Christianity and the rood screen in Western Christianity, behind which today women are not allowed during the Eucharist), along with the other clergy. As Gryson notes, "undeniably they were considered a part of the clergy. Indeed, no other document attributes to women a rank as high in the ecclesiastical hierarchy as that of widows who sat in front."[68]

In the democratic twenty-first century, it is interesting to note that the widows, in exact parallel to the instructions concerning the ordination of the bishop, priests, and deacons, are to be ordained from among "those who are chosen" (*quae eligitur*) by the congregation, that is, all the clergy were elected by the people.

Once ordained, the widow had a wide range of pastoral duties oriented toward women. She was to teach the women catechumens (*quae introeunt, efficiat ut sciant . . .*), instruct the ignorant, teach women prisoners (*doceat reas*), encourage and lead in prayer the virgins, admonish and try to win back those women who have gone astray, visit sick women, anoint women being baptized and supervise the deaconesses. (It is clear that in this document the "widows who sit in front" had the status that in other documents the deaconesses did, and vice versa.)

> Let her who is chosen be *ordained* a widow (*Ordinetur in viduam illa, quae eligitur*). . . . Let her *instruct* the ignorant (*erudiat ignorantes*), convert and teach the prisoners (*doceat reas*) . . . and she should supervise the deaconesses.[69]

§256 Widows Administer "Extreme Unction" to Men

Still, in the early third-century *Didascalia* (Syria) it is clear that at least some of the ministrations of the widow, other than teaching, were directed at men as well as women, for the extant Syriac and ancient Latin manuscripts clearly say brothers, *fratres*. Also, many scholars, Cardinal Jean Daniélou, for example, see in this praying and laying on of hands the administration of the Sacrament of the Dying, Extreme Unction:

> Why, O undisciplined widow, when you see your fellow widows or brothers (*conviduas . . . fratres*) lying in infirmity, do you not hasten to your members, that you may fast and pray over them and impose hands?[70]

§257 Widows Likened to Altars, Virgins Priests of Christ

In fourth-century letters written by Pseudo-Ignatius, widows are likened to altars. But what is quite startling is that virgins were said to be like priestesses of Christ. The term used was not *presbytera* but rather *hiereia* (same root as in "hierarchy"). In the whole of the New Testament, no individual Christian was ever specifically identified as a priest (*hiereus*), only pagan and Jewish priests were. Christians as a whole might have been called a "royal priesthood" (*basileion hierateuma*),[71] but Christian "priests" were called "presbyters" (*presbyteros*). *Hiereus* designated a cultic leader, which the early Christians claimed not to have; only with the passage of time did Christians associate church leadership with cultic leadership and the term "priest" (*hiereus* in Greek, *sacerdos* in Latin). Thus, it is striking that a Christian woman would be called a *hiereia* of Christ.

> Honor those who continue in virginity, as the priestesses of Christ (*hiereias Christou*); and the widows that persevere in gravity of behavior, as the altar of God.[72]

§258 Women Deacons

The Catholic Church in the West spoke of the sacrament of Holy Orders, in the plural, meaning the offices of bishop, priest, and deacon to which individuals were chosen and "ordered" by the community to serve the community in those three capacities. Beginning already with the New Testament, women were "ordered," "ordained" to the office of deacon.

§259 Women and Men Deacons Given Pauline Instructions

Already in the lifetime of Paul (d. 63 C.E.), the office of deacon was established.[73] Women as well as men served in this "*ordained*" office. Later when the Pauline First Epistle to Timothy was written (probably toward the end of the first century) women and men deacons were both required to have parallel qualities:

> Deacons likewise must be serious, not double-tongued, not addicted to much wine, not greedy for gain; they must hold the mystery of the faith with a clear conscience. And let them also be tested first; then, if they prove themselves blameless, let them serve as deacons. In the same way, the women deacons must be serious, no slanderers, but temperate, faithful in all things.[74]

§260 Phoebe a Deacon

Paul also named, and honored, a specific woman deacon. Here Paul referred to Phoebe as a deacon (*diakonos*), not as a deaconess (*diakonissa*).[75] Though the term "deacon" may not have had the formalized official quality during Paul's lifetime (d. 67 C.E.) that it acquired later, as in the perhaps late first-century letters to Timothy, Paul did address his letter to the Philippians to the *episkopois kai diakonois*.[76] Since the latter term is usually translated "deacon," it is appropriate to translate Phoebe's *diakonos* as "deacon" as well.

Clement of Alexandria, who wrote during the latter part of the second century, perhaps only decades after the letters to Timothy were composed, clearly refers to women deacons (*diakanōn gvnaikōn*, in *Stromata* 3, 6, 53:3–4.[77] Clement's student Origen, in commenting on Paul's letter to the Romans and its reference to Phoebe, states: "This text teaches with the authority of the Apostle that even women are instituted deacons in the Church [*feminas in ministeris Ecclesiae constitui*, in the extant Latin translation; *kai gynaikas diakonous tēs ēkkliēsias kathistasthai* in the original Greek[78]]. . . . And thus this text teaches at the same time two things: that there are, as we have already said, women deacons in the Church [*et haberi, ut diximus, feminas ministras in Ecclesia*, in Latin; *kai einai, hōs eipamen, gynaikas diakonous en tē ēkklēsia*, in reconstructed Greek[79]], and that women, who have given assistance to so many people and who by their good works deserve to be praised by the Apostle, ought to be accepted in the diaconate [*in ministerium*, Latin; *eis diakonian*, reconstructed Greek]":

> I commend to you our sister Phoebe, a deacon of the church at Cenchreae.[80]

§261 Phoebe a Ruler over Paul

Paul also refers to Phoebe as a "ruler" (*prostatis*), not as a "helper," as it is usually, and unwarrantedly, translated; the word appears nowhere else in the New Testament and always means ruler, leader, or protector in all Greek literature. Paul used a verb form of the word in 1 Thessalonians 5:12 (*proistamenous*), and it is translated as "rule over," as are also similar verb forms in I Tim 3:4, 5; 5:17, where the references are to bishops, priests, and deacons![81]

> Give her [Phoebe], in union with the Lord, a welcome worthy of saints, and help her with anything she needs, for she has been a ruler (*prostatis*) over many, indeed over me.[82]

§262 Martha a "Deacon"

In the Fourth Gospel's account of Yeshua's attending a dinner in Bethany,[83] Martha was said to have served at the table (*diēkonei*), in the same work assigned to the early "deacons."[84] As Raymond E. Brown points out, John was "writing in the 90s, when the office of *diakonos* already existed in the post-Pauline churches (see the Pastoral epistles) and when the task of waiting on tables was a specific function, to which the community or its leaders appointed individuals by laying on hands. In the Johannine community, a woman could be described as exercising a function which in other churches was the function of an 'Ordained' person."[85] In a different story, Luke 10:40–41, Martha again is described as serving at table (*diakonian . . . diakonein*). It is perhaps almost as possible that Luke, here writing ten or twenty years before the Fourth Gospel, may have had a similar awareness of the ecclesial connotation the word *diakonia* acquired early in Christianity, especially since it was the same Luke who shortly thereafter wrote of the first "deacons" in the Acts of the Apostles, that they were "to serve at table (*diakonein*) . . . and that they laid hands (*cheiras*) on them."[86]

> Six days before the Passover, Yeshua went to Bethany, where Lazarus was, whom he raised from the dead. They gave a dinner for him there; Martha served (*diēkonei*).[87]
>
> Now Martha who was distracted with all the serving [*diakonian*] said, "Lord, do you not care that my sister is leaving me to do all the serving (*diakonein*) myself?"[88]

§263 Deaconesses are Ordained

Although the status of women in the Christian Church gradually deteriorated after the first generation of the church (e.g., from Yeshua, to Paul, to the late pastoral epistles, to Timothy, etc.), there are records of the ordination of deaconesses (*diakonisses*) in the fourth century in the East and perhaps in the second century in the West. In the fourth-century *Apostolic Constitutions* (probably from Syria) the bishops were charged to *ordain* deaconesses:

> Ordain (*procheirisai*) also a woman deacon (*diakonon*) who is faithful and holy.[89]

§264 Ordination Prayer for Deaconesses

Also in the *Apostolic Constitutions*, the prayers are given for the ordination of a bishop, then a priest, a deacon, a deaconess, a subdeacon, and a lector, followed by regulations concerning confessors, widows, virgins, and exorcists; concerning all the latter, it was explicitly stated that they are *not* ordained, clearly implying that the former six were. Precisely the same terms, prayers, and actions (laying on of hands, etc.) were used for the deaconess as for the bishop, priest, and deacon. If these were sacramentally ordained, so was the deaconess:

> Concerning a deaconess (*diakonissa*), I Bartholomew make this constitution: O bishop, thou shalt lay thy hands upon her (*epitheseis autē tas cheiras*) in the presence of the presbytery, and of the deacons and deaconesses, and shalt say: O Eternal God, the Father of our Lord Yeshua Christ, the Creator of man and of woman, who didst replenish with the Spirit Miriam, and Deborah, and Anna and Huldah; who didst not disdain that Thy only begotten Son should be born of a woman; who also in the tabernacle of the testimony, and in the temple, didst ordain women to be keepers of Thy holy gates, do Thou, now also, look down upon this Thy servant, who is to be ordained (*procheirizomenēn*) to the office of a woman deacon (*diakonian*), and grant her Thy Holy Spirit, and "cleanse her from all filthiness of flesh and spirit," that she may worthily discharge the work which is committed to her to Thy glory, and the praise of Thy Christ, with whom glory and adoration be to Thee and the Holy Spirit for ever. Amen.[90]

§265 Women Clerics

The Council of Nicaea (325 C.E.) somewhat earlier referred to deaconesses as *clerics*:

> Likewise, however, both deaconesses (*diakonissōn*) and in general all those who are numbered among the clergy [*kanoni* in the Greek, *clericos* in the Latin] should retain the same form.[91]

§266 Deaconesses at Chalcedon

Somewhat later the Council of Chalcedon (451 C.E.) stated a regulation concerning the *ordination* of deaconesses and spoke of the deaconess's ministry, her "liturgy" (*leitourgia*):

> A woman should not be ordained (*cheirotonēsthai* in the Greek, *ordinandam* in the Latin) a deaconess before she is forty. And if after receiving ordination (*cheirothesian*) she continued in her ministry (*leitourgia*).[92]

§267 Women in "Orders"

In the West, even the misogynist Church Father Tertullian (160–225 C.E.) wrote:

> How many men and women there are whose chastity has obtained for them the honor of ecclesiastical orders (*in ecclesiasticis ordinibus*)![93]

§268 Second-Century Women Deacons

A very early second-century letter from Pliny to the emperor Trajan (reign 98–117 C.E.) refers to two women deacons (*ministrae*, the Latin translation then for *diakones*), who were apparently the leaders and most knowledgeable persons in their local church, which was then being persecuted:

> I judged it so much the more necessary to extract the real truth with the assistance of torture, from two maidservants [*ancillis*], who were called deacons [*ministrae*]: but I could discover nothing more than depraved and excessive superstition.[94]

§269 Deaconesses Teach

Although after New Testament times the deaconess was authentically ordained as part of the clerical hierarchy, her official ministry was normally limited to women, surely a regression from the time of Phoebe and Priscilla. Nevertheless, her responsibilities did include religious teaching, as is seen in the early third-century *Didascalia* (it is perhaps indicative of still further slippage that in the parallel passage of the fourth-century *Apostolic Constitutions* the words "instructs and teaches" are missing):

> And when she who is being baptized has come up from the water, let the deaconess receive her, and *teach and instruct* her how the seal of baptism ought to be kept unbroken in purity and holiness. For this cause, we say that the ministry of a woman deacon is especially needful and important. For our Lord and Savior also was ministered unto by women *ministers*. . . . And thou also hast need of the ministry of a deaconess for many things.[95]

§270 Sixth-Century Deaconesses

A sixth-century Western Church Father, Pseudo-Jerome, gave testimony of the continuing teaching office of the Eastern deaconesses in his commentary on Romans 16:1–2, where he states that Phoebe "is a deacon (*in ministerio*) of the church in Cenchreae":

> As even now among Orientals, deaconesses may be seen to minister (*ministrare*) to their own sex in Baptism, we have found some early women who have privately taught in the ministry of the word (*ministerio verbi*) e.g., Priscilla, whose husband was called Aquila.[96]

§271 Deaconess Likened to the Holy Spirit

Perhaps the highest praise of the deaconess in Christian documents comes from the *Didascalia*, where she is likened to the Holy Spirit! In this passage she is also listed before the priest:

> Let him be honored by you as God, for the bishop sits for you in the place of God Almighty. But the deacon stands in the place of Christ; therefore he should be loved by you. And the deaconess shall be honored by you as a type of the Holy Spirit (*eis typon hagiou pneumatos*, as translated in the fourth-century *Apostolic Constitutions*); and the presbyters shall be to you in the likeness of the Apostles; and the orphans and widows shall be reckoned by you in the likeness of the altar.[97]

§272 Decline of Deaconesses

Thus, at the time of the New Testament women were deacons, just as men were.[98] By the late fourth century the women deacons were called deaconesses, coming after deacons in status; nevertheless they were truly ordained and were classified as clerics. This was true mostly in the East; in the West the development of the "order" was much weaker. Still, even though the deaconess was largely expected to minister to other women, that restriction was not always maintained.

However, with the decline of the Roman Empire, sociological changes set off a decline in the order of deaconess, as reflected in the following council statements:

> Let no one proceed to the ordination of deaconesses anymore.[99]

> We abrogate completely, in the entire kingdom, the consecration of widows who are named deaconesses.[100]

> No longer shall the blessing of women deaconesses be given, because of the weakness of the sex.[101]

By the twelfth century, the order of deaconess almost totally disappeared from the church, both East and West.[102]

§273 Women as Presbyters (Priests)?

The presbyters (Greek *presbyteros*, elder, whence English "priest" is derived) of the New Testament were the leaders of the Christian churches, as, for example, in Ephesus. The writer of the deutero-Pauline First Epistle to Timothy speaks a great deal about "bishops,"[103] men deacons,[104] women deacons,[105] widows as a category of church "officers,"[106] men presbyters,[107] and women presbyters![108] The author notes that Timothy was "ordained" by the elderhood, or presbyterate (*presbyteriou*,[109] just four verses before the reference to the women presbyters, *presbyteras*,[110]), and a little later speaks of the honor and criticism of male presbyters.[111] It is right in the middle of this discussion of presbyters that the author speaks of how Timothy, probably a leader set above the rest of the presbyterate, possibly even a "bishop" (*episkopos*[112]), should deal with a man presbyter (*presbyterō*) and women presbyters (*presbyteras*). Thus, in 1 Tim 5:1–2 the words *presbyterō* and *presbyteras* are usually translated as "an older man" and "older women," but in this context of a discussion of the various "officers" of the church, a perfectly proper translation, which, if not more likely, is at least possible, would be "male presbyter" and "woman presbyters":

> Do not rebuke a male presbyter (*presbyterō*) but exhort him as you would a father; treat younger men like brethren, women presbyters (*presbyteras*) like mothers, younger women like sisters.[113]

§274 Episcopal Women?

(1) Though in New Testament times there was no "monarchical episcopacy," *episkopoi* (literally "overseers") did appear late in the period as sort of chairpersons of committees of presbyters. Many scholars argue that the "elect lady" (lady *kyria*, as parallel to lord, *kyrios*) to whom the Second Epistle of John is addressed, and her "elect sister," whose children sent greetings, must have been "symbols" of churches. But they were perhaps just as properly understood as real persons.[114] Judging from the content of the letter, the elect lady was responsible not only for her natural children but also for the Christians in her charge (a house church as with Priscilla, Nympha, etc.?); did she not then have the function of an "overseer," *episkopa*, even though the title was not mentioned, but rather *kyria* was? Her sister also?

We must also recall that the writer of the Epistles of John belonged to the same group of the "orthodox" portion of the Community of the Beloved Disciple (Mary Magdalene) who both had a long tradition of favoring women in the Fourth Gospel, which I contend was originally written by Mary Magdalene. The final Redactor felt he had to disguise her authority by using a pseudonym, the Beloved Disciple. Might the same kind of word-play be operating here with *eklektē kyria*?

> The elder to the elect lady (*eklektē kyria*) and her children, whom I love in the truth, and not only I but also all who know the truth. . . . I rejoiced greatly to find some of your children following the truth, just as we have been commanded by the Father. And now I beg you, lady, (*kyria*), not as though I were writing you a new commandment, but the one we have had from the beginning, that we love one another. . . . For many deceivers have gone out into the world, men who will not acknowledge the coming of Jesus Christ in the flesh: such a one is the deceiver and the anti-Christ. Look to yourselves that you may not lose what you have worked for, but may win a full reward. Any one who goes ahead and does not abide in the doctrine of Christ does not have God; he who abides in the doctrine has both the Father and the Son. If any one comes to you and does not bring this doctrine, do not receive him into the house. . . . Though I have much to write to you, I would rather not use paper and ink, but I hope to come to see you and talk with you face to face, so that our joy may be complete. The children of your *elect sister* greet you.[115]

(2) Already within the same century when John's epistle was probably written, namely, the second century, Church Father Clement of Alexandria spoke of "elect persons" as a designation for officers of the church, which included not only bishops but also widows, supporting the contention that the "elect" lady of 2 John could properly be understood as a generic term for church officers:

> However, there are many other precepts written in the sacred books which pertain to elect persons (*prosōa eklekta*): certain of these are for priests (*presbyterois*), others indeed for bishops (*episkopois*), others for deacons, still others for widows (*kērais*), all of which should be discussed at another time.[116]

§275 Women Authors of "Scripture"

I have already argued for women writers of what has become Christian Scripture, namely, Proto-Luke and Proto-Fourth Gospel. In addition, as already noted, a number of reputable scholars present strong cases in favor of Priscilla being the author of the canonical Letter to the Hebrews. But, barring the discovery of new documentary evidence, Priscilla can never be more than a strong candidate, among other strong candidates, for the authorship of the Letter to the Hebrews. However, the case is not nearly so tentative with some other "scriptural" documents, namely, the several apocryphal New Testament Acts of Apostles, that is, the Acts of "John," "Peter," "Paul," "Andrew," "Thomas," and the "Acts of Xanthippe and Polyxeus." No thought was given to the possibility of female authorship for these documents until the 1978 doctoral dissertation, "The Social World of the Apocryphal Acts," by Stevan Davies of the Religion Department of Temple University. In a most persuasive marshaling of evidence and development of argumentation, Davies showed that these documents give every indication of having been written both for women and by women.

§276 The Apocryphal Acts of the Apostles

To begin with, these Apocryphal Acts were all written between 160 and 225 C.E. in Greek, in Greece or Asia Minor, except for the Acts of Thomas, which was written in Syriac in Roman Syria, immediately adjacent to Asia Minor. They all breathe deeply a spirit of sexual asceticism, that is, they assume that being Christian entailed being celibate, the sexual act being described as abominable, filthy, unspeakable, and so forth. This anti-sex attitude, of course, permeated much of the history of Christianity. The form it took in the Apocryphal Acts was doubtless more intense than that found in Paul's epistles, but it surely was matched by some of the writings of the Desert Fathers, Jerome, Augustine (who in the *Confessions* set up his mutually exclusive choice between the joys of sex and Christ), and others. But in a society that tended to make married women subordinate to their husbands, being celibate allowed women to become their own mistresses, as men were their own masters. Hence, in this regard sexual continence was a force of both liberation and egalitarianism for these Christian women.

> The Apocryphal Acts . . . were written from within a particular community of Christians, a community somewhat outside the normal boundaries of society in the ancient world, a community which placed an exceptionally high value on sexual continence. It is our contention that the Acts derive from communities of continent Christian women, the Widows of their church, who were both adherents of apostles and participants in a stable church structure.[117]

§277 Women Models in the Apocryphal Acts

Throughout the Apocryphal Acts women are often central figures, outside of the apostles themselves, clearly the most striking and praiseworthy. They usually are not the stereotypically weak woman, but rather are strong, stereotypically "male," *vir*-ile, exercising great *vir*-tue, even disguising themselves as males, such as Thecla in the *Acts of Paul*.[118] Women performed various miracles, even raising dead men, which was done by no male other than the apostles, making those women female quasi or equivalent apostles.

> The figures of Drusiana, Cleopatra, Maximilla, Mygdonia, and Thecla are all impressive models of piety intended to be suitable for the emulation of Christians and, in particular, Christian women. There are no comparable role models in the Apocryphal Acts for Christian men. Stratocles, Marcellus, Lycomedes, the various men converted by Paul before his death, etc., are either flawed or of secondary importance in the narrative, or are not developed as narrative characters to any substantial extent. The great difficulty in Christian life is, time and time again, said to be the problem of continent living. This problem is always viewed from the standpoint of a woman who must leave her husband. At no time in the Apocryphal Acts does a man encounter substantial difficulties in leaving his wife. Married men are converted to the faith, if at all, either after their wives have converted or simultaneously with their wives.[119]

§278 Thecla Popular with Christian Women

The *Acts of Paul and Thecla*, in which some scholars argue is a historical core, was extremely popular in the early church, as was evidenced by the existence of not only the original Greek but also five different Latin translations plus Syriac, Armenian, Slavonic, and Arabic translations. In a manner typical of the Apocryphal Acts, Thecla was converted to Christianity by a wandering apostle, St. Paul. She and he assumed that her conversion meant her refusing to marry her fiancée. Eventually this precipitated all sorts of tortures and attempted executions of Thecla. Throughout these many trials, it is interesting to note, the women of the city were vocally in support of her. Once the various trials and tortures began, on no less than seven occasions the women as a group cried out for Thecla:

> (1) But the women were panic-stricken, and cried out before the judgment-seat: "An evil judgment! A godless judgment!" ... (2) But the women with their children cried out from above, saying: "O God, an impious

judgment is come to pass in this city!" . . . (3) The women said: May the city perish for this lawlessness! Slay us all, Proconsul! A bitter sight, an evil judgment!" (4) And the crowd of the women raised a great shout. . . . (5) And the women mourned the more, since the lioness which helped her was dead. . . . (6) But as other more terrible beasts were let loose, the women cried aloud, and some threw petals, others nard, others cassia, others amomum, so that there was an abundance of perfumes. And all the beasts let loose were overpowered as if by sleep, and did not touch her. . . . (7) But all the women cried out with a loud voice, and as with one mouth gave praise to God saying: "One is God, who has delivered Thecla!" so that all the city was shaken by the sound.[120]

§279 *Thecla Baptizes Herself*

Besides having shown extraordinary courage and being the object of many saving miracles, Thecla did something else worthy of note. She baptized *herself*. Most documents indicate that only men baptized, although deaconesses assisted in the East in the early centuries of Christianity. The protest against this restriction is most obvious in the *Acts of Paul and Thecla*, where the baptism story of Thecla, who in the midst of her trials, is told.

> When she had finished her prayer, she turned and saw a great pit full of water, and said: "Now is the time for me to wash." And she threw herself in, saying: "in the name of Jesus Christ I baptize myself on the last day!"[121]

§280 *Thecla Teaches Christian Doctrine*

Although beginning already in the later New Testament period, women were increasingly restricted from teaching Christian doctrine,[122] apparently many Christian women were aware of women's earlier freer involvement in Christian teaching, and in the *Acts of Paul and Thecla* registered a strong protest. Thecla not only instructed non-Christians in Christian doctrine and converts them but also did so at the behest of St. Paul.

> So Thecla went in with her and rested in her house for eight days, instructing her in the word of God, so that the majority of the maidservants also believed; and there was great joy in the house. . . . And Thecla arose and said to Paul: "I am going to Iconium." But Paul said: "Go and teach the word of God!" . . . After enlightening many with the word of God she slept with a noble sleep.[123]

§281 Thecla a Model for Christian Women

This baptizing and teaching by Thecla (who was listed as a saint by the Roman Catholic Church until 1969!), coupled with the great popularity of the *Acts of Paul and Thecla*, obviously provided a model for other Christian women to follow, as could be seen by the great disturbance of the late second-century North African Christian writer Tertullian.

> But the impudence of that woman who assumed the right to teach is evidently not going to arrogate to her the right to baptize as well, unless perhaps some new serpent appears, like that original one, so that as the woman abolished baptism, some other should of her own authority confer it. But . . . certain Acts of Paul, which are falsely so named, claim the example of Thecla for allowing women to teach and to baptize. . . . How could we believe that Paul should give a female power to teach and to baptize, when he did not allow a woman even to learn by her own right?[124]

§282 Women Authors of the Apocryphal Acts

After a lengthy and penetrating analysis, Stevan Davies concludes in his dissertation that, because so many factors point to female rather than male authorship of the Apocryphal Acts,

> Occam's Razor ought henceforth to cut the other way, that female authorship of the Apocrypha Acts ought to be assumed in the absence of any convincing arguments to the contrary. Were the Acts authored by men they would be men without high official position in the church, devoted to the lifestyle of sexual chastity but eager to associate with women, determined to promulgate a positive view of the female sex and to create models of exemplary women, greatly concerned with the financial well-being of Widows and Virgins of the Lord, devoted to wandering charismatic apostles, willing to hide their own identities while putting words in the mouths of Apostles of the first century, and prone to adopt the ancient love romance as the model for their own literary efforts. For women these traits are characteristic.

If anyone can bring evidence for the existence of men of this sort and argue that they, and not literate Widows or Deaconesses, composed the Acts, then the hypothesis of female authorship will be refuted. Until that time Christian women should be given credit for the creativity which remains embodied in their compositions, the Apocryphal Acts of the Apostles. . . .

Just as women of the present day seek to obtain fully equal standing with men in Christian churches, so did the Christian women of the second century. If our argument that the Apocryphal Acts originated in communities of continent Christian women can achieve general acceptance, Matristics will become a possibility.[125]

§283 The Holy Spirit a Women

The *Acts of Thomas*, an early third-century Gnostic Christian apocryphal writing, contains several lengthy prayers and one brief one, which addresses or refers to the Holy Spirit in feminine imagery. The three lengthy prayers are all *epicleses*, namely, prayers calling the Holy Spirit to descend upon the liturgical matter, usually the bread and wine used in the Eucharist. The first orthodox text is from Hippolytus in the early third century, like the *Acts of Thomas*. In the latter, two of the *epicleses* are invocations of the Holy Spirit at a Eucharist, but one is connected with Confirmation, which is also customary in orthodox Catholic Christianity. The connections between the feminine Wisdom, the Mother (*Mater Magna*, the Goddess), love, the Eucharist, the dove (symbol of the Goddess, and of the Holy Spirit, discussed in §84), and the Holy Spirit are all obvious.

> O Jesus Christ . . . we glorify and praise thee and thine invisible Father and thy Holy Spirit and the Mother of all creation.[126]

> And the apostle took the oil and pouring it on their heads anointed and chrismed them, and began to say:

> "Come, holy name of Christ that is above every name;
> Come, power of the Most High and perfect compassion;
> Come, thou highest gift;
> Come, compassionate mother;
> Come, fellowship of the male;
> Come, thou (fem.) that dost reveal the hidden mysteries;
> Come, mother of the seven houses, that thy rest may be in the eighth house;
> Come, elder of the five members, understanding, thought, prudence, consideration, reasoning,
> Communicate with these young men!
> Come, Holy Spirit, and purify their reins and their heart
> And give them the added seal in the name of the Father and Son and Holy Spirit."[127]

> And spreading a linen cloth, he set upon it the bread of blessing. And the apostle stood beside it and said: "Jesus, who hast made us worthy to partake of the Eucharist of thy holy body and blood, behold we make bold to approach thy Eucharist, and to call upon thy holy name; come thou and have fellowship with us!" And he began to say:

"Come, gift of the Most High;
Come, perfect compassion;
Come, fellowship of the male;
Come, Holy Spirit;
Come, thou that dost know the mysteries of the Chosen;
Come, thou that hast part in all the combats of the noble Athlete;
Come, treasure of glory;
Come, darling of the compassion of the Most High;
Come, silence
That dost reveal the great deeds of the whole greatness;
And make the ineffable manifest;
Holy Dove
That bearest the twin young;
Come, hidden Mother; Come, thou that art manifest in thy deeds and dost
    furnish joy
And rest for all that are joined with thee;
Come and partake with us in this Eucharist
Which we celebrate in thy name,
And in the love-feast
In which we are gathered together at thy call."

And when he had said this, he marked the Cross upon the bread and broke it, and began to distribute it. And first he gave to the woman, saying: "Let this be to thee for forgiveness of sins and eternal transgressions!" And after her he gave also to all the others who had received the seal.[128]

And when they were baptized and clothed, he set bread upon the table and blessed it and said: "Bread of life, those who eat of which remain incorruptible; bread which fills hungry souls with its blessing . . . we name over thee the name of the mother of the ineffable mystery of the hidden dominions and powers, we name over thee the name of Jesus."[129]

§284 PAULINE WRITINGS

§285 Authentic Paul's Positive Attitude toward Women

In attempting to assess Paul's attitude toward women, one must note the distinction between those Pauline letters which are universally accepted as Paul's and those which are generally or widely held by scholars not to be attributable directly to Paul. Those letters which are indisputably Paul's and which have something significant to say about women are: Romans, 1 Corinthians, Galatians, and, to a much lesser extent, 1 Thessalonians. Those letters which are very generally held by scholars to have been written after Paul's death (in 67?) by a disciple of his and which also spoke of women are the so-called pastoral letters: 1 Timothy, 2 Timothy, and Titus. The authorship of two other Pauline letters that speak of women, Ephesians and Colossians, is disputed. Whatever the relative merits of the various arguments for or against Paul's authorship, it seems clear that, as we have them, these two letters cannot be attributed to Paul in the same direct sense as the undisputed letters are: either Paul gave much more freedom to his amanuensis—he never physically wrote his own letters—than was his usual custom, or disciples pieced together fragments of lost Pauline letters, or some other like theory.

Hence, the attitudes toward women exhibited in the pastoral letters almost certainly provide no evidence for Paul's attitude, and those in Ephesians and Colossians probably do not. Those in Romans, 1 Corinthians, and Galatians do, with one important exception in Corinthians that is discussed below. The first two groups of letters, the so-called deutero-Pauline letters, even though not penned by Paul, of course still are part of the canon of the New Testament and hence are considered later in this book.

The passages listed above wherein Paul teaches women as freely as men, treats them as co-workers in the spreading of the Gospel, and refers to them as apostle, deacon, and ruler are all evidence of a positive attitude toward women. The pertinent passages in four of the undisputed letters of Paul and perhaps also Colossians, as well as a speech attributed to Paul in Luke's Acts of the Apostles, also add further evidence of a positive attitude. The oldest of the letters is 1 Thessalonians (c. 50 C.E.), then Galatians (c. 54 C.E.), 1 Corinthians (c. 56 C.E.), Romans (c. 57 C.E.), and Colossians (c. 62 C.E.?).

§286 Paul in Female Imagery I

The first point is a small one, Paul's use of feminine imagery to describe himself. He did so in at least three instances. In the letter to the Thessalonians he refers to himself as a nursing mother (*trophos*, used in feminine form here).

> But we were gentle when we were with you, like a nursing mother (*trophos*) taking care of her children.[130]

§287 Paul in Female Imagery II

In the second instance, Paul repeats the image of the nursing mother feeding her child milk rather than solid food, though the term *trophos* was not used here.

> I treated you as sensual men, still infants in Christ. What I fed you with was milk, not solid food, for you were not ready for it.[131]

§288 Paul in Female Imagery III

In the third instance, Paul uses the imagery of giving birth to refer to himself, a clear indication that the most female of activities was not something he felt he as a male should disdain as alien to him, quite the contrary.

> I must go through the pain of giving birth to you all over again, until Christ is formed in you.[132]

§289 Female Equality

The next point is vastly more significant. Paul states that in the Christian sphere the religious distinction between male and female, along with the religious distinctions which existed between Jew and Gentile (or Greek, as he puts it here) and slave and free, all of which existed in Judaism, no longer existed. All were equal!

Paul, who here is said by many scholars to be using the phraseology common in the early Christian baptism liturgy, obviously made his own its explicit rejection of the threefold daily rabbinic prayer, discussed earlier (see §6), thanking God for not having made the man praying a Gentile, a woman, or a slave. As noted, the rabbinic prayer was recorded, in somewhat varying form, in three ancient sources. They are the Tosephta, a collection of rabbinic teachings from 200 B.C.E. to 200 C.E.; the Palestinian Talmud; and the Babylonian Talmud; both of the latter containing similarly early material and other teachings down to 400–500 C.E. In the Babylonian Talmud, the prayer is attributed to Rabbi Meir (early second century C.E.), who claims he faithfully passed on what he learned from his teacher Rabbi Akiba (50–135 C.E.). Given the tendency of the disciples of rabbis to memorize and pass on huge amounts of previous traditions, it is highly likely this threefold prayer was in one or several of its variant forms in use in Paul's lifetime (which even overlapped Akiba's by seventeen years). The striking similarity of Paul's (and the early Christian formulary's) inversion in Galatians 3:28 is so close as to constitute a final proof that the threefold rabbinic prayer was well known in the middle of the first century of the Christian Era.

> Praised be God that he has not created me a Gentile! Praised be God that he has not created me a woman! Praised be God that he has not created me a slave![133]

> All [are] baptized in Christ, you have all clothed yourselves in Christ, and there are no more distinctions between Jew and Greek, slave and free, male and female, but all of you are one in Christ Jesus.[134]

§290 Female Equality II

This rejection of distinction "in Christ Jesus" is repeated in three other Pauline passages, once referring only to the distinction between Greek and Jew,[135] once to Greeks-Jews and slaves-free,[136] and once to an even longer list,[137] which normally is not translated with the reference to male and female. However, there are a number of ancient Greek and Latin manuscripts, including the first-century "Clermont" manuscript, which does contain the words male and female, and at the head of the list.[138]

> Here there cannot be [male and female,] Greek and Jew, circumcised and uncircumcised, barbarian, Sythian, slave, free person, but Christ is all, and in all.[139]

§291 Adam, Source of Sin

A small but interesting point should be noted about Romans 5:12–14 and 1 Corinthians 15:21–22. In both instances, Paul refers to the first sin in Eden. In doing so, he attributes the sin to Adam, only to balance the sin by a single man with redemption by Christ. This is understandable since Adam in the Genesis story is the "first" man. However, such an explanation is quite different from much of the interpretation prevalent just before and during Paul's time, which made, not Adam, but Eve the source of sin and death.[140] It is also different from the deutero-Pauline 1 Tim 2:14, where it is said: "It was not Adam who was led astray but the woman who was led astray and fell into sin." The authentic Paul was clearly aware of Eve's having been "seduced" by the serpent,[141] but he did not make her the source of sin and death; that responsibility he laid on Adam.

> Well then, sin entered the world through one man, and through sin death, and thus death has spread through the whole human race because everyone has sinned. Sin existed in the world long before the Law was given. There was no law and so no one could be accused of the sin of "law-breaking," yet death reigned over all from Adam to Moses, even though their sin, unlike that of Adam, was not a matter of breaking a law.[142]
>
> Death came through one man and in the same way the resurrection of the dead has come through one man, just as all men die in Adam, so all men will be brought to life in Christ.[143]

§292 Marriage and Sex Affirmed

The last passages positive toward women to be treated are found in the indisputably Pauline letter, 1 Corinthians; it contains four significant passages.

One[144] was treated above; the second[145] is analyzed below (§299) along with other ambivalent passages. The third,[146] which prohibits women from speaking in assemblies and is clearly negative in its attitude toward women, is widely held, however, not to be authentically part of Paul's letter, but an insertion by an early scribe paraphrasing 1 Tim 2:11–12. Briefly, the major evidence is as follows: (1) This passage directly contradicts Paul's earlier statement[147] that women may speak in assembly; (2) this passage is obviously out of place, having nothing to do with what immediately precedes and follows it and when it is removed, the text reads logically and smoothly; (3) Paul would never base a Christian argument on the Law, as does 1 Corinthians 14:34; and (4) the thought of this passage is very similar to that of the deutero-Pauline 1 Tim 2:11–12, that it is a gloss from the deutero-Pauline circles inserted into the 1 Corinthians manuscript is quite likely.[148] Since this passage is almost certainly not Paul's, it too will not be treated here, but later with the other deutero-Pauline material (§309).

The fourth passage in 1 Corinthians is basically positive in its attitude toward women. In it, Paul says yes to the legitimacy of marriage and sexuality within marriage (there were encratic groups at the time who opposed marriage and the use of sex). Paul emphasizes the equal sexual rights and responsibilities of the husband and wife in marriage, and stresses that he personally prefers, not commands, celibacy. Because the section is long, the whole of chapter 7 will be quoted and commented on briefly in sections.

In the first section, Paul answers a man who apparently had a strong sexually ascetic bent. Paul's insistence on the propriety of marriage and the equal sexual rights of both wife and husband stem from rabbinic Judaism. The notion of sexual continence for the sake of prayer, however, is found already in the second century B.C.E. Testament of Naphtali (8.8): "There is a season for a man to embrace his wife, and a season to abstain therefrom for his prayer." However, Paul's stress on the mutuality of the consent goes beyond the early rabbinic rules, which, although generally stressing marital sexual mutuality, allows rabbinic students to absent themselves for thirty days against their wives' will to study the law,[149] the later (fifth century C.E.) Talmud extends the time to three years.[150]

> Now for the questions about which you wrote. Yes, it is a good thing for a man not to touch a woman; but since sex is always a danger, let each man have his own wife and each woman her own husband. The husband must give his wife what she has the right to expect, and so too the wife to the husband. The wife has no rights over her own body; it is the husband who has them. In the same way, the husband has no rights over his body; the wife has them. Do not refuse each other except by mutual consent, and then only for an agreed time, to leave yourselves free for prayer; then come together again in case Satan should take advantage of your weakness to

tempt you. This is a suggestion, not a rule: I should like everyone to be like me, but everybody has his own particular gifts from God, one with a gift for one thing and another with a gift for the opposite.

There is something I want to add for the sake of widows and those who are not married: it is a good thing for them to stay as they are, like me, but if they cannot control the sexual urges, they should get married, since it is better to be married than to be tortured.[151]

§293 The "Pauline Privilege"

The next section of 1 Corinthians 7 concerns divorce. Paul repeats Yeshua's novel (to Judaism) egalitarian prohibition of divorce and remarriage. He then proceeds on his own account to emend it to allow divorce and remarriage to save the Christian faith of the Christian partner of a mixed marriage; Paul, too, is evenhanded in his allowances and expectations for both the wife and husband.

For the married I have something to say, and this is not from me but from the Lord: a wife must not leave her husband, or if she does leave him, she must either remain unmarried or else make it up with her husband, nor must a husband send his wife away.

The rest is from me and not from the Lord. If a brother has a wife who is an unbeliever, and she is content to live with him, he must not send her away; and if a woman has an unbeliever for her husband, and he is content to live with her, she must not leave him. This is because the unbelieving husband is made one with the saints through his wife, and the unbelieving wife is made one with the saints through her husband. If this were not so, your children would be unclean, whereas, in fact, they are holy. However, if the unbelieving partner does not consent, they may separate; in these circumstances, the brother or sister is not tied: God has called you to a life of peace. If you are a wife, it may be your part to save your husband, for all you know; if a husband, for all you know, it may be your part to save your wife.[152]

§294 Paul on Celibacy

The final portion of 1 Corinthians 7 is an extended discussion of Paul's personal (he distinctly says his own and not Yeshua's) opinion on the advantages of celibacy. There seem to be two main reasons: first, the Second Coming of Christ was imminent (in his later letters Paul saw it to be postponed); second, and closely connected, the unmarried can devote more time and attention to "the things of the Lord," prayer and good works. Nevertheless, Paul is firm in his rejection of any condemnation of marriage, which apparently some in the Corinthian Christian community were looking for.

In this section on celibacy Paul maintained a relative evenhandedness for the most part. Verses 29–31 are addressed to men alone; there was no parallel addressed to women. Verses 36–38 are addressed to men, but they are more or less paralleled by verses 39–40, which are addressed to women. The Greek for verses 36–38 is so ambiguous that they could refer to a man giving his daughter in marriage, or a man marrying a maiden (both possibilities are provided below). In either case, it is apparently the man who decides whether the woman is to marry or not. Of course, the widowed woman in verses 39–40 also makes the parallel decision about whether to marry or not. Though the situations are not exactly the same and the tilt is in fact in favor of the man, there is nevertheless a relative evenhandedness.

> About remaining celibate, I have no directions from the Lord but give my own opinion as one who, by the Lord's mercy, has stayed faithful. Well then, I believe that in these present times of stress this is right: that it is good for a man to stay as he is. If you are tied to a wife, do not look for freedom; if you are free of a wife, then do not look for one. But if you marry, it is no sin, and it is not a sin for a young girl to get married. They will have their troubles, though, in their married life, and I should like to spare you that.
>
> Brothers, this is what I mean: our time is growing short. Those who have wives should live as though they had none, and those who mourn should live as though they had nothing to mourn for; those who are enjoying life should live as though there were nothing to laugh about; those whose life is buying things should live as though they had nothing of their own; and those who have to deal with the world should not engrossed in it. I say this because the world as we know it is passing away.
>
> I would like to see you free from all worry. An unmarried man can devote himself to the Lord's affairs, all he need worry about is pleasing the Lord; but a married man has to bother about the world's affairs and devote himself to pleasing his wife; he is torn two ways. In the same way an unmarried woman, like a young girl, can devote herself to the Lord's affairs; all she need worry about is being holy in body and spirit. The married woman, on the other hand, has to worry about the world's affairs and devote herself to pleasing her husband. I say this only to help you, not to put a halter round your necks, but simply to make sure that everything is as it should be, and that you give your undivided attention to the Lord.
>
> Still, if there is anyone who feels that it would not be fair to his daughter to let her grow too old for marriage, and that he should do something about it, he is free to do as he likes: he is not sinning if there is a marriage. On the other hand, if someone has firmly made his mind up, without any

compulsion, and in complete freedom of choice to keep his daughter as she is, he will be doing a good thing. In other words, the man who sees that his daughter is married has done a good thing but the man who keeps his daughter unmarried has done something even better.

[An alternate reading of the above paragraph is as follows:

In the case of an engaged couple who have decided not to marry: if the man feels that he is acting properly toward the girl and if his passions are too strong and he feels that they ought to marry, then they should get married, as he wants to. There is no sin in this. But if a man, without being forced to do so, has firmly made up his mind not to marry, and if he has his will under complete control and has already decided in his mind what to do, then he does well not to marry the girl. So that man who marries does well, but the one who doesn't marry does even better.]

A wife is tied as long as her husband is alive. But if the husband dies, she is free to marry anybody she likes, only it must be in the Lord. She would be happier, in my opinion, if she stayed as she is, and I, too, have the Spirit of God, I think.[153]

§295 Humanity in God's Womb

In the speech Paul made before Greek Gentiles in Athens he used paraphrases of Greek poetry, the first of which projected God in as feminine an image as possible, that of a pregnant woman. Paul spoke of all humanity as existing within God as does a fetus within its mother's womb, since "it is in him [God] that we live, and move, and exist."[154] It is difficult to see how this image was not that of a fetus in a womb, especially since Paul then immediately paraphrased another Greek poet (perhaps Aratus, third century B.C.E.), by saying, "We are all his [God's] children." It would appear that Paul deliberately used the imagery of God as mother (not at all strange to Greeks) but retained masculine genders in the pronouns referring to God, giving an androgynous cast to the image of God here.

> Yet, in fact God is not far from any of us, since it is in him that we live, and move, and exist, as indeed some of your own poets have said: "We are all his children." Since we are all the children of God.[155]

§296 Conclusion

All told, one would have to describe Paul's attitude toward women expressed in this section as basically positive, evenhanded toward women and men. At the same time, his attitude toward sex and marriage, in general, is moderately negative, the sources of which would include the following: (1) the anticipated imminent Second Coming of Christ, already mentioned; (2) an anti-sex and marriage attitude in a limited part of contemporary Judaism, as reflected in the Essenes (who saw sex as a source of religious uncleanness); (3) ascetic attitudes in contemporary Hellenism. Paul himself indicated that Yeshua was definitely not a source, suggesting that those later Gospel sayings stressing celibacy were placed on Yeshua's lips by later church tradition.

NOTES

1. Acts 1: 14.
2. Acts 2:1–4.
3. Acts 5:14.
4. Acts 8:3.
5. Acts 9:1–2.
6. Acts 22:4–5.
7. Acts 16:13.
8. Acts 13:50.
9. Acts 16:14–15.
10. Acts 17:4.
11. Acts 17:12.
12. Acts 17–34.
13. 2 Tm 4:19, 21.
14. Rom 16:15.
15. Rom 16:13.
16. Rom 16:3.
17. Rom 16:6, 12.
18. Migne, *Patrologia Graeca*, vol. 51, col. 668–69.
19. Rom 16:7.
20. Rom 16:1–2.
21. Phil 4:2–3.
22. Acts 12:12.
23. 1 Cor 1:11.
24. Acts 16:14–15, 40.
25. Rom 16:1–2.
26. Col 4:15.
27. Phlm 1–2.
28. Rom 16:3, 5.
29. 1 Cor 16:19.
30. Acts 18:1–3.
31. Acts 18:18–19.
32. Rom 16:3.
33. 1 Cor 16:19.
34. 2 Tm 4:19.
35. Rom 16:3–5.

36. See Ruth Hoppin, *Priscilla, Author of the Epistle to the Hebrews* (Hicksville, NY: Exposition Press, 1969).

37. Acts 18:24–26.

38. 2 Tm 4:19.

39. Migne, *Patrologia Graeca*, vol., col. 191–92.

40. Acts 9:36–42.

41. John Chrysostom, *The Homilies of St. John Chrysostom, Nicene, and Post-Nicene Fathers*, series 1, (Grand Rapids, MI: Eerdmans, 1956), 11:555.

42. See Bernadette Brooten, "'Junia . . . Outstanding among the Apostles' (Romans 16:7)," in Leonard Swidler and Arlene Swidler, eds. *Women Priests: A Catholic Commentary on the Vatican Declaration* (New York: Paulist Press, 1977), 141, for a totally convincing scholarly analysis which argues that Junia was a woman apostle.

43. Rom 16:6–8.

44. Lk 2:36–38.

45. Lk 1:41–45.

46. *Marialis cultus*, 37. See §155 for an analysis of and the text of the "Magnificat" and Lk 1:46–55.

47. Acts 1:13–14, 2:1–4.

48. Jl 3:15.

49. Acts 2:14, 16–18.

50. Acts 21:7–9.

51. Eusebius, *Ecclesiastical History*, 3:31.

52. 1 Cor 11:5.

53. Rv 2:20–23.

54. Kerygmata Petrou, *New Testament Apocrypha*, 2:117.

55. Acts 18:26.

56. Ti 2:3.

57. See §159 for an analysis of the text and Lk 2:36–38.

58. Lk 8:1–3 and Mk 15:40–41.

59. Acts 9:36, 39–40, 41.

60. Acts 4:35.

61. Acts 6:1–3.

62. Acts 6:3–6. In Greek, *epethekai autois tas cheiras*; this laying on of hands often signified an "ordination" in the Christian Church; it is often thought to be so intended here. It, and variations, often appeared in the ordination of deaconesses, and even widows.

63. I Tm 5:9–10.

64. Ignatius, *Letter to the Smyrnians*, 13.1.

65. Tertullian, *De virginibus velandis*, C.9.

66. Polycarp, *Letter to the Philippians*, 4.3.

67. *Statuta ecclesiae antique*, C.12.

68. Gryson, *The Ministry of Women in the Early Church* (Collegeville, MN: Liturgical Press, 1976), 66.

69. *Testamentum Domini*, 1.40 and I. E. Rahmani, ed. *Testamentum Domini* (Syriac text with Latin trans.) (Mainz, 1899), 95ff.

70. *Didascalia* 3.8.3.

71. 1 Pt 2:9.

72. F. Funk and F. Diekamp, *Patres apostolici* (Tübingen, 1913), 2:142.

73. See Phil 1:1.

74. 1 Tm 3:8–11. Though the Greek word for "women deacons" is *gynaikas*, women, most scholars, as well as most Greek fathers of the church, e.g., John Chrysostom, Theodore of Mop-

suestia, and Theodoret of Cyrrhus (see Gryson, *Ministry of Women in the Early Church*, 87), agree that in this context, the necessary characteristics for bishops, deacons, and women deacons are being listed. It has the meaning of women deacons; those who argue that it refers to the deacons' wives overlook the lack of a parallel with bishops' wives in chapter 3, verses 1–7, whereas, in every other regard, there are matching parallels.

75. *Diakonissa* is a Greek word that appears only in the late fourth-century Syrian document, the *Apostolic Constitutions*, which incorporated most of the text of the early third-century Syrian *Didascalia*, whose original Greek text was lost. However, wherever the *Apostolic Constitutions* quoted the *Didascalia* it used the term "woman deacon" (*hē diakonos*), that is, the feminine article with the regular noun "deacon." Otherwise it uses the neologism *"diakonissa."* See Gryson, *Ministry of Women in the Early Church*, 138.

76. Gryson, *Ministry of Women in the Early Church*, 121.

77. See Gryson, *Ministry of Women in the Early Church*, 30.

78. As reconstructed by Gryson, *Ministry of Women in the Early Church*, 134.

79. As reconstructed by Gryson, *Ministry of Women in the Early Church*, 134.

80. Rom 16:1.

81. See J. Massyngberde Ford, "Biblical Material Relevant to the Ordination of Women," *Journal of Ecumenical Studies* 10, no. 4 (Fall 1973): 676–77.

82. Rom 16:2. *Gar autē prostatis pollōn egenēthē, kai emou autou* for she ruler of many has been and of me myself.

83. Jn 12:2.

84. Acts 6:1–6.

85. Raymond E. Brown, "Roles of Women in the Fourth Gospel," *Theological Studies* (December 1975): 690.

86. Acts 6:2–6.

87. Jn 12:1–2.

88. Lk 10:40.

89. *Apostolic Constitutions* 3.16.1 and Alexander Roberts and James Donaldson, eds. *The Ante-Nicene Fathers* (Grand Rapids, MI: Eerdmans, 1951), 7:431.

90. Roberts and Donaldson, *Ante-Nicene Fathers*, 7:492.

91. J. D. Mansi, *Sacrorurn conciliorum nova et amplissa collectio* (Florence: 1757–1798), 2:676ff.

92. Mansi, *Sacrorum conciliorum nova et amplissa collectio*, 7:364.

93. Migne, *Patrologia Latina*, vol. 2, col. 978.

94. Pliny, *Letters*, ed. William Melmoth (Cambridge, MA: 1963), 2:405.

95. *Didascalia* 3.12.

96. Migne, *Patrologia Latina*, vol. 30, col. 743.

97. *Didascalia* II.26.5–8.

98. Rm 16:1–2 and 1 Tm 3:12.

99. Council of Orange (441 C.E.), Canon 26.

100. Council of Epaon (517 C.E.), Canon 21.

101. Council of Orleans Il (533 C.E.).

102. For an excellent history of ecclesial women in the early centuries of Christianity, see Mary Lawrence McKenna, *Women of the Church: Role and Renewal* (P. J. Kenedy & Sons, 1967). For a collection of all the pertinent Greek and Latin texts, see Josephine Mayer, ed. *Monumenta de viduis diaconissio virginibusque tractantia*, 1938, in series *Florilegium Patristicum*, ed. B. Geyer and J. Zellinger (Bonn: Peter Hanstein, 1904), 71ff.

103. 1 Tm 3:1–7.

104. 1 Tm 3:8–13.

105. 1 Tm 3:11.

106. 1 Tm 5:9–10.

107. 1 Tm 4:14; 5:1–2, 17–22.

108. 1 Tm 5:2.

109. 1 Tm 4:14.

110. 1 Tm 5:2.

111. 1 Tm 5:17–19.

112. 1 Tm 3:1.

113. 1 Tim 5:1–2.

114. For a similar view, see Ernst Gaugler, *Die Johannesbriefe* (Zurich: EVZ-Verlag, 1964), 283.

115. 2 Jn 1, 4–5, 7–10, 12–13.

116. Migne, *Patrologia Graeca*, vol. 8, 675.

117. Stevan Davies, "The Social World of the Apocryphal Acts" (diss., Temple University, 1978), 73.

118. A portion of which is sometimes referred to as the *Acts of Paul and Thecla*, or even *Martyrdom of the Holy Proto-Martyr Thecla*.

119. Davies, "The Social World of the Apocryphal Acts," 92.

120. *Acts of Paul and Thecla, New Testament Apocrypha*, 2:360–63.

121. *Acts of Paul and Thecla, New Testament Apocrypha*, 2:362.

122. Cf. 1 Tm 2:11–12.

123. *Acts of Paul and Thecla, New Testament Apocrypha*, 2:363–64.

124. Tertullian, *De Baptismo* 17.4.

125. Davies, "The Social World of the Apocryphal Acts," 154–45, appendix.

126. *Acts of Thomas*, in *New Testament Apocrypha*, ed. Edgar Hennecke and Wilhelm Schneemelcher, 2:465 (Philadelphia: Westminster Press, 1966).

127. *Acts of Thomas*, in *New Testament Apocrypha*, 456–57.

128. *Acts of Thomas*, in *New Testament Apocrypha*, 470–71.

129. *Acts of Thomas*, in *New Testament Apocrypha*, 512.

130. 1 Thes 2:7.

131. 1 Cor 3:1–2.

132. Gal 4:19.

133. Tosephta Berakhoth 7, 18.

134. Gal 3:27–28.

135. Rm 10:12.

136. 1 Cor 12:13.

137. Col 3:11.

138. See Augustinus Merk, ed. *Novum Testamentum Graece et Latine* (Rome: Pontific Instituti Biblicic, 1959) and Joan Morris, *The Lady Was a Bishop* (New York: Macmillan, 1973), 122–23.

139. Col 3:11.

140. See the second century B.C.E. Ben Sira 25:24: "Sin began with a woman, and thanks to her we all must die"; the first century B.C.E. *Book of Adam and Eve*: "And Adam said to Eve: 'Eve what have you wrought in us? You have brought upon us great wrath which is death'"; the first century B.C.E. *Book of the Secrets of Enoch*: "And I took from him a rib, and created him a wife, that death should come to him by his wife"; and the Tannaitic work, i.e., from 200 B.C.E. to 200 C.E., the Tosephta, Shabbath 2, 10(112): "The first man was the blood and life of the world . . . and Eve was the cause of his death."

141. 2 Cor 11: 3.

142. Rom 5:12–14.

143. 1 Cor 15:21–22.

144. 1 Cor 3:2.

145. 1 Cor 11:2–16.

146. 1 Cor 14:33b–35.

147. 1 Cor 11: 2–16.

148. See Robin A. Scroggs, "Paul and the Eschatological Woman," *Journal of the American Academy of Religion* (September 1972): 284.

149. Mishnah Kethuboth 5, 6.

150. Talmud bKethuboth 62b.

151. 1 Cor 7:1–9.

152. 1 Cor 7:10–16.

153. 1 Cor 7:25–40.

154. This was said by Clement of Alexandria to be a paraphrase of the sixth century B.C.E. Greek poet Epimenides.

155. Acts 17:28–29.

Appendix II

§297 Ambivalent Elements
in Christian Tradition

§298 AUTHENTIC PAUL'S AMBIVALENT
ATTITUDE TOWARD WOMEN

§299 To Differentiate Male and Female

The last authentic Pauline passage dealing with women is 1 Corinthians 11:2–16. This is a notoriously difficult passage to understand, so much so that scholars often debate what is even a correct translation. Verse 3 is a case in point. Professor Robin A. Scroggs argues, persuasively, that the Greek word used here for "head," *kephalē*, is not used in the metaphorical sense of chief or authority, but rather in the sense of "source," like the head waters of a river.[1] Hence, when Paul wrote that man is the *kephalē* of woman, he is alluding to the Genesis 2 story of Eve being made from the side of Adam, that Adam was her "source." This understanding is reinforced by verse 8, where Paul wrote that "woman came from man."[2]

Paul appeared extraordinarily preoccupied with an attempt to maintain visible distinctions between women and men. The women's liberation movement moving through the Greco-Roman world (see above, pp. 9ff.) would, of course, have had the tendency to blur many of the traditional distinctions. Such developments would allow subterranean homosexuality more public scope; homosexuality, moreover, had already played a significant role in earlier Greek culture. Paul, as a devout Jew, was absolutely opposed to homosexuality; he railed against it elsewhere, for example, in Romans 1:26–27 and 1 Corinthians 6:9–10. Paul's insistence on the one hand on women retaining long hair and having their heads covered (or shaving their heads!) and on the other hand on long hair on men being contrary to nature sounds very much like the voice of the frustrated older generation in the face of the 1960s generation gap. His final statement epitomized his exasperation at "not being able to tell them apart": "To anyone who might still want to argue: it is not the custom with us, nor in the churches of God." If this understanding of this portion of the passage is not off the mark, then Paul is not trying to make women subordinate, but is resisting what he sees as an open door to homosexuality, which is another problem entirely. Thus, this whole passage is largely an attempt by Paul to maintain this visible distinction of long hair and covered heads for women and the opposite for men by means of a rather abstruse paraphrase of, or Midrash on, the Genesis 2 story of the creation of Adam and Eve, plus some self-admittedly ineffectual arguments from "nature."

Two other points should also be noted about this very difficult passage. One, Paul says man is the image and manifestation or glory (*doxa*) of God, but woman is the manifestation or glory (*doxa*) of man, meaning woman was made from the side of man according to Genesis 2. Paul does *not* say woman is the image of man, for according to Genesis 1, she is the image of God. Paul here is still straining to find some scriptural basis for insisting on the head covering for women. His continuing with weak arguments and his final gasp of exasperation show he is aware he is not being very clear or persuasive. This lack of clarity reaches its peak in 1 Corinthians 11: 10 with its reference to angels. Though there have been many proffered explanations of the meaning of this text, no one is completely satisfied with any of them.

There are at least three particularly troublesome areas in verse 10. One concerns the word *exousia*. It often is translated as meaning "the woman ought to have a sign of 'submission' on her head."[3] Another interpretation is, however, possible. Jean-Marie Aubert states: "But the word 'exousia' has the basic meaning of freedom of action, of power, which would give the exact opposite meaning to St. Paul's phrase: 'the woman ought to have a sign of power on her head. . . . ' Therefore, far from being a symbol of power submitted to by the woman (= submission), the veil would be a symbol of her spiritual power exercised in the assembly."[4]

Concerning the second problem area, the phrase "because of the angels" (*dia tous angelous*), André Feuillet suggests that the angels in the context refer to the male clergy gathered around, who should not be distracted by the woman's uncovered hair. He adds, "When the woman prays and prophesies she finds herself associated with the angels. . . . She finds herself thus placed in a privileged position which morally obliges her . . . to have on her head a sign of the power she received from Christ."[5]

Lastly, as noted in §228, Paul, when speaking of women being veiled when prophesying (clearly, from the context, in church), obviously presumes that women do properly pray and prophesy out loud in church.[6]

Thus, upon analysis this obscure passage may not express as strong a negative attitude toward women as a superficial reading might lead one to think. On the other hand it could hardly be described as promoting the liberation of women. Still, there is an evenhandedness in 1 Corinthians 11:11–12, which speaks about women and men needing each other and coming from and being born from one another. But Paul's concern to maintain the visible distinction between women and men (no unisex!), has, perhaps unwarrantedly, beclouded his reputation of having a positive attitude toward women.

§300 Paul's Faulty Exegesis of Genesis

Still, one further matter in Paul's argument here is disturbing. He speaks as though the Hebrew text of Genesis 2 says that the male human being was created first and that the female was created from the male. Paul must have been familiar with the Hebrew, and hence would have known that the Hebrew says that God first took some *adamah* (earth), breathed his spirit into it and created *ha adam*, literally, "the earthling," as yet ungendered. Then follows an etiological story about the origin of the male and female genders, with the rib being taken from the side of the sleeping ungendered earthling and formed into *ishshah*, the female, and when *ha adam* woke from its sleep, it had been transformed into the male, *ish*. Paul should have known that, for the other rabbis discuss these issues with these understandings. Why did Paul go with his baseless line of argument? Is it possible that he really didn't know Hebrew very well? It hardly seems possible. Whatever the reason, he nevertheless makes a glaring exegetical error here.

> You have done well in remembering me so constantly and in maintaining the traditions just as I passed them on to you. However, what I want you to understand is that Christ is the source (*kephalē*) of every man, man is the source of woman, and God is the source of Christ. For a man to pray or prophesy with his head covered is a sign of disrespect to his source. For a woman, however, it is a sign of disrespect to her source if she prays or prophesies unveiled; she might as well have her hair shaved off. In fact, a woman who will not wear a veil ought to have her hair cut off. If a woman is ashamed to have her hair cut off or shaved, she ought to wear a veil.

> A man should certainly not cover his head, since he is the image of God and reflects God's glory (*doxa*); but woman is the reflection of man's glory (*doxa*). For man did not come from woman; no, woman came from man; and man was not created for the sake of woman, but woman was created for the sake of man. That is the argument for women's covering their heads with a symbol of the authority over them, out of respect for the angels. However, though woman cannot do without man, neither can man do without woman, in the Lord; woman may come from man, but man is born of woman, both come from God.

Ask yourselves if it is fitting for a woman to pray to God without a veil; and whether nature itself does not tell you that long hair on a man is nothing to be admired, while a woman, who was given her hair as a covering, thinks long hair her glory?

To anyone who might still want to argue: it is not the custom with us, nor in the churches of God.[7]

Thus, the undisputedly Pauline materials yield a number of positive actions and attitudes toward women, plus a very confused passage which, depending on the translation, at worst is quite negative toward women, and at best is perhaps best described as not really negative toward women, but not positive either, and further confounded by a fundamentally faulty exegesis concerning *ha adam*.

§301 DEUTERO-PAULINE AND OTHER AMBIVALENT AND NEGATIVE ATTITUDES TOWARD WOMEN

As noted above, the Pauline authorship of the letter to the Ephesians is strongly disputed by scholars and the letter to the Colossians even more so; further, the two letters to Timothy and the one to Titus are almost unanimously considered not to have been written by Paul, but by some later disciples of his. None of the statements about women in this deutero-Pauline material is positive in its attitude; at most some of them are ambivalent, several are quite negative.

§302 Household Tables

Both the statements about women in Ephesians[8] and Colossians,[9] as well as those in Titus[10] and the First Letter of Peter,[11] have a basic similarity: they give expression to the "household tables." This is a set of rules governing "proper" duties of the various strata in a household. It is said to have originated with Zeno the founder of Stoicism at the end of the fourth century B.C.E. and had, in the ensuing period, become the common property of all the schools of Hellenistic ethics, including Hellenistic Judaism. The various "strata" with superordinate and subordinate responsibilities vis-à-vis each other included husbands and wives, parents and children, masters and slaves. In each of the four instances listed dealing with women, slaves being subordinate to their masters is also mandated; three times children are also charged with obedience to parents; twice (Titus and 1 Peter) submission to civil authorities is likewise exhorted. Although the undisputed Pauline writings required respect for civil authority[12] and a sort of good order in general, they nowhere adopt the "household tables," which figure so prominently in these later extra-Pauline New Testament writings. In general, these later writings reflect a settling down of Christianity, a growing more conservative and organized for the "long haul." That shift away from Yeshua's radicalness in his attitude toward women, and Paul's openness to them, to the late New Testament uncritical acceptance of one popular (probably largely middle and lower class), negative Hellenistic morality toward women placed women, or to be more precise, wives, for unmarried women are not discussed here, in a clearly unequal, subordinate position.

§303 Ephesians 5:21–33

The author followed the Stoic household tables but provided Christian symbolism, motivations, or scriptural quotations for each pair: wives-husbands,[13] children-parents,[14] slaves-masters.[15] The husband-wife relationship is compared with the relationship of Christ and the church, with the requisite love of the husband for his subordinate wife being enjoined, a sublime comparison for a married couple, but one that only reinforces the subordination of the wife.

> Wives should regard their husbands as they regard the Lord, since as Christ is the head of the Church and saves the whole body, so is a husband the head of his wife; and as the Church submits to Christ, so should wives to their husbands, in everything. Husbands should love their wives just as Christ loved the Church and sacrificed himself for her to make her holy. He made her clean by washing her in water with a form of words, so that when he took her to himself she would be glorious, with no speck or wrinkle or anything like that, but holy and faultless. In the same way, husbands must love their wives as they love their own bodies; for a man to love his wife is for him to love himself. A man never hates his own body, but he feeds it and looks after it; and that is the way Christ treats the Church, because it is his body, and we are its living parts. For this reason, a man must leave his father and mother and be joined to his wife, and the two will become one body. This mystery has many implications; but I am saying it applies to Christ and the Church. To sum up; you, too, each of you, must love his wife as he loves himself; and let every wife respect her husband.[16]

§304 Colossians 3:18 to 4:1

Though the author has just declared[17] that in the "religious sphere," that is, "in Christ," there is no distinction between slave and free,[18] he is unwilling to translate that into immediate social action, for he then uncritically accepts the

Stoic household tables and admonishes wives, children, and slaves to obey their husbands, parents, masters. Again, the requisite concern of the superior for the inferior is enjoined and provided with Christian motivations; but the subordination of the wife to the husband, and so forth, remains in place.

> Wives, give way to your husbands, as you should in the Lord. Husbands, love your wives and treat them with gentleness. Children, be obedient to your parents always, because that is what will please the Lord. Parents, never drive your children to resentment or you will make them feel frustrated.

> Slaves, be obedient to the men who are called your masters in this world; not only when you are under their eye, as if you had only to please men, but wholeheartedly, out of respect for the Master. Whatever your work is, put your heart into it as if it were for the Lord and not for men, knowing that the Lord will repay you by making you his heirs. It is Christ that you are serving; anyone who does wrong will be repaid in kind and he does not favor one person more than another. Masters, make sure that your slaves are given what is just and fair, knowing that you, too, have a Master in heaven.[19]

§305 Titus 2:3–9

The author adopted the Stoic household tables and applied them not only to the typical family but also to the "household of God." The subordination of wives again stands clear.

> Similarly, the older women should behave as though they were religious, with no scandal mongering and no habitual wine-drinking, they are to be the teachers of the right behavior and show the younger women how they should love their husbands and love their children, how they are to be sensible and chaste, and how to work in their homes, and be gentle, and do as their husbands tell them, so that the message of God is never disgraced. In the same way, you have got to persuade the younger men to be moderate and in everything you do make yourself an example to them of working for good: when you are teaching, be an example to them in your sincerity and earnestness and in keeping all that you say so wholesome that nobody can make objections to it; and then any opponent will be at a loss, with no accusation to make against us. Tell the slaves that they are to be obedient to their masters and always do what they want without any argument; and there must be no petty thieving, they must show complete honesty at all times, so that they are in every way a credit to the teaching of God our Saviour.[20]

§306 1 Peter 3:3–7

The author enjoined obedience to civil authority,[21] to slave masters,[22] and to husbands, thus also following the Stoic "household tables." The wife was urged to obey partly to convert her husband to Christianity. An asceticism in dress is urged on the wives (apparently seeing feminine, though not masculine, physical beauty as evil), much as is also in 1 Tim 2:9–10; nothing parallel is urged on the husbands. Again, along with slaves, wives are held to be subordinate.

> For the sake of the Lord, accept the authority of every social institution: the emperor, as the supreme authority, and the governors as commissioned by him. . . .
>
> Slaves must be respectful and obedient to their masters, not only when they are kind and gentle but also when they are unfair. . . .
>
> In the same way, wives should be obedient to their husbands. Then, if there are some husbands who have not yet obeyed the word, they may find themselves won over, without a word spoken, by the way their wives behave, when they see how faithful and conscientious they are. Do not dress up for show: doing up your hair, wearing gold bracelets and fine clothes; all this should be inside, in a person's heart, imperishable: the ornament of a sweet and gentle disposition, this is what is precious in the sight of God. That was how the holy women of the past dressed themselves attractively, they hoped in God and were tender and obedient to their husbands; like Sarah, who was obedient to Abraham, and called him her lord. You are now her children, as long as you live good lives and do not give way to fear or worry.
>
> In the same way, husbands must always treat their wives with consideration in their life together, respecting a woman as one who, though she may be the weaker partner, is equally an heir to the life of grace. This will stop anything from coming in the way of your prayers.[23]

§307 Things Get Worse: 1 Timothy

The deutero-Pauline First Letter to Timothy contains three sections dealing with women, one positive, one negative, and one ambivalent. For the positive statement, see §273.

The author has a lengthy statement about widows which is really three-layered. He speaks first of women whose husbands have died but who have relatives who can care for them. Secondly, he mentions those widows who had no one to support them; here the church should step in. Thirdly, he describes the widows who become members of the ecclesial order of widows (see §250).

A downgrading of sex and marriage is apparent here: a second marriage makes a woman unfit to become an "ecclesial widow"; an opposition is set up between a legitimate desire for marriage and "dedication to Christ" (literally, "for when they may have grown wanton against Christ they wish to marry"). This seems to be an echo of Paul's plea for sexual continence over against marriage in 1 Corinthians 7, though the author of 1 Timothy reluctantly concludes it is actually better that young widows marry again.

> Be considerate to widows; I mean those who are truly widows. If a widow has children or grandchildren, they are to learn first of all to do their duty to their own families and repay their debt to their parents, because this is what pleases God. But a woman who is really widowed and left without anybody can give herself up to God and consecrate all her days and nights to petitions and prayer. The one who thinks only of pleasure is already dead while she is still alive: remind them of all this, too, so that their lives may be blameless. Anyone who does not look after his own relations, especially if they are living with him, has rejected the faith and is worse than an unbeliever.
>
> Enrolment as a widow is permissible only for a woman at least sixty years old who has had only one husband. She must be a woman known for her good works and for the way in which she has brought up her children, shown hospitality to strangers and washed the saints' feet, helped people who are in trouble and been active in all kinds of good work. Do not accept young widows because if their natural desires get stronger than their dedication to Christ, they want to marry again, and then people condemn them for being unfaithful to their original promise. Besides, they learn how to be idle and go round from house to house; and then, not merely idle, they learn to be gossips and meddlers in other people's affairs, and to chatter when they would be better keeping quiet. I think it is best for young widows to marry again and have children and a home to look after, and not give the enemy any chance to raise a scandal about them; there are already some who have left us to follow Satan. If a Christian woman has widowed relatives, she should support them and not make the Church bear the expense but enable it to support those who are genuinely widows.[24]

The third passage of 1 Timothy dealing with women is perhaps the most negative of the New Testament in its attitude toward women. Like 1 Peter 3:2–4, it expresses a hostile attitude toward women's physical beauty, though again nothing is said about men's. Women, apparently in general, are told they do not have this author's permission to teach or exercise authority over men; they are told to keep silence. Recalling Paul's reference to women "praying and prophesying" in the Corinthian Church,[25] Klaus Thraede remarks: "Apparently at the beginning of the second century [when 1 Timothy is thought to have been written] there were still communities in which Christian women collaborated in the worship service, although we could not say whether in 'prayer and prophecy,' or even in scriptural preaching. In any case, what could be learned about the Pauline communities from 1 Cor was confirmed *a posteriori*. Now, about a half century later, in the name of Paul, this custom was disallowed."[26] The basis for this order is the Jewish apocalyptic interpretation of the Fall which lays the blame at Eve's feet (rather than Adam's, as is done in the undisputed Pauline letters, see §300), and they are relegated to pious motherhood to gain salvation, all of which flies in the face of earlier statements and actions of Paul, as recorded in the Acts of the Apostles and his undisputed letters.

§308 Continued Faulty Exegesis of Genesis

Again, it is puzzling how the author of this letter was so clearly distorting of the text of the Genesis garden of Eden story, much like the earlier authentic Paul so distorted the Hebrew text as to argue that God created the male first (see §284), which mistake this author repeated as well. Here the author also made another egregious error when he wrote that "Adam was not deceived, but the woman was deceived." If one asks what the image of the woman is and what the image of the man is in the Genesis text, the answer is dramatically different from what has been the typical male sexist projection onto the text, including that of the author of the letter to Timothy here. The author wrote, "Adam was not deceived, but the woman was deceived and became the transgressor," implying that if the serpent had attempted to deceive the male, it would not have succeeded, but could attain its goal only by approaching the less intelligent human, the woman.

Of course, the text says precisely the opposite. In the text the woman carries on a deep conversation with the serpent about a life and death subject and finally "sees that the fruit was good to eat, and ate." She talked and thought about the action, then made an "executive decision" and acted. What does the text say about the male in all this? After the woman's decision and action, the text says simply that "she gave the fruit to her husband, and he ate." No deep thought about a life or death issue, no dialogue, no "executive decision." The male simply "took and ate." The image of the male in the text here is that the male is merely a stomach, whereas the woman is a thinking, probing, deciding, acting, and leading person. The next scene in the text depicts God as walking in the garden and calling for Adam and asking, "'Have you been eating of the tree I forbade you to eat?' The man replies, 'It was the woman you put with me; she gave me the fruit, and I ate it.'" This is hardly the image of a leader; it is the image of a wimp and whiner. But relating what the text actually projected of the woman and the man in the Genesis story was not the aim of the author of Timothy; rather he was looking for something to

confirm the subordination of women to men, and so he twisted the round peg
of the text into the square hole of his intention.

> Women should adorn themselves modestly and sensibly in seemly apparel,
> not with braided hair or gold or pearls or costly attire but by good deeds,
> as befits women who profess religion. Let a woman learn in silence with
> all submissiveness. I permit no woman to teach or to have authority over
> men; she is to keep silent. For Adam was formed first, then Eve; and Adam
> was not deceived, but the woman was deceived and became a transgressor.
> Yet woman will be saved through bearing children, if she continues in faith
> and love and holiness, with modesty.[27]

§309 An Interpolation

As noted in §221, 1 Corinthians 14:33b–35 is almost certainly an interpolation inserted into the authentic Pauline letter to the Corinthians. It bears an
extraordinary resemblance to 1 Tim 2:9–15, just quoted. There is one difference, however. The 1 Timothy passage restricts all women to silence in
church, whereas this 1 Corinthians passage appears to refer specifically to
married women, for the women are told to ask their husbands for information. Thus, it treats at least married women as perforce unlettered inferiors, a
puzzling attitude in a Hellenistic world where there were so many women
readers and writers; perhaps the author thought of the women as all converts
from Judaism, where women, as noted earlier, for the most part were discour-
aged from reading, as reflected in the influential saying of the first century
C.E., Rabbi Eliezer, who claimed he taught only what he learned from his
teachers; he went so far as to say: "Rather should the words of the Torah be
burned than entrusted to a woman. . . . Whoever teaches his daughter the
Torah is like one who teaches her lasciviousness."[28]

> As in all the churches of the saints, the women should keep silence in the
> churches. For they are not permitted to speak, but should be subordinate, as
> even the law says. If there is anything they desire to know, let them ask their
> husbands at home. For it is shameful for a woman to speak in church.[29]

§310 Mothers and Grandmothers

In 1 Timothy, the deutero-Pauline author states that women would gain salvation by childbearing and child-rearing. This notion is similar to the rabbinic
saying that a woman merits by sending her husband and sons off to synagogue to study Torah and waiting for them,[30] and finds concrete fulfillment
in 2 Timothy 1:5, where the author subtly praises Timothy's grandmother and
mother for having embraced the Christian faith and passing it on to him who,
as an ordained man, will exercise church leadership.

How different from the earlier authentic Pauline situation where Phoebe, Lydia, Priscilla, Junia, and many other women are mentioned for themselves and their own accomplishments and leadership and not simply because they mothered a Christian son. The womanly model held up in the two letters to Timothy, and their probable interpolation into 1 Corinthians 14:33b–35, and 1 Peter is dramatically distinct from that presented in Luke's Acts of the Apostles and the undisputed Pauline letters. In the early materials the women are respected, vigorous, assertive co-workers; in the later writings they are silenced, subordinated, passive followers.

> Then I am reminded of the sincere faith which you have; it came first to live in your grandmother Lois, and your mother Eunice, and I have no doubt that it is the same faith in you as well.[31]

§311 "Undefiled by Women"

Revelation, the last book of the New Testament, often called the Apocalypse, a transliteration of the Greek word *apocalypsis*, meaning "revelation," was most probably written in its several parts by several unknown writers sometime during the latter part of the first century. The section attacking the woman prophet in the Christian church in Thyatira[32] is analyzed in §239. The bulk of the book is full of visions and images, centrally including three images of women. The first is Israel,[33] who gives birth to the Messiah. The second is the state of Rome, which is depicted in quite lurid terms as a great whore.[34] The third is the Christian Church, the New Jerusalem, descending from God in heaven.[35] The impression given is that women are either the best or the worst; they never seem to be truly, equally human with men. But (one of) the author(s) reflects his basically negative attitude toward women in Revelation 14:4, where he speaks of the 144,000 who are *undefiled* by women, that is, they have no sexual intercourse with them. There is no talk of women being defiled by men: sex defiles, but only sex by women.

> There in front of the throne they were singing a new hymn in the presence of the four animals and the elders, a hymn that could only be learnt by the hundred and forty four thousand who had been redeemed from the world. These are the ones who have kept their virginity and not been defiled with women.[36]

NOTES

1. Robin A. Scroggs, "Paul and the Eschatological Woman Revisited," *Journal of the American Academy of Religion* (September 1974): 543–44. Scroggs provides ample statistics of the Greek usage.

2. It is interesting to note that Yeshua refers only to the Genesis 1 account of creation, where the creation of male and female is described in a totally egalitarian manner, whereas Paul used only the Genesis 2 account, which has traditionally, though incorrectly, been interpreted in a woman-subordinating manner.

3. New American Bible.

4. Jean-Marie Aubert, *La Femme antiféminisme et christianisme* (Paris: Cerf/Desclee, 1975), 39.

5. André Feuillet, "Le signe de puissance sur la tête de la femme, 1 Cor 11, 10," *Nouvelle Revue Théologique* 95 (1973): 950.

6. Providing one of the strong arguments (§288) against 1 Cor 14:33b–35 being authentically Paul's.

7. 1 Cor 11:2–16.

8. Eph 5:21–33.

9. Col 3:18–25.

10. Ti 2:3–9.

11. 1 Pt 3:1–7. The First Letter of Peter, which was clearly not written by Peter, but perhaps by Silvanus, or Silas, mentioned in 1 Pt 5:12, a frequent companion of Paul.

12. Rom 13:1–7.

13. Eph 5:21–33.

14. Eph 6:1–4.

15. Eph 6:5–9.

16. Eph 5:21–33.

17. Col 3:11.

18. And in some manuscripts also between male and female, cf. §271.

19. Col 3:18 to 4:1.

20. Ti 2:3–9.

21. 1 Pet 2:13–17.

22. 1 Pet 2:18–20.

23. 1 Pet 2:13, 18; 3:1.

24. 1 Tm 5:3–16.

25. 1 Cor 11:5.

26. Klaus Thraede, "Frauen im Leben frühchristlichen Gemeinden," *Una Sancta* (1977): 292–93.

27. 1 Tim 2:9–15.

28. Mishnah, Sota 3,4.

29. 1 Cor 14:33b–35.

30. Talmud bSotah 21a.

31. 2 Tim 1:5.

32. Rv 2:20–29.

33. Rv 12:1–17.

34. Chapters 17, 18, 19.

35. Chapter 21.

36. Rv 14:3–4.

Appendix III

§312 Christian Tradition's
Negative Elements

The Christians who wrote about things Christian after the close of the New Testament, from the beginning of the second century C.E. until the end of the eighth century, are referred to as the Fathers (*Patres*) of the church. For the most part they wrote in Greek and Latin, and to a much lesser extent in Syriac and other languages. Along with the decrees of the first seven universal, or ecumenical, councils of about the same period, their writings constitute a most important body of Christian religious literature reflecting on and applying the Bible message, Hebrew Bible and New Testament. In many ways the importance of this literature in Christianity is like that of rabbinic literature in Judaism.

As with rabbinic literature, with which it is basically contemporaneous, patristic literature reflects a largely negative, non-egalitarian attitude toward women. A number of positive statements concerning women from this patristic writing have been presented in this book. For the sake of a semblance of balance, an extremely brief survey of the negative attitudes toward women expressed by the Christian Fathers is presented here.

§313 CHRISTIAN MOTHERS

To begin with, there is no talk of "Christian Mothers," no "Mothers of the Church," as there is of Christian Fathers and Fathers of the Church, even though, for example, a significant number of the writings in the volumes of Migne's *Patrologia Latina* devoted to Jerome are, in fact, written by Christian women.[1] There is much written about the early Christian monastics of the third and subsequent centuries who founded monasticism in the deserts of

Egypt and elsewhere. But practically all of it is about the Desert Fathers. There is not even a term "Desert Mothers," even though Christian women

> took their part in every phase of the monastic movement in Egypt, and some lived the eremitical life as recluses in the desert, while communities of women came into existence earlier than those of men, and in Egypt were to be found as early as the middle of the third century.[2]

Anthony of Egypt (251–356 C.E.) is usually reckoned as the founder of Christian monasticism. And yet:

> We are told that St. Anthony, when he renounced the world, placed his sister, for whom he was responsible, in a "house of virgins," a nunnery, when, as yet, there were no similar institutions for men.[3]

One of Anthony's younger contemporaries, Pachomius, also of Egypt (290–346 C.E.), was the first to write a "rule" which monastics followed and hence is said to be the founder of communal monasticism (Anthony and his followers were hermits; they lived singly). It is recorded of Pachomius that he

> built a convent for his sister Mary, on the bank of the Nile opposite to Tabennisi, where his own monastery was, and there *she established a nunnery, of which she was the abbess.*[4]

Women continued to flock to the monastic life in great numbers. A dozen women's monasteries were founded shortly after the one by Mary the sister of Pachomius, and they continued to multiply, for in the city of Antinoë alone, Palladius (365–425 C.E.), who visited Egypt before 400 C.E., reported that there were twelve women's monasteries, and one of them was ruled by a woman, Amma Talis, who had already spent eighty years in asceticism.[5]

Around the same time, the Egyptian abbot Shenoudi (333–450 C.E.) founded two monasteries, one with 2,200 men, and one with 1,800 women. And in the same period, it is reported by Palladius that in the city of Oxyrhynchus, twelve miles south of Cairo, there were as many as 20,000 nuns![6]

Even earlier, in Syria, where perhaps several of the Gospels were composed, as well as the *Didascalia* (early third century), which speaks at length of deaconesses,

> we find women ascetics also to the fore . . . and in the Christian Church of the third century we find "Daughters of the Covenant" (*B'nāth Q'yāmā*) alongside of the Sons. In the *Martyrdom of Shamōna and Guria* . . . is an account of the persecution of Diocletian against the Churches in which the *B'nāth Q'yāmā* and the cloistered nuns are described as standing in bitter exposure.[7]

Thus, there were thousands of Christian women ascetics and monastics along with and even before the Desert Fathers, but, outside of rare places, hardly a word is read of them and they are never called Desert Mothers. In fact, the greatest recognition given them by their male contemporaries, and indeed by themselves, so low had the self-esteem of Christian women fallen, is that they had become "manly." One such "Desert Mother," Sara, once said to the male monks: "It is I who am the man and ye who are the women!"[8]

§314 THE GREEK FATHERS

As mentioned above, the Christian Fathers, for the most part, wrote either in Greek or Latin. The Greek Fathers came from the eastern part of the Roman Empire, while the Latin Fathers came from the West. Quotations are presented below from six of the most outstanding Greek fathers from the second to the fifth century, providing an overview that is typical of the largely, though not exclusively, negative attitude toward women held by the Greek Fathers— of course, if Christian women de-sexed themselves and became "manly" they were treated as quasi equals.[9]

§315 Clement of Alexandria (150–215 C.E.)

Clement of Alexandria was probably born in Athens, but after having studied philosophy and Christianity, he became a Christian and eventually became the head of the Catechetical School of Alexandria, Egypt. In general, Clement had a rather balanced and positive attitude toward life, in a period that was marked by extremes, of which the Egyptian Gnostics and ascetics were examples. He seems to have allowed women into his lectures and spoke occasionally of their equality of nature and capacity for wisdom.[10] But much more often he treated women far more restrictively than men, which treatment is typified by his paean of praise for that symbol of manliness, the beard: man is strong, active, uncastrated, and mature; woman is weak, passive, castrated, and immature:

> His beard, then, is the badge of a man and shows him unmistakably to be a man. It is older than Eve and is the symbol of the stronger nature. By God's decree, hairiness is one of man's conspicuous qualities, and, at that, is distributed over his whole body. Whatever smoothness or softness there was in him God took from him when he fashioned the delicate Eve from his side to be the receptacle of his seed, his helpmate both in procreation and in the management of the home. What was left (remember, he had lost all traces of hairlessness) was manhood and reveals that manhood. His

characteristic is action; hers, passivity. For what is hairy is by nature drier and warmer than what is bare; therefore, the male is hairier and more warm-blooded than the female; the uncastrated, than the castrated; the mature, than the immature. Thus it is a sacrilege to trifle with the symbol of manhood [the beard].[11]

§316 Origen (185–254 C.E.)

Origen, raised as a Christian in Alexandria, was a brilliant student of Clement of Alexandria and became his successor as head of the Catechetical School. Origen was an extraordinary intellectual who was also endowed with a certain impetuosity; at one point he was prevented from seeking martyrdom only by his mother's hiding of his clothes; at another point, in a literal application of Matthew 19:12,[12] he castrated himself. Not unexpectedly, his attitude toward women is rather negative. Woman is antithetic to the divine, she is fleshly:

> What is seen with the eyes of the creator is masculine, and not feminine, for God does not stoop to look upon what is feminine and of the flesh.[13]

> It is not proper to a woman to speak in church, however admirable or holy what she says may be, merely because it comes from female lips.[14]

§317 Dionysius the Great (190–264 C.E.)

Dionysius of Alexandria was Origen's successor as head of the Catechetical School of Alexandria and became bishop of Alexandria in 247 C.E. Holding to the Hebraic laws of ritual impurity which Yeshua rejected (see §12), Dionysius forbade Christian women from entering a church during their menstruation, implying, of course, a spiritual as well as a bodily impurity; naturally such women were cut off from receiving communion; they were literally excommunicated:

> The one who is not entirely pure in soul and body must be stopped from entering the Holy of Holies.[15]

§318 Epiphanius (315–403 C.E.)

Epiphanius was a native of Palestine who became the bishop of Cyprus and later of Salamis. He was a very vigorous advocate of monasticism and of orthodoxy, as he understood it, and was quick to believe evil of others. Thus, he attacked one group he accused of according divine honor to Mary, Yeshua's mother, and, assuming that women were responsible for that action, revealed clearly his male supremacist attitude:

For the female sex is easily seduced, weak, and without much understanding. The devil seeks to vomit out this disorder through women. . . . We wish to apply masculine reasoning and destroy the folly of these women.[16]

§319 John Chrysostom (347–407 C.E.)

John Chrysostom was such an extraordinary preacher (especially in Antioch) that he was called "golden mouthed," *chrysostomos*. He was made Patriarch of Constantinople in 398 C.E. Despite his unusually deep and tender relationship late in his life with the deaconess Olympia, he often expressed an extremely low opinion of marriage and women in general. In writing to a monk who was thinking about the possibility of marriage, Chrysostom used rather savage language, indicating that he thought women, especially beautiful ones, were, if not evil, "at least" filthy:

> Should you reflect about what is contained in beautiful eyes, in a straight nose, in a mouth, in cheeks, you will see that bodily beauty is only a white-washed tombstone, for inside it is full of filth.[17]

After denigrating marriage as good only to keep men from "becoming members of a prostitute,"[18] Chrysostom violently attacks remarriage after widowhood. His language indicates a male supremacist, ownership attitude toward women that in the golden mouth of a sainted Patriarch of Constantinople is rather breathtaking:

> We are thus made, we men: through jealousy, vainglory or whatnot, we like above all what nobody has owned and used before us and of which we are the first and only master.[19]

Chrysostom did not see women as completely useless in marriage outside of satisfying male libido. Women had their function, but it was no more than that of a supportive servant, enabling the man to do active, creative things. The tone of paternalism and condescension is almost overpowering:

> Since private affairs are part of the human condition, as well as public ones, God has doled them out: all that takes place outside, he has trusted to man, all that is within the house, to woman. . . . This is an aspect of the divine providence and wisdom, that the one who can conduct great affairs is inadequate or inept in small things, so that the function of woman becomes necessary. For if he had made man able to fulfill the two functions, the feminine sex would have been contemptible. And if he had entrusted the important questions to woman, he would have filled women with mad pride. So, he gave the two functions, neither to the one, to avoid humiliating the other as being useless, nor to both in equal part,

lest the two sexes, placed on the same level, should compete and fight, women refusing authority to men.[20]

§320 Cyril of Alexandria (376–444 C.E.)

Cyril, bishop of Alexandria, was a very clear, precise, orthodox dogmatic theologian, but, at the same time, a violent, self-righteous, unscrupulous protagonist of his own views. He militarily attacked the Jews of Alexandria, driving thousands of them from their synagogues and homes. As might be expected from a hostile ideologue, he also held a very low estimate of women. In a country with a long tradition of literate women (see above, pp. 8–9) he nevertheless held that women were uneducated and not able to understand difficult matters easily.[21] In explaining why Mary Magdalene did not immediately recognize Yeshua after his resurrection,[22] Cyril put down women in general:

> Somehow the woman [Mary Magdalene], or rather, the female sex as a whole, is slow in comprehension.[23]

In a way, this attitude is especially puzzling, since, when Cyril became bishop at Alexandria, the most celebrated non-Christian mathematician and philosopher of the Neoplatonic School in Alexandria was a woman, Hypatia. But in a neurotic sort of way the two elements fit together, for Hypatia, known for her "great eloquence, rare modesty, and beauty," attracted many students and naturally opposed much of what the authoritarian, violent Cyril stood for. Her existence as a proof of the falsity of Cyril's image of woman's uncomprehending nature was swiftly cut off by Christian monks who dragged her from her chariot into a Christian church, stripped her naked, cut her throat, and burned her piecemeal; Cyril was deeply complicit, indirectly if not directly.[24]

§321 THE LATIN FATHERS

Farther to the west in the Roman Empire the predominant language was Latin. Hence, the early Christian writers there are referred to as Latin Fathers. The attitude toward women follows the same pattern as among the Greek Fathers, namely, quite negative, although not totally so. For example, if a woman "gave up" her sex by remaining a virgin or a widow and embraced an ascetical life, Jerome had strong praise for her:

> As long as woman is for birth and children, she is different from man as body from soul. But when she wishes to serve Christ more than the world, then she will cease to be a woman and will be called man (*vir*).[25]

Again, only a selection of typical quotations of the negative attitude of several of the important Latin Fathers, including the four "Doctors of the Church" *par excellence* (Ambrose, Jerome, Augustine, Gregory the Great), from the second through the sixth century will be presented here.

§322 Tertullian (160–225 C.E.)

Tertullian lived in Carthage, in North Africa, and was a prolific, vigorous, even polemical writer who had such a pervasive influence that he has been called the Father of Latin Theology. His polemical approach, in thought as well as style, led him into an extreme anti-Judaism in theology and such a rigorism in morality that he eventually left the Catholic Church and joined the rigorist Montanist movement. His polemicism and moral rigorism also found expression in extremely anti-woman treatises and statements in which he tended to see "materialism" as the basic evil in the world, sex as the most central dimension of that basically evil "matter," and woman as the personification of fundamentally evil sex. Men, of course, were innocent victims of the wiles of women.

The following quotation from Tertullian's Catholic period, like the deutero-Pauline first letter to Timothy and the Jewish pseudo-epigraphical and rabbinical writings, blames woman for bringing sin and death into the world, and adds to that guilt the responsibility for the death of the Son of God! He wrote to a Christian woman that surely she would not wear cheerful clothes, but rather, somber ones,

> walking about as Eve, mourning and repentant, in order that by every garb of penitence she might the more fully expiate that which she derives from Eve, the ignominy, I mean, of the first sin, and the odium (attaching to her as the cause) of human perdition. "In pains and anxieties dost thou bear (children), woman; and toward thine husband (is) thy inclination, and he lords it over thee." And do you not know that you are (each) an Eve? The sentence of God, on this sex of yours, lives in this age: the guilt must of necessity live, too. You are the devil's gateway; you are the unsealer of that (forbidden) tree: you are the first deserter of the divine law: you are she who persuaded him, whom the devil was not valiant enough to attack. You destroyed so easily God's image, man. On account of your desert, that is, death, even the Son of God had to die.[26]

§323 Ambrose (339–397 C.E.)

Ambrose, "Doctor of the Church," was chosen by the Catholic laity of Milan to be their bishop even though he was not yet baptized. His many accomplishments include playing a major role in the conversion of Augustine to Christianity. His attitude toward women clearly was that they were inferior to men:

> Whoever does not believe is a woman, and she is still addressed with her physical sexual designation; for the woman who believes is elevated to male completeness and to a measure of the stature of the fullness of Christ; then she no longer bears the worldly name of her physical sex, and is free from the frivolity of youth and the talkativeness of old age.[27]

§324 Ambrosiaster

Commentaries on the thirteen Pauline epistles were attributed to Ambrose until the time of Erasmus in the sixteenth century, who recognized them as spurious and therefore named their unknown author Ambrosiaster. In these commentaries the same Ambrosian attitude toward women, that they are inferior to men, is expressed. In commenting on 1 Corinthians 11, Ambrosiaster writes:

> Although man and woman are of the same essence, nevertheless the man, because he is the head of the woman, should be given priority, for he is greater because of his causal nature and his reason, not because of his essence. Thus the woman is inferior to man, for she is part of him, because the man is the origin of woman; from that and on account of that the woman is subject to the man, in that she is under his command. . . . The man is created in the image of God, but not the woman. . . . Because sin began with her, she must wear this sign [the veil].[28]

§325 Jerome (342–420 C.E.)

Jerome, born in Aquileia in northeastern Italy, studied in Rome, embraced an ascetical life, and spent much of his life in the Holy Land. He became a giant of a scholar in Sacred Scripture. He had a number of women disciples, but they all had to adopt a life of extreme asceticism, so as to "become a man (*vir*)."

Jerome obviously had grave difficulties with his own sexuality; in the midst of the most extreme ascetic life in the desert, Jerome was filled with wild sexual fantasies:

> Although in my fear of hell I had consigned myself to this prison where I had no companions but scorpions and wild beasts, I often found myself amid bevies of girls. My face was pale and my frame chilled with fasting, yet my mind was burning with desire and the fires of lust kept bubbling up before me when my flesh was as good as dead.[29]

At times, he gratuitously projected debaucheries on women whom he did not even know and about whom he had no information, as, for example, in his letter to a Christian ascetic woman in Gaul in which he describes in lurid detail her imagined behavior, such as her mincing gait, pretended ascetic dress, carefully ripped to display the white flesh beneath, her shawl which she allows to slip and quickly replaces to reveal her curving neck.[30] Professor Rosemary Ruether remarks on this letter:

> All this is pure fantasy, since Jerome has never met the woman. Descriptions such as these, which fill Jerome's letters, leave the reader with a dilemma as to how to understand such ascetic enthusiasm that compels such remarkable pruriency toward women, known and unknown alike. This most probably should be taken as the by-product of violent libidinal repression that generates its own opposite in vivid sensual fantasizing under the guise of anti-sensual polemics. In this, his views and psychology do not differ essentially from those of the other Church Fathers, although he was more skilled than most in rhetorical expression.[31]

Most Christian Fathers thought of marriage as having two ends, namely, to produce Christian offspring and to "allay concupiscence," so as to avoid fornication. Under the influence of a pervasive dualism, which thought of spirit alone as good and of matter as evil, all sense pleasure, especially that most intense one, the sexual, was thought of as evil, at least to some degree. Hence, the second end of marriage, the satisfaction of the sexual appetite, was only a concession to human weakness, really not a good, but a necessary evil. In the context of such a discussion, Jerome drew the logical conclusion of this position and, in the process, revealed again his fear and hatred of women:

> If it is good not to touch a woman, then it is bad to touch a woman always and in every case.[32]

Although Jerome encouraged women to embrace the Christian "religious" life, that is, the ascetic life, he in no way allowed them to take any leadership roles in religion, or anywhere else, for that matter. Following the "Pauline" stance, Jerome insisted that "it is against the order of nature or law for women to speak in an assembly of men."[33] But in another place he became much more vicious in his misogynist hatred of women who would play a leading role in religion:

> What do these wretched sin-laden hussies want! . . . Simon Magus founded a heretical sect with the support of the harlot Helena. Nicholas of Antioch, the contriver of everything filthy, directed women's groups. Marcion, sent on to Rome before him, a woman, to infatuate the people for him. Apelles had Philomena as companion for his teaching. Montanus, the proclaimer of the spirit of impurity, first used Prisca and Maximilla, noble and rich women, to seduce many communities by gold, and then disgraced

them with heresy. . . . Even now the mystery of sin takes effect. The two-timing sex trips everyone up.[34]

§326 Augustine (354–430 C.E.)

Augustine was, without question, the greatest of the Latin Fathers and the most influential of the Doctors of the Church. He was born in North Africa, eventually became a Christian and the bishop of Hippo in North Africa. Before his conversion to Christianity, Augustine became a devotee of Manichaeism, an explicitly dualistic philosophy-religion, which greatly stressed the essential evil of matter, which notion Augustine largely carried over with him into Christianity, and, through his massive influence, into the rest of Western Christianity.

Augustine also had severe difficulties with his sexuality, which is reflected in his Christian writings about sex and about women. Augustine took a common-law wife, to whom he remained faithful for fifteen years and whom he obviously loved deeply. At his mother's insistence he drove away his common-law wife (whose name, tellingly, we never learn), though she also loved him intensely, so Augustine could take a legal wife with a more suitable social background; instead, he took another mistress, probably in some kind of quasi-covert revenge against his mother, Monica, with whom he had a love-hate relationship, and who played a dominant, even domineering, role in his life.

The basic dualism that Augustine absorbed from his years as a Manichee turned up in his problem of what to do with his sexuality. When teetering on the edge of embracing Christianity, Augustine was plagued by what appeared to him as an obvious either-or choice: either choose Christ or choose sexual satisfaction. For Augustine the two were mutually exclusive; sexual desire was a disorder engendered by sin.[35]

> I feel that nothing so casts down the manly mind from its height as the fondling of woman and those bodily contacts which belong to the married state.[36]

Against this background it is not surprising to find Augustine going far beyond Paul[37] and directly contradicting Genesis 1:27 (see §291), in saying that woman is not made in the image of God, only man is!

> How then did the apostle tell us the man is the image of God and therefore he is forbidden to cover his head, but that the woman is not so, and therefore she is commanded to cover hers? Unless according to that which I have said already, when I was treating of the nature of the human mind, that the woman, together with her own husband, is the image of God, so

that the whole substance may be one image, but when she is referred to separately in her quality as a helpmeet, which regards the woman alone, then she is not the image of God, but, as regards the man alone, he is the image of God as fully and completely as when the woman too is joined with him in one.[38]

Augustine's dualism, his fixation on sex, and his consequent abhorrence of women find expression in the following:

A good Christian is found in one and the same woman: to love the creature of God (*quod homo est*), whom he desires to be transformed and renewed, but to hate in her the corruptible and mortal conjugal connection, sexual intercourse, and all that pertains to her as a wife (*quod uxor est*).[39]

In another place, Augustine likens men to the superior portion of the soul and women to the inferior, on what grounds we are not told; it is simply assumed to be obviously true, with the consequence that a woman leader is said to be a perversion of nature:

Just as the spirit (*mens interior*), like the masculine understanding, holds subject the appetites of the soul through which we command the members of the body, and justly imposes moderation on its helper, in the same way the man must guide the woman and not let her rule over the man; where that indeed happens, the household is miserable and perverse.[40]

Elsewhere, Augustine makes the same point about women necessarily being followers and subordinate to men, but in so doing likens women now not even to the inferior part of the soul but to flesh, that epitome of dualistic evil:

Flesh stands for woman, because she was made out of a rib. . . . The apostle has said: Who loves his woman loves himself; for no one hates his own flesh. Flesh thus stands for the wife, as sometimes also spirit for the husband. Why? Because the latter rules, the former is ruled; the latter should govern, the former serve. For where the flesh governs and the spirit serves, the house is upside down. What is worse than a house where the woman has governance over the man? But that house is proper where the man commands, the woman obeys. So, also, is that person rightly ordered where the spirit governs and flesh serves.[41]

§327 (Pseudo) Augustine and Canon Law

Just as Ambrose's negative writings on women fostered the attribution to him of additional writings negative toward women which were written by a writer

Erasmus named Ambrosiaster, so also were other writings negative toward women incorrectly attributed to Augustine. This Pseudo-Augustine we now know is the same person as Ambrosiaster. The reason for reproducing a Pseudo-Augustine quotation here is not to exemplify this historical curiosity, but rather because it typifies the massive influence these anti-woman writings of Augustine, authentic or pseudonymous, had, not only on all subsequent theology, but also on church law.[42] Thus, the following statement attributed, incorrectly, to Augustine was used by Gratian in his twelfth-century collection of church law, which became so fundamental for subsequent canon law. Partly because of it and Augustine's authority, women were severely restricted:

> Woman certainly stands under the lordship of man and possesses no authority; she can neither teach nor be a witness, neither take an oath nor be the judge.[43]

§328 Gregory the Great (540–604 C.E.)

Gregory was an upper-class Roman who sold his property, gave the proceeds to the poor, and became a Benedictine monk. In 590, he was made pope, and because of his extraordinary administrative abilities, he laid the foundation for the medieval papacy. He was also a prolific writer, receiving in posterity the title of the fourth Latin Doctor of the Church. His religious writings were nonspeculative in nature, being given over mostly to moral lessons and allegorical interpretations of the Scriptures. His attitude toward women basically continued that negative pattern which was largely established by the Christian Fathers before him. One example will suffice to exhibit the continuation of that anti-woman pattern. In commenting on Job 14:1, where it is written, "Man, born of woman, is short of life and full of woe," Gregory found misogynist meanings that most would not have suspected were intended by the writer of Job:

> In Holy Scripture [the word] "woman" stands either for the female sex (Cal 4:4) or for weakness, as it is said: A man's spite is preferable to a woman's kindness (Sir 42:14). For every man is called strong and clear of thought, but woman is looked upon as a weak or muddled spirit. . . . What then is designated in this passage by the word "woman" but weakness, when it says: Man born of woman? just as when it is said even more clearly: What measure of strength can he bear in himself who is born from weakness?[44]

§329 PERORATION

As shameful and shoddy as most of the past two thousands years of Christian history has been in its treatment of women, and given the extraordinary model of feminism that was given by our "Founder" Yeshua, I am unwilling to close this volume with these dismal appendeces of misogynism. Rather, I invite Adele Hebert to present her "Adele's Accolade":

Adele's Accolade

Yeshua loved women so much!
Thank God no woman was made mute.
Thank God no woman decided to kill innocent baby boys.
Thank God no woman was ever rebuked harshly by Yeshua.
Thank God no woman was ever called a name by Yeshua.
Thank God no woman was ever silenced.
Thank God no woman ran away.
Thank God no woman denied knowing Yeshua.
Thank God no woman was ever predicted to be part of the plot to murder Yeshua.
Thank God no woman pronounced Yeshua's death sentence.
Thank God no woman was part of the beating, mocking, whipping, or crucifixion.
Thank God no woman ever hurt Yeshua in any way.
Yeshua loved women so much!
Thank God one woman said, "Yes!"
Thank God another woman said, "No!"
Thank God for women prophets.
Thank God women told and retold and retold their stories; they were given a voice.
Thank God for the caring, nurturing, generous women who followed, fed those men three years.
Thank God for the timid, trembling woman who dared to touch his hem.
Thank God Yeshua called women forward to receive healing, then gave them a voice.
Thank God for the bold woman who asked for crumbs.
Thank God Yeshua defended the children, called them, hugged them, blessed them.
Thank God for the woman who anointed Yeshua's feet and wiped them with her hair.
Thank God for the Samaritan woman who told her whole village.
Thank God for the named women in the genealogy of Matthew.
Thank God we are now called daughters, sisters, and friends.
Thank God children shouted, "Hosanna!"
Thank God Yeshua touched women, even those with blood, even a dead girl.
Thank God Yeshua made us equal in marriage and divorce.
Thank God Yeshua forgave women.
Thank God the Holy Spirit is feminine.

Thank God for the parallel stories about women.

Thank God for servant girls speaking, and pregnant women praising.

Thank God Yeshua wept.

Thank God for the woman who dared to share her dream.

Thank God Yeshua uplifted widows for what little they can give.

Thank God Yeshua revealed his being the Messiah to a woman.

Thank God women were honored, uplifted, blessed, healed, and heard.

Thank God Yeshua gave women a voice!

Thank God women and children were important.

Thank God Mary Magdalene was the Beloved Disciple.

Thank God for the faithful women who were there at the cross, and the empty tomb.

Thank God Yeshua chose a woman/women to be the first to see the Risen Lord.

Thank God Yeshua chose a woman/women to "Go and Tell!"

Thank God she/they ran and told.

Thank God women were there in the upper room.

Thank God women received the Holy Spirit!!

Thank God for the women who had the first house churches.

Thank God women were teachers, co-workers, and apostles.

Above all, Yeshua gave women a voice!![45]

NOTES

1. For example, Paula. See §267 for a discussion of female authorship of other extra-canonical Christian writings of early Christianity.

2. Margaret Smith, *Studies in Early Mysticism in the Near and Middle East* (London: Sheldon Press, 1931), 35; repr. Amsterdam: Philo Press, 1973.

3. Smith, *Studies in Early Mysticism*, 36.

4. Smith, *Studies in Early Mysticism*, 36. Italics added.

5. Palladius, *Historia Lausiaca*, Eng, trans. W. K. L. Clarke (New York: Macmillan, 1918), 59.

6. Palladius, *Paradise of the Fathers*, trans. E. A. Budge (Leipzig: W. Drugulin, 1907), 1:337.

7. Smith, *Studies in Early Mysticism*, 44.

8. Palladius, *Paradise of the Fathers*, 2:257.

9. See Rosemary Ruether, "Misogynism and Virginal Feminism in the Fathers of the Church," in *Religion and Sexism*, ed. Rosemary Ruether (New York: Simon & Schuster, 1974), 150–83.

10. *Stromateis* 4, 8, 9.

11. Clement of Alexandria, *Paedagogus* 3.3.

12. "There are eunuchs who have made themselves that way for the sake of the Reign of Heaven. Let anyone accept this who can."

13. Origen, *Selecta in Exodus* 18.17, Migne, *Patrologia Graeca*, vol. 12, col. 296–97.

14. Origen, quoted in George H. Tavard, *Woman in Christian Tradition* (Notre Dame, IN: University of Notre Dame Press, 1973), 68.

15. Dionysius of Alexandria, Canonical Epistle, chap. 2, Migne, *Patrologia Graeca*, vol. 10, col. 1282.

16. Epiphanius, Adversus Collyridianos, Migne, *Patrologia Graeca*, vol. 42, col. 740–41.

17. John Chrysostom, Letter to Theodora, chap. 14, *Sources chrétiennes*, 117:167.

18. John Chrysostom, *On Virginity*, chap. 25, *Sources chrétiennes*, 125:175.

19. John Chrysostom, On the One Marriage, *Sources chrétiennes*, 138:191.

20. Chrysostom, On the One Marriage, 183 and *Homily Quales ducendae sint uxores*, in *Opera*, 3:260–61.

21. Migne, *Patrologia Graeca*, vol. 74, col. 692.

22. Jn 20:14.

23. Cyril of Alexandria, Migne, *Patrologia Graeca*, vol. 74, col. 689.

24. Socrates, *Historia ecclesiastica*, 7:15.

25. Jerome, *Comm. in epist. ad Ephes.* 3.5, Migne, *Patrologia Latina*, vol. 26, col. 567.

26. Tertullian, *De cultu feminarum* 1. 1, *The Fathers of the Church*, 40:117–18.

27. Ambrose, *Expositio evangelii secundum Lucam*, liber 10, n161, Migne, *Patrologia Latina*, vol. 15, col. 1844.

28. Ambrosiaster, Migne, *Patrologia Latina*, vol. 17, col. 253.

29. Jerome, Epistle 22.7.

30. Jerome, Epistle 117.

31. Ruether, *Religion and Sexism*, 172.

32. Jerome, Epistle 48.14.

33. Migne, *Patrologia Latina*, vol. 30, col. 732.

34. Jerome, Migne, *Patrologia Latina*, vol. 22, col. 1152–53.

35. See Tavard, *Woman in Christian Tradition*, 115.

36. Augustine, *Soliloquies* 1.10.

37. 1 Cor 11:2–12. See §280.

38. Augustine, *De Trinitate*, 7.7, 10.

39. Augustine, *De sermone Domini in Monte* 1.15, Migne, *Patrologia Latina*, vol. 34, col. 1250.

40. Augustine, Migne, *Patrologia Latina*, vol. 34, col. 205.

41. Augustine, Migne, *Patrologia Latina*, vol. 35, col. 1395.

42. For a thorough analysis of the whole problematic, see Ida Raming, *The Exclusion of Women from the Priesthood* (Metuchen, NJ: Scarecrow Press, 1976).

43. (Pseudo) Augustine, Migne, *Patrologia Latina*, vol. 35, col. 2244. For Gratian, see *Corpus Iuris Canonici* c. 14, C 33, q 5; ed. A. Friedberg, 2 vols. (Leipzig, 1879–1881); repr. Graz, (1955), 1:1254.

44. Gregory, Migne, *Patrologia Latina*, vol. 75, col. 982–83.

45. Adele Hebert, "Adele's Accolade." Hebert is an independent scholar from Valleyview, AB, Canada. Her e-mail address is adele_h@telus.net.

Index

273

About the Author

Leonard Swidler, Professor of Catholic Thought and Interreligious Dialogue at Temple University in Philadelphia since 1966, is co-founder with his wife Arlene Anderson Swidler in 1964 of the *Journal of Ecumenical Studies*, and the founder and President of the Institute for Interreligious and Intercultural Dialogue. He has authored or edited over seventy books.